Teacher Extraordinary

DESIGN FOR SILVER MEDALLION
*Original in possession of
West London Institute*

Teacher Extraordinary

JOSEPH LANCASTER
1778–1838

Mora Dickson

The Book Guild Limited
Sussex England

F92

For
SANDY

'The Gospel day, the latter Glory, will *begin with Children,*
with their Education.'
(Joseph Lancaster to his father, Sept 1814. AAS)

The Book Guild Limited
Temple House, 25 High Street,
Lewes, Sussex
First published 1986
© Mora Dickson 1986
Set in Linotron Plantin
Typesetting by CST, Eastbourne
Printed in Great Britain by
Antony Rowe Ltd.
Chippenham, Wiltshire

ISBN 0 86332 170 4

CONTENTS

Illustrations by the author

Previous Publications

New Nigerians
Baghdad and Beyond
Israeli Interlude
A Season in Sarawak
Assignment in Asia

A World Elsewhere
Count Us In
A Chance to Serve

Longhouse in Sarawak
Beloved Partner
The Inseparable Grief
The Powerful Bond
The Aunts

ILLUSTRATIONS

ACKNOWLEDGMENTS

I would like, first of all, to thank Sir Edgar Vaughan of London and Professor Edward F. Wall of the College of the Holy Cross, Worcester, Mass., both of whom have worked in great detail on specific aspects of Joseph Lancaster's life and work, for the generous way in which they have shared with me the results of their meticulous research.

Equally I thank Mr G. F. Bartle, archivist at the British & Foreign School Society Archives Centre in the West London Institute – the successor in unbroken line of Lancaster's Borough Road school – for his kindness and help.

By the gracious permission of Her Majesty The Queen I have been able to quote from material in the Royal Archives, Windsor Castle.

The British Library have been kind enough to let me use material from the Place Papers in their possession and I have made considerable use of both printed and manuscript material in the Friends Library and Dr William's Library in London.

Archivists in both public and private collections have been, as always, very helpful. In particular I would like to thank Battersea District Library, the Central Library, Bristol, the County Record Office, Bedford, for access to the Whitbread Papers, for permission to quote from which I have to thank S. G. Whitbread Esq. The City of Birmingham Public Libraries Department, the Central Library, Canterbury, the County Library, Dover, have all taken trouble to supply me with information, and the Local Studies Library, Southwark produced both topographical and pictorial material. In Ireland the Public Record Office of Ireland. The Public Record Office of Northern Ireland, and the Belfast Education and Library Board were all kind enough to photocopy manuscript material in their possession and give me permission to quote from it. The archivist at Guy's Hospital supplied information about Joseph Fox. The National Portrait Gallery not only gave permission to quote from the letter to Sam Sharwood and the David Holt appeal in their possession but also to reproduce the portrait of Joseph Lancaster by J. Hazlitt. The Department of Manuscripts, National Library of Scotland supplied material, and the libraries of the University of Keele and University College, London, allowed me to quote from the Wedgwood Fox letters and the Brougham Papers respectively.

In the United States of America archivists and institutions were equally generous. Special thanks must go to the American Antiquarian Society, Worcester, Mass., and the Historical Society of Pennsylvania for putting at my disposal the very large quantities of manuscript material in their Lancaster collections and allowing me to quote extensively from them. The Rare Book Dept, Boston Public Library and the Museum and Library of Maryland History, Baltimore were both very helpful, as were Martin Luther King Memorial in the District of Columbia and New York Public Library. The Butler Library, Columbia University, New York gave me permission to quote from the deWitt Clinton-Lancaster letters. Haverford College PA have allowed me to quote from a letter in their Quaker Collection and both the Friends' Historical Library, Swarthmore College PA and the Sterling Memorial Library, Yale University made access to manuscript material easy.

The Bibliothèque de la Ville de Montréal, Canada supplied me with photocopies of relevant material.

Thanks are also due to the Cambridge University Press, Methven, and the Harvard University Press for permission to quote from the books referred to published under their imprints.

To all those, and many others who gave me encouragement, I tender my grateful thanks.

Part
1

UNITED KINGDOM

'London Street Boy — after G. Doré'

Chapter 1

EARLY DAYS

'All youth are influenced by example, and, like sheep, follow their leaders.' 'Improvements . . .' 3rd edition 1805

When Joseph Lancaster was born in Kent Street, Southwark, on November 25th 1778, England had the reputation of being the worst educated nation in Europe. For most of the young and poor education took place in the factory or the sweat shop, or on the streets. There was no equivalent to the parochial schools which had spread across Scotland in the eighteenth century. English Charity Schools and common day schools, providing a little learning for small numbers of poor children, proved lamentably inadequate when faced with urban expansion and the rise in population. In 1805 the State recognised no responsibility for the education of the two-hundred-thousand children of paupers directly under its care. School mastering was, in general, a despised occupation; often left to those who were handicapped or deformed or who had proved themselves failures in the struggle to gain a livelihood.

Southwark, known as the Borough because it was the only city suburb to return two members of Parliament, was an area in transition. Fields and orchards interspersed the filthy, crowded dwellings lining the streets and courts. There was no water or sanitation. Towards the end of the American war many speculative builders had been ruined and the road from the new Blackfriars Bridge to the Obelisk was edged with melancholy, half-finished shells of houses, macabrely known as 'carcases'. The Borough High Street, carrying passenger coaches and goods waggons to and from Kent, Surrey and Sussex across London Bridge, was one of the oldest roads in the metropolitan area. Off it, Kent Street abounded in rookeries and thieves' kitchens.

Cheek by jowl, in similarly squalid conditions, respectable tradesmen and their wives made for their families 'decent and comfortable' homes. On their hard work, and that of the labouring poor, depended what prosperity the area boasted. Southwark was an old dissenting stronghold. Many of these men and women were literate, readers of books and newspapers, concerned with events being enacted on a stage larger than just that of the Borough itself.

Richard and Sarah Lancaster were one such couple. Richard Lancaster's own father had been a splintmaker in Warwick. He came from a Quaker background but he did not have his own children brought up as Friends. The mother was a member of the Established Church. When he was seventeen Richard enlisted as a soldier. He saw continental service, fighting with the Foot Guards at Minden.

Richard Lancaster married Sarah Foulkes and in due time ten children were born. The father's industry and his care for this growing family brought him to the attention of his Colonel who, impressed by his obvious qualities, freed him from many military duties so that he could develop a business as a cane sieve maker, based on a small shop kept by Sarah in the neighbourhood of St George's Fields. Eventually the Colonel obtained release from the army with an extra pension for Richard Lancaster.

This event took place in 1784. Richard Lancaster was forty-two, his youngest son Joseph six.

On leaving the Army Richard Lancaster began again to attend the Established Church, probably St George the Martyr near the

Marshalsea at the end of Kent Street, where at least four of his children were baptised. But he was a man who did not take his religion lightly or unthinkingly and, although all his life he retained a partiality for 'the most pious and consistent ministers of that church', he came to feel that the Anglican clergy as a whole had departed from what he saw as the true principles of Christian ministry. He joined a dissenting chapel; from which unfortunately he was later driven out. Perhaps the breadth of his views and the natural tolerance of his character made him unacceptable as a member of any particular congregation in those days of fierce and heartfelt denominational rivalry.

Richard Lancaster was a quiet and humble man. He needed to express his love of God in loving his neighbour. Separated from membership of any religious society, he began to go with a group of devout friends and fellow tradesmen on visits to hospitals, prisons and poorhouses. The group also travelled to small country congregations on Sundays; some of them from ten to twenty miles from London, ready to pay coach hire but not refreshment or the wear of shoes. On these expeditions Richard Lancaster never pushed himself forward; but neither did he decline, if asked, to take a service or comfort a mourner. 'He had been too long a soldier', Joseph wrote later, 'to play the coward in any good cause.' On some of those occasions Richard Lancaster took his youngest son with him.

Joseph Lancaster was a pious, bookish little boy. Coming from such a background it was not surprising. But he still had the 'mercurial restiveness of youth' and was later to show an optimistic cheerful temperament and the resilience of the true adventurer. He also had courage. He knew the life of the streets, where hordes of ragged urchins fended for themselves as best they could. There is a story that, seeing a crowd of ragamuffins throwing stones at a sparrow tied to a stick, he rebuked them for their cruelty and stood his ground until the bird escaped. He loved and admired his father.

Richard Lancaster, for his part, had determined to use the small extra means his Army pension brought him to give his children some education. A number of Joseph Lancaster's enemies later discounted his scholastic background as valueless and it was true that it was modest. But it gave him an experience of the schooling available for the child of humble parents which was to prove very useful.

At quite an early age he went in succession to two dame schools, kept by respectable females in reduced circumstances. He did not learn much; but at least the first taught him to read, the gift that he came to believe the most valuable that could be given to any child. It opened to him a world into which he entered with whole-hearted appetite, devouring not only the Bible but anything and everything on which he could lay his hands. It also enabled him to take up the duty of reading aloud the newspaper to his father after their dinner.

Thirty years on he recalled the excitement of wars and rumours of wars; the thunderstruck reaction of the English to the fall of the Bastille, 'especially that class of people who had been accustomed to view the French as living slaves of a despot and hated them with all the force of national prejudice;' and the hopes that, after all, the French might really become the true disciples of liberty.

Joseph's next school, to which he went with some of his brothers, was kept by an old man who had been in the Army and continued to enforce military discipline among his boys. He must have been a non-commissioned officer, perhaps a sergeant, for he gave commands in a stentorian voice which he expected to be instantly obeyed, and he had worked out complicated evolutions to be gone through when school was dismissed. Joseph Lancaster, son of a soldier though with Quaker ancestors, enjoyed this call to parade and precision, seeing it as 'natural to children who love noise and the promptitude of alacrity'.

This martial master wore green spectacles and one day in the street some boys from a rival school mocked him, calling him 'Green Eyes'. He followed them and complained to their teacher of this gross impertinence, this 'infraction of the public peace'. Feebly, the teacher said that if he could find the offenders they would be punished. 'Sir', retorted the veteran, 'If they were my boys I would drum them out of the Regiment!' How much knowledge was acquired in this establishment is not clear, though some improvement was noted before 'Green Eyes' moved away from the neighbourhood. Certainly the next school gave Joseph Lancaster nothing; two lessons in three months was a good average. The master was noted for his laziness and the youngest Lancaster very soon left. Both of those teachers used monitors; the first from a habit of military order, the second from his own laziness.

None of these experiences lasted very long. Joseph Lancaster must have been about eleven or twelve years old when they finally came to an end and he went to work in his father's business. With the small amount of money he earned he found for himself a teacher of 'superior attainments' with whom he studied in the evenings.

When he was about ten years old something happened which was to influence profoundly Joseph Lancaster's future religious life. One day his father sent him on an errand and on his way home he saw a hearse and a number of coaches drawn up at the gate of a Quaker burying ground. Always ready to inform himself the small boy went in and stood quietly behind the group of family mourners. The coffin rested beside the open grave. A profound silence lay over everything. Curious, Joseph waited for the words of committal and farewell. Nothing happened. The silence deepened. He found his perception of it changing. He no longer waited for speech, but could feel the spiritual communication within the silence itself. After a while the mourners left and Joseph Lancaster went home awed.

He told his father what he had seen and the other strange things he had noticed in the burying ground; the lack of gravestones, so different from more orthodox cemeteries where he liked to wander and spell out the epitaphs. Sarah Lancaster, according to her son, was the 'living chronicle of the family', but it was only now that Richard Lancaster revealed that he himself came of Quaker stock; that both he and his father and grand-father had been born Friends.

Richard Lancaster seems to have disclosed this information with some reluctance for he later opposed, though with gentle-ness, his son's slow progress towards a Quaker profession. He did speak of the basic Quaker principle of the 'Light Within' and admit that when he met Friends he would use the plain speech of 'thee' and 'thou', but otherwise pleaded ignorance. On the boy's pressing he told him where a Friends Meeting was to be found and from that time Joseph occasionally attended, though he was not again touched by the sense of a Living Spirit as he had been in the graveyard.

He disliked his father's business. But his affection for his father remained undimmed, though he found it impossible to talk to him except in the most superficial way. The sibling next in age to himself was an older sister, Sarah. The brothers must all have left home to make their own ways in the world. It may even have been George, four years older than Joseph, apprenticed to trade, who died about this time. Isolated in his inner searchings, with little idea of what the future might hold for him, Joseph's real life lay in books.

He was an omnivorous reader, curious about the world and interested in every scrap of information he could discover. He gained access to a library, borrowed books from neighbours and at last, with the support of his father, found himself in the business of buying and selling. With his wages he acquired reading matter, devoured it and then, with Richard Lancaster's permission, put the books and pamphlets for sale in the window of the shop. Occasionally he bought a novel or a play that he considered corrupting in order to destroy it. Among the books which he read were Thomas Clarkson's Evidences for the Abolition of the Slave Trade, John Locke's Thoughts Concerning Education and Thomas Paine's Rights of Man. In this way the boy amassed knowledge and formed a small personal library. In view of his later financial improvidence it is interesting to note that this first venture into the commercial market was obviously a success.

He also tried to write. In a comment in his own Improvements in Education Joseph Lancaster described the first attempts of a lad of about thirteen to write for publication. The boy in question was almost certainly himself. 'Some years ago a lad . . . took it into his head to write paragraphs for newspapers: he did so, but all his paragraphs were returned to him unprinted. Previously to this he had attempted to write a selection of anecdotes: in this he did not persevere. He attempted to write a sermon, and left it nearly finished . . . His next attempt was an 'Answer' to Paine's *Rights of Man* which was followed by a new system of Physic, a Democratical pamphlet, a Defence of Revealed Religion. In all these attempts he wasted many quires of paper, rose in the morning early, neglected his meals and was often wholly swallowed up in the subject in which his mind was engaged . . .'

Introverted, perhaps lonely, brooding over philosophies and ideas which seemed to bear little resemblance to the bustling, harsh, often desperate, world of the Borough around him, Joseph Lancaster, at the age of fourteen, came to feel that only in solitude could he find the way to the spiritual fulfilment that he had glimpsed for a moment in the Quaker graveyard. Like many a young man before and after him, he saw no means of reconciling his longing for holiness with the actuality of everyday life as it had to be lived in the courts of Kent Street and the back alleys off Newington Causeway. Only by getting away, by retiring to a cave or a hermitage in the country and living off the land, would it be possible to discover God and his own soul.

The logic of this thinking was that he must leave home; a major step which he did not feel capable of undertaking alone. He made a confidant of a young neighbour of the same age, whose own ideas on the subject turned out to be a great deal more practical and worldly than Joseph's. However, when the possibility was first discussed, this lad appeared knowledgeable about suitable places to make for and dazzled the simple Joseph with his description of the wonders of the country and his romantic pictures of the beauty of the road. It was agreed that they should leave on August 3rd 1793. Joseph Lancaster was fourteen and a half.

He was torn between his love for his parents, the recognition that he was going to cause them pain, and his vision of the search for ultimate truth. The vision won. All his life it was to win.

At nine in the evening, with an aching heart, carrying very little money, his Bible and his 'Pilgrim's Progress', he took a last look at his much loved home and set out. He left behind a letter which he admitted 'explained nothing'. It called on the Lord to render all things well but '. . . appeared only to render all things more ambiguous'. It hinted at a duty to God but the conduct it made no attempt to explain 'could not be considered otherwise than very undutiful to excellent parents'.

The two lads hurried across London towards Highgate. It was a warm night. The uphill road and the emotion of their surreptitious departure resulted in their being overcome with sleepiness soon after they had passed through the village. They lay down for an hour under some trees, then pressed on in the direction of St Albans. They had only gone about ten miles when a discussion arose as to their financial resources. It was at this point that the erstwhile friend revealed his conviction that Joseph had money of his own. But Joseph was travelling on faith, and had never considered that it might not be sufficient for the days that lay before him. Indeed his companion turned out to be considerably richer than he was. With disgust on one side and relief on the other, the two lads parted company.

The weather was beautiful; the lush countryside lay drowsing under the summer sun. Joseph Lancaster, who had never before been so far out of the city, was enchanted by it. He changed his direction and began to walk west. Passing through Slough towards evening, he saw Windsor Castle on the horizon with the Royal Standard above it and found it a sight to stir both patriotic and romantic feelings. Tired, but content, he slept under a hedge.

He woke, however, with thoughts of home and parents and a realisation of the enormity of what he had done. For a short while he determined to go back and even turned his steps that way. Then a sense of the adventure and excitement of being on a journey and the fascination of fresh discoveries, took charge of him and he started once again towards the West. The town of Bristol, the slaving port in which Thomas Clarkson had sought so much of his 'evidence', was in his mind.

Going through Reading, hungry, thirsty and footsore, he asked for water outside an inn. Another foot traveller, with more ale than he wanted, gave the lad his tankard. Possibly he saw his innocence and inexperience; he guessed him to be a runaway apprentice. In any case this new friend suggested that they travel on together and for two days they did so at his expense till they parted at Chippenham, the one to go to Bristol, the other to Bath.

Joseph arrived in Bristol with his shoes in ribbons, badly in need of sustenance and shelter. He was also rather confused. The country cot and the simple solitary life that he had left London to find seemed as far off as ever. He made enquiries about ships bound for Africa. There was one but it would not be at anchor till morning. Had he managed to go on board that evening his life would have taken a very different turn.

A lad looking for a ship was a familiar enough sight in a great seaport. Kindly strangers suggested he apply to an American vessel moored at hand. He did so and received a welcome from the sailors leaning over the side. But the Captain was not on board and no immediate decision could be made. Night was coming on. Joseph was a well-grown boy, tall for his age. A man standing near by said: "Come with me to the Rendezvous and you'll get a ship at once."

He had no idea what was meant, though if he had had he might still have accompanied this helpful stranger. They went together to the inn, had a good supper of bread and cheese, and Joseph Lancaster found himself entered for service as a volunteer in the Royal Navy.

The next morning, on board a small boat, they took passage down the Avon and drew up beside the Union tender; a brig with a few guns, captain Lieutenant North, one hundred and ten men in her company.

Joseph's feelings about this development in his fortunes were ambivalent. It was true that instead of the solitude he sought he found himself among a 'shipload of Philistines'. Their idleness and profanity shocked him. But he was not as dismayed as might have been expected. His eye was still keen for the beauties of the scenery in the estuary and, though he felt himself to be surrounded by impious heathens, he was not afraid to make his own views known. The sailors must have thought him a queer fish but perhaps his courage in being prepared to reprove them for swearing made an impression on them too. Some said they had a parson come among them and that he ought to preach.

No sooner mentioned than the idea of a jest at the expense of the newcomer began to grow. Next morning the Lieutenant and his second-in-command went on shore leaving the mate and a midshipman in charge. There were whispers of a sermon from the boy. The mate came up to Joseph and said that he must preach to them. Joseph declined. A kindly seaman warned him quietly that if he did not things might be worse for him. Though he had accompanied his father, Joseph had never preached before. The thought of doing so to such a congregation filled him with nervous apprehension. But the crowd closed in and the mate urged him roughly once again to give them a sermon.

Summoning his courage Joseph said that if he were to do so he must have a quiet room, his Bible and an hour to study. It was agreed. The men were all ordered on deck so that he could have the space below to himself.

Joseph Lancaster never forgot the painful impressions of that moment. He felt himself unfit to preach and had no idea what to say. Though he chose a verse as a text, his mind was blank when he tried to think about it. In the circumstances it was a bold choice: 'Why do the heathen rage, and the people imagine a vain thing.'

All too quickly the hour went by. The boy was called up to the quarter deck where a hundred men were assembled. He was shown an elevated place before the main mast. Mate and midshipman sat on either side of him. He was appalled. He managed to announce his text, and then his voice failed him.

Jeers and laughter broke out among the company. It was, after all, what they had been waiting for. Agitated, and with a rising indignation, Joseph climbed down from his platform. Jostling and laughing the men crowded round him, taunting him to go on.

Suddenly his anger took charge and he boldly refused to allow his religion to be held up to ridicule. At this unexpected firmness one or two sailors began to look ashamed. Someone shouted to the men to be orderly. Almost before he knew what was happening Joseph found himself once again on his platform, but this time with very different feelings. Forgetful of his former diffidence, fuelled by passion and the consciousness of a cause to be defended, the words flowed out of him. For an hour the ship's company stood silent while he spoke and when he finished they surrounded him again; this time to ask him to conclude with prayer.

Of course, after this, he was known as 'Parson'. In a sense he had passed an initiation test. Whatever he said, it was an astonishing feat for a young lad away from home for the first time. He must have spoken with a directness which, in spite of themselves, penetrated the armour of these tough, unlettered men. Indeed his later oratory, occasionally too forceful and common for more aristocratic audiences, would point to where, even in embryo, his powers lay.

From now on he met much kindness. Books were lent to him. He was given a new coat to replace his threadbare one. Two men in particular, Pember, who had been sent to sea by his parents in Bristol to get him away from an undesirable girl and who sadly died a year later on His Majesty's Ship 'Cambridge', and Richard Boger, midshipman, took him under their protection. Though perhaps in the case of Pember this is not a wholly accurate description, for he seems in turn to have confided most of his own family troubles to the young 'Parson'.

The Union tender dropped down the Bristol Channel to Swansea where she joined a convoy of merchant vessels and some other Royal Navy ships, three hundred sail in all. It was a glorious sight and Joseph Lancaster appreciated it to the full. With the ship under way the atmosphere on board had become active and cheerful. Everything about the scenery was new to him. When he considered his own future his thoughts were gloomy ones but the resilience of his nature made it impossible to ignore the exciting and interesting aspects of the experience.

The whole convoy set off for Plymouth, passing Lundy Island in the late afternoon. As the sun set, however, the wind changed. Signal guns were fired and the fleet tacked for shelter in Milford Haven.

The storm was a bad one. A sloop was wrecked and all her crew lost. The tender had her top mast carried away. During the night hammocks were drenched by heavy seas sloshing in and out between decks. To the contempt of seasoned seamen, the landsmen were terrified. One or two even exclaimed, "Parson, Parson, now do pray for us". They had to wait in Milford Haven for repairs. Joseph Lancaster managed to get hold of paper and ink to write to his parents and the letter went off in the shore boat.

Back in the Lancaster home sorrow and alarm had disrupted family life. On the first day, when it was discovered that Joseph was nowhere to be found, the parents could think of no explanation except that he had been detained with neighbours and had spent the night with them. When, late at night, he had still not come home a search was made and the note, which must have been ambiguously placed as well as ambiguously written, was discovered. It explained nothing. Richard and Sarah Lancaster had a sleepless night. Only on the second day, when the absence of the neighbour's lad was also noticed, did they begin to think that their Joseph had been led astray. His mother, who knew that he had been deeply impressed by Clarkson's pamphlet on the slave trade, thought he might be making for the West Indies.

During this time of grief and uncertainty Thomas Urwick an elderly dissenting minister travelling home to Clapham, happened to come into the Lancasters' shop to make a purchase. He could not but be aware that Sarah Lancaster was deeply upset and asked her kindly what the matter was. At this sympathetic enquiry Mrs Lancaster burst into tears and, calling her husband, revealed the whole story. They had lost their youngest son and did not know if he was alive or dead. They thought he had been seduced by a friend and suspected he might have gone to sea; it was after all where many young boys who left home ended up.

Thomas Urwick had influential connections and he clearly took to this worthy couple. He gave them his address and told them that if they heard from their son, and their suspicion that he might be at sea proved justified, then they should let him know. He had friends at both Portsmouth and Plymouth of sufficient importance to get Joseph returned if he had been pressed into the Royal Navy.

It was nearly two months before the Union tender arrived at Plymouth, a voyage usually done in one week from Milford Haven. Health examinations took first priority and Joseph Lancaster, among others, found himself sent to the hospital ship, though for what ailment is not recorded. As he left the tender Lieutenant North said, "Parson, I wish you well"; and the midshipman in charge of the group saw that Joseph's exploits as a preacher were made known to his new shipmates.

The letter from Milford Haven, giving Plymouth as the tender's destination, had arrived in Southwark and the Lancaster parents had hastened to make its contents known to Thomas Urwick. He in turn gave them a letter of introduction to Jasper Barron Esq, landowner, related to the Port Admiral's Captain at Plymouth, and at that very moment on a visit to London from Devon.

Jasper Barron promised to help and his relative, Captain Berger of His Majesty's Ship 'Cambridge', on being appealed to, instituted a search for this runaway boy. It took some time, his transfer to the hospital ship having complicated matters. However, one day to his great surprise, and that of others, Joseph was summoned to the Captain's cabin on His Majesty's Ship 'Cambridge' and there, in front of a number of high-ranking officers and Joseph Barron Esq, was asked if he would like to quit sea life. He replied, "Yes," adding as an explanation a word about the wickedness he had witnessed. The Captain, appearing not to resent this slur on his Service, murmured, "The Boy speaks sense".

Nevertheless some aspects of naval life were not wholly distasteful. During the time at Plymouth the surrender of Toulon had taken place and the Fleet celebrated this event with spectacular and thunderous cannonades and feux de joie. This Joseph thoroughly enjoyed, wishing that it were always possible to fire off the guns in such an innocent and pleasurable manner.

Mr Barron sent him fresh clothes, linen and shoes. They

happened to be the property of a short thin man, and black. Joseph Lancaster's arms and legs stuck out of the ends of sleeves and trousers, and his substantial frame could barely be accommodated within the tight coat. The crew of the hospital ship thought he now had the appearance, as well as the reputation, of a parson and urged him, in the few days before he regained his liberty, to preach again. He refused.

Nine weeks after he had left home Joseph Lancaster was taken off the ship by Mr Barron. He had hardly slept the night before. He was given a hearty meal, which he much enjoyed having found ship fare very inadequate, and Mr Barron drove him in his own chaise to Ashburton where, with a present of several guineas and advice about how to get the stage at Exeter, he put him on the road to London. It was probably Joseph Lancaster's first personal experience of the power of patronage.

The journey home took four or five days. At Exeter he wrote to his parents. It was a letter of apology, gratitude for deliverance, affection and promises of future good behaviour. But it gave no explanation, any more than earlier letters had, of why he had felt impelled to leave home in the first place. The experience had taught him that education opened doors and boldness brought its own rewards. It is possible too that the generosity with which material, and especially financial, help had been bestowed on him, shaped his later conviction that money existed to be used for the general good and not to be loved for its own sake.

Shortly after his return Joseph went to Clapham with his parents to express personal thanks to Thomas Urwick. The ageing man, he was sixty-six, must have found something exceptional in the young boy for this meeting started a friendship which was, in a few years, to result in very practical support.

Joseph Lancaster returned to his father's business. He had never cared for it as an occupation but now he felt a strong sense of filial duty tied him to the little shop. He was still uncertain where his future lay, though his adventure had persuaded him that 'right usefulness in society would best satisfy his MAKER'. He had discovered that solitude was not for him though, paradoxically, deep within him a core of solitariness still drew him to the Quaker silence as a means of approaching the God in whom he profoundly believed.

Only after some time did Sarah Lancaster reveal to her son

that in their grief at his absence his parents, like Hannah with the infant Samuel, had made a vow to dedicate him to the Lord if they got him back. He then discovered that many friends, including Thomas Urwick, also felt that Providence had selected him for the Ministry. While his well-wishers busied themselves with plans to get him to college or a dissenting academy Joseph, now burdened by family obligation, remained uncommitted, privately exploring a different path. Only his youth was an obstacle to the zeal of his friends '. . . and a very happy obstacle it proved!'

Books were still his guide and consolation. He read Thomas à Kempis. A neighbour lent him 'No Cross, No Crown' by William Penn. The two men could not have been more doctrinally different in their approach to spiritual matters, yet both sought to attain to the inward and both spoke to Joseph Lancaster's condition. 'The one drove in the nail, the other fixed it.' Between them they decided his religious profession for the rest of his life; a profession that was constantly to appear totally, and often catastrophically, at variance with his outward behaviour.

A Quaker neighbour offered the works of George Fox and Robert Barclay. Joseph began to go again to Meeting, but he found little satisfaction in it, unable to reconcile the inward spiritual truth which he sought with an appearance of prosperity and smugness. Though it was in the silence that he had first found illumination, his need to learn more made him also want to hear preaching. He and his father still went to listen to those clergy of the Established Church whom they admired and this background, together with his natural thirst for information, caused Joseph Lancaster to long for vocal exposition of Quaker doctrine. On enquiry he was told that Thomas Scattergood, a Friend from Philadelphia, was frequently to be heard at the White Hart Meeting House.

He went there and found a preacher of weight and power to whom his heart was attracted. It was not unusual for American Friends to make religious visits to England and soon he had listened to David Sands from New York State and William Savory, also from Philadelphia. These men gave him the knowledge and doctrine on which to base the religious life that he sought. Returning to the wholly silent Meeting of Horsleydown in Southwark, he found the silence once again filled with meaning.

A tacit struggle was going on in the Lancaster home. Joseph was torn between filial duty and inclinations which ran counter to his father's wishes. Richard Lancaster, who had for some time watched his son's increasing involvement with the Quakers tolerantly, now began to feel it was prejudicing his own plans to train him for the Ministry. He did not welcome Joseph's return to the sect to which his grandfather had belonged. There were arguments; then an uneasy truce.

One day a neighbour brought news that a respectable teacher, known to them all, was looking for an assistant. Joseph leapt at the chance. Richard Lancaster, probably with some relief, agreed. Though continuing to live at home, Joseph Lancaster now had a job of his own.

The master whom he joined was an intelligent, upright man and a good mathematician, for whom the school was a means of livelihood only. To pay an assistant and make any profit at all he had to 'live by the average'. As in all common day schools numbers fluctuated wildly. If the weather was bad, family circumstances straitened, starvation threatening, or the need to earn money paramount, the schoolroom was almost empty. Nor was it necessarily the same children who returned. No means of regulation was possible outside the school, nor thought of within its walls. Where in lean weeks individual attention could be given, when pupils proliferated the days were not long enough for the teacher to hear each child repeat the required lessons, nor would the 'average' permit the employment of an extra assistant.

For Joseph Lancaster this situation offered continual frustration. When he ventured to complain he was told, "You can do no more than time permits. Shine them over the surface and let everyone appear to do the full quantity".

It was during this period, when he was about sixteen, that an incident occurred which was to prove of great significance. Walking along a street, as usual deep in a book, he passed a girl standing in a shop door. She watched him and suddenly, with passionate intensity, exclaimed, "Oh that I could read!" The cry arrested the young man. Something in the tone of it moved his heart. The instincts of a teacher already beginning to stir in him, awoke to respond. Because prayer came naturally, he prayed there and then that it might be given to him to teach children to read. It was an all-embracing petition. For the first time he felt the misery and rejection of every unlettered child and it seemed to Joseph Lancaster that next to the plea 'What shall we do to be saved?' the girl's exclamation was the most profound that a human being could utter.

He remained assistant at the school for eighteen months, then the ill health which was to dog his footsteps for the rest of his life brought him home again. Richard Lancaster packed him off to recuperate with a friend who owned a fishing smack bringing turbot and plaice to the London market from the seas off the coast of Holland. The next venture, on the recommendation of a kindly Friend, was as an assistant teacher at a boarding school for Friend's children in Essex. It does not seem to have been a great success. There were twenty-six pupils and the wife managed the domestic concerns well, though she 'watched the comings and goings of farthings as if farthings were angels', a trait which the new assistant did not share. But the master, John Kirkham, had little talent as a teacher. He was a devout Quaker who had been a gentleman's servant. According to Joseph Lancaster '. . . he had passed from an extreme of paltry Gaiety to its contrast and few minds are strong enough to go from one Profession to its opposite without some effervescence of feeling, some exuberance of conduct'. When he wrote those words, thirty years later, they had the ring of personal experience.

One thing of importance, however, did happen at Colne. In November 1796 a Friend wrote to Joseph Lancaster, 'and on beholding the change in thy outward appearance . . . I have desired for thee as myself that the inward work the most work the most necessary work may keep pace therewith'. Away from home, in the company of devout Friends, Joseph Lancaster took the significant step of assuming the dress and plain language of the peculiar people called Quakers. The state of the spirit within was to remain a continuing, and increasingly exasperating, concern of Joseph Lancaster's Quaker friends, but there was an irony in Josiah Knight's comment. For Joseph Lancaster had been for a long time preoccupied with his soul's relation to its God, and was to remain so; it was his outward actions and demeanour which were to fail to keep pace with his inner heart-searching.

In the Spring of 1797 he was home again, back in his father's business and the buying and selling of books. Though he appears to have had no sense of vocation as yet, at least his religious profession was decided and it must have been clear to Richard

Lancaster that his hopes for his son in this direction were not to be fulfilled. In November 1799 Joseph Lancaster applied for admission to Horselydown Monthly Meeting, Southwark. On January 13th, 1801, with their usual deliberation, the Quakers formally accepted him as a member by convincement. Much had happened in that interval. In spite of appearances it was to be a coming together of opposites which was to lead over the years to vexation and anguish on both sides.

At this time Joseph Lancaster was an unusual young man, singular rather than in any sense outstanding. He was diffident and bookish, with no certainty as to where his future lay. He was still attracted by the idea of going to Africa and even went so far as to make enquiries about a passage there.

He came from a background of decent, hard working petty tradesmen, where life was a continual struggle to keep poverty and starvation at bay. It must have seemed strange to friends and neighbours that, at the age of eighteen, he was not yet earning his own living. Trade was in a declining state. His brothers were finding it difficult to make ends meet. Within the Lancaster family, however, Joseph occupied a privileged position. He was a loved youngest son granted freedom from normal constraints because it was expected that he would be able to do better for himself. His siblings could read and write, but their interest in learning extended little further, and there may indeed have been some jealousy of the latitude allowed young Joseph. But Richard Lancaster probably saw in this boy the success of his policy of giving his children what education he could afford and the possible realisation of some of his own dreams. Joseph held the centre of the domestic circle; round him his parents and his sisters revolved.

This was not a radical young man. He had tried to 'Answer' Thomas Paine, not agree with him. For all his reading and his desire for solitude and a simple life, philosophical theories and abstract arguments did not greatly appeal to him. He wanted to be an orthodox Quaker, even though he found himself out of sympathy with many of that persuasion. The quiet withdrawn exterior hid a passionate nature, as yet barely realised. His family affections, which were to remain a lode star all his life, indicated a generous and loving heart.

The winter of 1797-98 was a bad one in England. There had been a poor harvest; trade was slack. Book selling suffered. Once again Joseph was caught up in the situation he most disliked, assistant to his father in cane sieve making. He knew only one other job that could bring him some money, so he asked Richard Lancaster if he could have a room in the house, probably by now at 9 Newington Causway, to start a pay school for neighbourhood children at reduced prices. Richard Lancaster agreed and on January 1st, two months after his nineteenth birthday, Joseph Lancaster opened his first school and found his vocation. He had two pupils.

'Rev Dr Andrew Bell — after portrait by W. Owen 1812'

Chapter 2

EXPERIMENTS IN EDUCATION

'. . . for whenever an efficient remedy is to be discovered a practical acquaintance with the precise nature of the evil must afford the modest clue to the discovery'
(*Joseph Lancaster's Autobiography Mss LAAS*)

In 1798 the Borough was not without educational establishments. The parish church of St George the Martyr had two Charity Schools, one for boys and one for girls, and there were several other such academies in Southwark, both anglican and dissenting. Indeed the Society for Promoting Christian Knowledge, under whose auspices the Charity School Movement began, reported that the first volunteer efforts arose in St George's Southwark where, in 1699, sixteen pounds a year was subscribed towards a school. It was in dame schools and common day schools in the neighbourhood that Joseph Lancaster had himself been educated.

The Charity Schools, associated with parishes and supported by voluntary contributions, had an honourable place in the history of the education of the poor in the eighteenth century. Saving souls to the Glory of God and training in habits of order and decency, they were the bastions of Church and State. When Patrons and Trustees exerted a continuing influence and visited regularly then within their limitations, which were the limitations of every other kind of school in the kingdom, the children were clothed and fed, and given 'a little safe instruction' in reading, writing, domestic tasks and trade skills. Where benefactors were dead or had lost interest, the children endured misery and inhumanity. In Charity Boarding Schools, working long hours at spinning or oakum picking for a miserable pittance which then enriched the superintendent, they often received no educational nourishment at all and precious little physical sustenance.

The poor were a fact of life; further than that, with their contribution of laborious toil, they were the necessary foundation on which the pyramid of a civilised community could be built. It was a minority who saw any reason to educate them; the majority feared that the slightest change in the status quo might disrupt the base on which society rested, with results that could only be disastrous. Charity children, well clothed and fed, marching to hear an annual charity sermon in the cathedral, were felt by many to be getting above themselves, likely to reject the manual labour which was their destiny. Neither did the minority desire to alter existing conditions, but contended that a modicum of simple education and discipline would result in more honest, upright and intelligent workmen and servants. Hard work and the service of God were the principal ends of Charity School education.

Nevertheless, in the first half of the eighteenth century when the Charity School Movement was growing rapidly, increasing numbers of the children of the labouring poor learned their letters with the King James Bible, that storehouse of literary beauty, human insight, profound thinking and social criticism, as their textbook. Methodism, based on reading the Scriptures, reinforced the slow development of a literate public; a development which in the end helped to raise the general standard of living.

It was to the credit of the Charity Schools that they made no distinction between boys and girls but were prepared to educate both. The grammar schools and the old boarding foundations, whatever their endowments might state, ignored female education and always translated the word 'children' in their statutes as meaning boys. As late as 1873 an article in the Westminster Review stated: 'A girl is not expected to serve God in Church and State, and is not invited to the university or grammar school, but she may, if poor, be wanted to contribute to the comfort of her betters as an apprentice or servant, and the charity schools are open to her.' But the Charity Schools might well have taken the view that female servants were less likely to have minds of their own if they remained illiterate. The fact is they did not and it was the endowment of those same schools that eventually helped to establish girls secondary education.

In the last half of the eighteenth century, however, the Charity School Movement had begun to lose its impetus. In England it was largely an urban phenomenon; with the rise of population and the rapid growth of towns, the old methods and standards were found sadly wanting. The numbers in school were a mere fraction of the ever-increasing offspring of the poor. In London, where it had been possible to appoint a better type of full-time teacher, forty was the average number of pupils in a Charity School. In rural communities it was twenty. With the dame school run for a small weekly fee by an elderly woman, often herself almost illiterate, and the common day school under a teacher who was frequently brutal or simply idle, the Charity School had become a sterile and unhappy institution.

Francis Place, a leather breeches maker who went on to become the valued adviser of radical politicians and a stern critic of Joseph Lancaster, wrote of his own life in a common day school about 1780. In 1798 such schools were virtually unchanged.

It was run by a man called 'Savage' Jones, because of the delight he took in punishing. The boys were taught to read and write, and some to count. On opposite sides of a big room the master and the usher each called out six boys in rotation. The first boy spelled his column or read his lesson and was then dismissed. The rest of the time he spent in idleness or mischief. Any failure was punished by two to twelve very severe strokes of the cane on the hand, which could result in swelling, pain and loss of use. No excuses were permitted. In a brutalising process the boys constantly challenged each other to show how they

could bear pain and sometimes provoked punishment deliberately. Punctuality to avoid such castigation was the only lesson
Francis Place learned.

In the grammar schools, with their curriculum based on the
classical languages and all other subjects extra, and the public
boarding schools, the situation was often not much better. The
only way to keep order was by terror.

Francis Place's family, like that of Joseph Lancaster, valued
education and Francis himself was an intelligent and able boy.
Later he and his brother attended a small school in Windsor
Court off the Strand run by Mr Bowes, a good man who was
greatly loved. His own learning was very ordinary but he took
pains to teach as well as he was able though the education in his
establishment was not so much better than that of 'Savage'
Jones. The boys' reading was heard and their sums examined
individually every other day. Spelling was on alternate days. But
the regime was mild and those, like Francis Place, whose own
brains drove them to learn, could educate themselves and benefit
from Mr Bowes' wisdom and advice.

There was a multitude of parents, however, who perceived
schooling as not only unnecessary but also a positive threat to the
earning power of the family. At a very early age the child could
begin to bring home a small financial contribution even if, in an
unpoliced metropolis, it were the result of begging or stealing.
The half guinea a quarter, which was the usual sum charged by a
day school master, was beyond the pockets of poorer parents and
a subject of bitter complaint even when it was not. The teacher
was dependent on his fees. He had little prestige and no power to
compel. Children often settled their own terms and came to
school if and when they pleased. The drunkenness of the school
master, caught in a situation for which he had no inclination, was
proverbial. Schools were frequently filthy and always appallingly
noisy. Clothes and bodies stank. Half the pupils fell asleep or
were in a state of waking stupefaction.

Most of the children in dame schools or common day schools
had parents, caring or uncaring; in the boarding Charity Schools
they were at the mercy of those who ran the establishments,
utterly dependent on their goodwill and that of any Visitors or
Patrons. There were, of course, good schools as well as bad but
at the end of the eighteenth century the school, as an institution,
ranked low in the public estimation and the teacher, without

training or status often came to this work because he had failed in everything else.

In 1780 it was the sight of troops of wild, ragged, undisciplined children making the Sabbath hideous for the staider inhabitants of Gloucester, celebrating their freedom not from schooling but from the deadly work which occupied twelve or fourteen hours of their weekdays, that persuaded the owner and editor of the Gloucester Journal, Robert Raikes, to put his prestige and his paper behind Sunday Schools.

Raikes had worked for many years to try to alleviate the terrible conditions in Gloucester gaols; in those abandoned ragamuffins he saw future fodder for the penitentiary and the hulks. Well into the next century it was still possible for ten-year-old George Barrett to be convicted at the Old Bailey, under the Shop Lifting Act, for a five shilling theft and consigned to Newgate under sentence of death; and it was not unusual for children of eleven or twelve to be sent to the hulks.

There had been examples of individual Sunday Schools before Robert Raikes was encourged to give publicity to a successful experiment of his own. The Gloucester Journal was highly respected and had a wider circulation than just its home town. The idea spread like wildfire and in 1785 a Sunday School Society was formed, embracing both anglicans and dissenters, strengthening local philanthropic efforts and a loose national framework. In 1786 Mrs Sarah Trimmer, who was to play an important part in Joseph Lancaster's life opened a Sunday School in Brentford and had an interview with Queen Charlotte about the possibility of similar schools at Windsor.

Sunday Schools were free. Robert Raikes paid a small sum, one shilling each, to four decent women to teach on the Sabbath; Mrs Trimmer inspanned the ladies of Brentford and their daughters and herself gave voluntarily of her own time. Whatever the pattern, the schools gave religious instruction and taught reading. Some added writing, though many considered this a dangerous art for the labouring classes to learn. Contacts were made, and if possible sustained, with the parents and where there was family distress the children might receive food and clothing.

The whole day was occupied by the Sunday School, with two or three hours of teaching in the morning, attendance at service in the church, and more hours of instruction in the early evening.

This innovation was instantly popular, not only with solid citizens as a way of humanising and controlling the riotous young poor, or with parents as a method of giving their offspring some education without losing their earning power, but with the children themselves. At early service in St Mary de Crypt Church, Gloucester, Robert Raikes was astonished to find himself surrounded by a group of ragged urchins: children flocked to Mrs Trimmer's Brentford schools: with great rapidity Sunday Schools were set up in different parts of the country and were as quickly filled. As with the early days of the Charity Schools, education, which popular opinion held to be unsuitable for the poor, was thirstily embraced by the poor themselves.

It was a remarkable phenomenon that the children, whose only free day it was, who were in many instances beyond any control and who, whatever the pressure from employers, parents or clergy, could not have been compelled to attend if they did not wish to, came to Sunday Schools in such great numbers. Nor was this all. Reports of an astonishing alteration in the manners and morals of those children began to come in, so widespread and so well-attested that it is impossible not to realise that a very real change was taking place. 'Where children had been ignorant, profane, clamorous, filthy and impatient of restraint they became quiet, decent and orderly.'

The French Revolution was to have as great an effect on the social climate of England as the loss of the American colonies thirteen years before had had upon the nation's trade. Thomas Paine's 'Rights of Man', published in 1791, brought sharply home to the British people that the Channel was no barrier to the spread of ideas. 'Jacobin' became once again a term of honour or oppobrium though it was fifty years since a Stuart pretender had actually threatened the throne. Men with energies to spare took sides. Jacobinism split the hitherto unified Sunday School Movement. The fear of infection led Government to harsh Acts, severe penalties and an increase of repression. General agitation and distress added to the numbers of the poor, and reduced the resources of those philanthropists on whom they depended for aid. The few who advocated schooling for the poor faced an opposition freshly convinced of its overwhelming dangers. In France the National Assembly was discussing education: universal, compulsory, gratuitous and secular. In England there was no Parliamentary interest in any such idea. The right of individual freedom was insisted on in education as in religion though for those who were not Anglican and possessed of some substance, and even for those who were, such freedom was of doubtful benefit.

Education had always been the prerogative of the Church. By the Act of Uniformity of 1662 every school master or teacher in England, instructing any youth, had to conform to the liturgy of the Church of England and be licenced by the Ordinary. Where the penal clauses were not strictly enforced there had long been some dissenting academies, but the numbers of them were small and their standards did not markedly differ from those of their anglican counterparts. Only in 1779, a year after Joseph Lancaster's birth, had Protestant dissenters become legally free to teach – except in universities or the great schools. During the following decade the same liberty was accorded to Roman Catholics.

Among those philanthropists whose concern was with the education of the poor there was a fear that the universal popularity of Sunday Schools might cause them to be seen by parents and employers as a convenient and economical substitute for day schools. To those who perceived education as a power for social amelioration Sunday Schools offered only a partial solution. In his 'Essay on Population', published in 1798, Malthus stated that it had become a national disgrace that the education of the lower classes should be left to a few Sunday Schools supported by subscriptions from individuals.

In 1796 the Reverend Dr Andrew Bell had come home from Madras, India, with a handsome competency said to be about £27,000; a comfortable fortune which shrewd financial management was to keep intact. He was forty-three and prepared to settle down and exploit whatever ecclesiastical patronage could be persuaded to come his way. A vicarage in Swanage suited his initial needs.

Though a Scot, Andrew Bell was ordained in Anglican orders. He was also a doctor; as it happened of medicine, though that was not the doctorate applied for when a friend had asked St Andrew's University for an honorary degree to give Andrew Bell some leverage in the world. Both men had hoped for a doctor of laws but the university had proved 'delicate' about the choice of those on whom it conferred the more prestigious honour and they had to be content with medicine. Andrew Bell made no secret of his disappointment. 'MD for one who had neither pursued nor studied the art of medicine had not the same respectable appearance after it (his name) which LLD would have been held to carry'.

He sailed for India in February 1787 with £128. 10s and some scientific instruments. Thanks to a plurality of chaplaincies with the East India Company's regiments and his own financial abilities he returned nine years later a wealthy man. The appointment which was to bring him fame, however, had been undertaken for no salary. He had offered his services as Superintendent of the Military Male Asylum at Madras where the offspring of British soldiers and Indian mothers were given a rudimentary education.

On the ship coming home, and in the first months of what was virtually retirement, Andrew Bell wrote a pamphlet describing events in the military orphanage of which he had been Director. It appeared in 1797 under the title 'An Experiment in Education, made at the Male Asylum at Madras, suggesting a system by which a School or Family may teach itself under the Superintendence of the Master or Parent'. He did not anticipate any great interest and the pamphlet had a limited sale among those concerned with parochial and Sunday School Education.

His experience had some unusual aspects. An energetic and gifted teacher he had been appalled to find himself in charge of an institution capable of holding two hundred boys where less than twenty inmates, under the supervision of an incompetent master and two weak ushers, did as they pleased in an atmosphere of chaos and apathy. Maddened by inefficiency and waste, Andrew Bell attempted to introduce reforms, only to find himself obstructed at every turn by the mutinous obstinacy of his staff. Any attempt at reorganisation was blocked. The school lacked even the minimum of materials needed to make teaching possible.

Out riding in the early morning one day, Andrew Bell passed a Malabar school where a group of Indian children, sitting on the ground, were writing in the sand. He was struck by their concentration and co-operation and the ease with which the use of a natural resource made it possible for all the children to be actively working at the same time. Back at the Asylum he determined to conduct an experiment. He collected sand, had it strewn on board specially set up, and described to his staff how to use this new method of teaching. Unwilling instructors under any circumstances, they saw no merit in such primitive tools and nothing but trouble for themselves in the unfamiliar turmoil created by this new broom.

A passionate and obstinate man, Andrew Bell was not to be balked by the deliberate non-cooperation of his assistants. If necessary he was willing to let them go. Instead he looked round for an intelligent and responsible boy.

The choice lighted on John Friskin who was about twelve years old. He was instructed in the new method and given the alphabet class. So well did this venture work that by the time Andrew Bell left India the Military Male Asylum was entirely, and successfully, organised on the basis of older boys teaching younger, with John Friskin superintending the junior assistants and the adult staff acting as administrators and general overseers. It was the details of this experiment that Andrew Bell committed to print.

The old century went out and the new was ushered in with years of great distress and scarcity. It was a time of anxiety and social dislocation, with a rapid rise in population and widespread need due to a succession of bad harvests. Winters were hard. Because of crop failure and taxation for the French war, prices had risen enormously. It was a period of political alarm and the harsh measures that such times produce. Joseph Lancaster charged his first pupils 4d a week; a bargain when compared with the half guinea a quarter which was normal in common day schools.

It had cost him about twenty shillings to set up his school. He bought some old boards and nails and, though not a very expert carpenter, sometimes using two or three nails where one would have done, he managed to fit up desks and forms. He had bills printed and distributed them among likely customers promising to teach reading, writing, arithmetic and the Holy Scriptures and stipulating that he must have one morning free to attend weekday Meeting.

This undercutting of the usual fees did not go unnoticed. An angry neighbour, also hoping to provide a pittance to live on by teaching, put a large handbill in a shop window opposite which read: 'Children taught as cheap as by the bookseller over the way'.

In the next weeks one more scholar joined the original two. Joseph, however, was not idle. Hearing of a family in danger of having their goods seized by the landlord for debt, he managed to collect £10 for them and offered to educate the children for very little. Slowly the school room began to fill. Joseph came again to his father with a request; could he have the use of a workshop instead.

He had not started a school because he wished to experiment with new educational theories; he started a school because he needed to earn his living and perhaps also because he remembered the cry of a girl in the street and his own reaction to it. But, if he was not already aware of it, it must soon have become clear to him that he had a talent for teaching.

Once again the children came, with the thirst for literacy already demonstrated by the response to Sunday Schools. By the summer of 1798 there were too many even for the workroom and he had to hire a large workshop in the Borough Road. Some time in 1799 the Lancaster family left the area and Joseph moved house to live in his own school building.

In the autumn of 1798 he had also started a First Day school, being concerned about the moral condition of his pupils. For this work he raised a subscription of £5, possibly from two members of Horsleydown Monthly Meeting who were to prove faithful friends and consistent supporters, Anthony Sterry an oilman, and Thomas Sturge a straightforward, unassuming shopkeeper. So that he could himself go to Meeting, Joseph employed a poor parent as teacher on Sunday afternoons and it became one of his weekly pleasures to return home for tea and serious talk with his large new family. The children brought their own bread and butter while he supplied the tea and sugar. The young man who had thought the fulfilment of his nature lay in solitude now found great happiness in the company of his pupils and committed himself with enthusiasm to working on their behalf.

For the next three years Joseph Lancaster raised small subscriptions among local Friends for the First Day school.

By the summer of 1799 the daily school had about one hundred and thirty pupils and was open six to eight hours a day. Not content only with teaching, Joseph went out when he could and preached the value of education to all who would listen, primarily to parents. Seeing the total poverty, so much worse than his own, in which many families lived he began more and more frequently to waive even the modest fee which he charged. When this happened it was an absolute rule that no pupil knew who paid and who did not. Joseph told impoverished parents to instruct their children, on hearing their names called when the weekly register of fees was made up, simply to answer that there was a parental arrangement. Sometimes even the child himself had no idea what this arrangement was.

That autumn, through the agency of Anthony Sterry, the generosity of two benevolent gentlemen and a timely building speculation by a Lambeth tavern keeper, James Hedger; Joseph Lancaster was able to move yet again out of his dilapidated workshop into a large building just off the Borough Road. It came to him rent and tax free for nine years and with a grant of land. Over the door he fixed a board which read: 'All that will, may send their children, and have them educated freely: and those that do not wish to have education for nothing, may pay for it if they please'. His financial priorities had changed in a way that did not find favour with Richard and Sarah Lancaster, though they recognised the qualities of their son's heart. Others later on were to pass harsher judgements on his fiduciary blindness.

Of Joseph Lancaster's ability to kindle, and to sustain, the interest of his pupils, however, there was no doubt. With such a fluctuating constituency it was difficult to be accurate about the numbers present at any one time. The Lancaster school suffered from the usual problems of other day schools for poor children. But it was clearly popular and the very situation that Joseph, when an assistant, had found so frustrating was now developing in his own establishment; single handed he was having to cope with well over one hundred children. 'Live by the average and do what you can', his former master had told him. As was to become clear, this plain young Quaker was not a man to whom averages meant a great deal.

Talents, hitherto unused, were beginning to blossom. He had experience of bad education, and a determination to do better. He must also have had the self-confidence to communicate to his pupils something of his own passionate belief in the importance of knowledge. He had a large physical presence, but the youthful earnestness beneath the flat Friend's hat could have made him a figure of fun had not the close contact with his children released an exuberant enjoyment in the pleasure of childhood. It may be that, serious, bookish, sheltered by devout parents, the youngest in a family for whom life was a hard struggle, the fun of street games and the excitement of group activities had up till now passed Joseph Lancaster by.

Perhaps he could have afforded an assistant, though this is by no means certain. But it is likely that he would, in any case, have been reluctant to share the exhilaration of this experience with anyone. One of his new found talents was for administration. To get anything done it was important to have order. Remembering Old Green Eyes he began to use commands, and probably monitors, as non-commissioned officers, to help enforce them. The din of war was in every street. Children could not pass through them to school without being attracted by martial music and marching soldiers. It seemed to them, as it did to Joseph, natural to bring something of this into the school and they found the enforcement of a regular discipline exciting precisely because it did imitate the glamour of the tramping troops outside.

But if the summer of 1799 had been full of discovery and enjoyment, the autumn of that year, in spite of the move into a new building, brought a harsh reality that was powerfully to affect Joseph Lancaster.

It was a winter of dreadful weather. Scarcity bit deep. The school role sank to thirty, many being absent because they were starving or because their clothes had been sold or pledged to pay for food. Unable to witness such need without doing what he could to help, Joseph began to provide large numbers of his pupils with hot dinners and some with extra clothing. If they wished to come to school few, if any, were ever refused because of an inability to pay. Instead he tramped the streets, raising what money he could from London Quakers. He went to market himself to choose the legs of beef, the sacks of rice, potatoes or millet; spending with abandon the Friends' liberality. The next winter was equally bad. This time he was not taken by surprise, issuing a handbill in November 1800 which said that Joseph Lancaster proposed to serve at least twenty-five pupils a hot meal four times a week for three months and appealing for support.

It was as well that he was no longer living in the family home. He now had an old Welshwoman as housekeeper and, in William Corston's phrase, had 'domesticated himself with his pupils'. He had opened his school to the children of debtors in the King's Bench prison and took some of the older lads to live with him.

Many pupils arrived before school hours and stayed on long after they were officially finished. Their young master entered whole-heartedly into whatever play they engaged in or, as seems more likely, invented activities with them infinitely more interesting than any they could make up themselves. In summer, on high days and the Thursday and Saturday half-holidays, they would all make excursions to villages round London, or run races, play trapball, scramble for apples in nearer fields or playgrounds.

So the bond was formed. 'They honoured him – he loved them'.

All the same he was still toying with the idea of going to Africa not because the school was failing but precisely because it was a success. In May 1800 a senior Friend, Frederick Smith, was writing to Joseph Lancaster the kind of letter that Friends through the years were so often to address to him advising him to 'continue the little, quiet, humble path that thou hadst been blest in far beyond thy expectations when thou first began thy employ': to be cautious and careful about the prospect of great things or large openings: to be content and avoid hankering after new opportunities. He did not think that the idea of going to Africa, to bring education to the African children, was a good one.

No doubt it was sound advice. The trouble was that it was not in the nature of the young man to whom it was given to heed it. All kinds of fresh powers were stirring in him and with them came ambition. He did not intend to hide his light under a bushel if, by burning publicly and brightly, it could be a beacon in a world of ignorance and need. There are hints in the letter that already Frederick Smith understood this. In the circum-stances it is surprising that, seven months later, Horsleydown Monthly Meeting formally accepted Joseph Lancaster into the Quaker fellowship.

Monitors had long been known in schools as assistants to masters. It lay in Joseph Lancaster's own temperament and in the quality of his relationship with his boys that, when the sheer necessity of numbers drove him to rely more and more on his senior pupils, he injected into the old role a new sense of confidence and shared adventure which gradually transformed it from a mechanical drudgery into a responsible office.

It did not happen overnight. Many experiments were made during the first three years, some of which proved useless. A good deal of money, which could ill be spared, was wasted. Sometimes there was a failure to recognise the real requirements of a particular situation. Only slowly, occasionally accidentally, solutions were stumbled on and a pattern gradually took shape. So are important discoveries more often made than by the blinding flash of revelation. It was probably while this process was still in the melting pot that, in 1800, a friend gave Joseph Lancaster a copy of Andrew Bell's book, 'An Experiment in Education' and he found in it reinforcement for his own ideas and suggestions which he could incorporate into the system he was developing. One of the latter was the use of sand tables.

About this time a handbill appeared on the streets of Southwark.

Education, on a liberal Plan;
At the Academy, No 1 James Street,
near the Borough Road, Southwark
Children are taught reading at . . . . . . 4d per week
writing with ditto . . . . . . 5d per week
Arithmetic and both ditto . . . . . . 6d per week

Writing books are sold at a very low price, and the use of Bibles, Grammars, Slates, Pens and ink, are found, Gratis.

Joseph Lancaster having studied the Benefit of Youth placed under his Care, has exerted himself to plan the Order of the School, as to hold out incitements for improvement in every progressive stage of Learning, by Commendation, Encouragement and Rewards, according to Merit.

Charitable Persons disposed to send Orphans, or Fatherless Children to this school, may expect to find it an agreeably run Asylum for them – and the parents of large Families may also find it worthy their attention.

The school house may be seen on the Right of the Road from Stones-End to the Obelisk, at a small distance from Belvedere Place.

Among the charitable persons disposed to help were Anthony Sterry the oilman and Thomas Sturge. Already interested in the education of poor children, each had agreed to pay a guinea a year for five or six pupils. By January 1801, when Joseph Lancaster felt that the time had come to offer an examination of accounts, he had institutionalised this arrangement by forming a subscription list, asking an annual contribution of a guinea per child; fifteen shillings to go on education, six shillings on school expenses, books, etc. Subscribers were entitled to nominate pupils. In a year or two he was to announce that the guinea would educate three children rather than one. Where the average yearly cost in a Charity School was fifteen guineas, one guinea, a purely arbitrary figure invented by Joseph Lancaster, seemed a bargain. For the first time his financial support included non-Quakers. The names of Zachary Macauley, Secretary to the Sierra Leone Company, William Wilberforce, crusading politician, and Henry Thornton, Member of Parliament for Southwark, were included in the 1801 subscription list. All three men were noted philanthropists who had made their weight felt in the affairs of the State. The young Quaker was beginning to attract influential friends.

Joseph Lancaster had no sense of financial prudence and little feeling that there should be some relation between income and rate of development; what he did have was a talent for organisation, a vision that went beyond the confines of the Borough and the ability to communicate it, and an instinctive understanding of young people. That they had a role to play in teaching each other he felt sure. He remembered also his own surprise, when he was first employed as an assistant, at the way in which half-forgotten knowledge was renewed and fixed in the memory by the act of teaching. But he recognised that children had limitations as well as strengths and set out to eliminate weakness as far as possible. 'Experience soon taught him that he could not commonly nor entirely depend upon such youth in general for discretion, wisdom and judgement: that they needed judicious training as well as skilful selection: that they must walk in precise line and be accustomed to that alone'. So the System was invented to substitute for wisdom and experience; and it was the System that was eventually to bring his lifework into disrepute.

The school rules were simple and straightforward.

SPEAK THE TRUTH
Be Honest
Be Obedient
Be Diligent
Be Attentive

> Be Neat and Clean
> Be Civil
> Be Silent in School
> Be Meek and Modest
> Come Early Always

Gradually, in those first years, under the guiding hand of Joseph Lancaster's own genius and personality, the infant Plan brought joyful order out of dismal chaos and injected into the lives of the children who flocked to his school a sense of purpose and opportunity. When the whole institution now swollen to two or three hundred; though in the matter of numbers Joseph was notoriously unreliable, went walking on one of their holiday expeditions led by their Master, it must have been an astonishing sight. Joseph named these 'rejoicing times'. Ranked in classes, in itself an innovation, and captained by their monitors, the ragged army holding banners, kites, balls and anything else that Joseph Lancaster considered would add to the enjoyment of the day, marched down the highways and out into the byways, exhibiting an order and discipline so different from the normal wild riotousness of both schools and streets that it seemed a miracle to those who watched them. And it was no longer a discipline of fear. These young people marched with pride and pleasure to spend the day in undiluted enjoyment. As with those who had crowded to the Sunday Schools twenty years before it was impossible to deny that they had changed. No wonder the curious began to take notice, the more earnest to make enquiries.

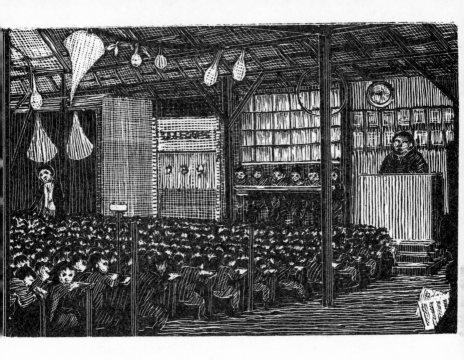

'Portion of Royal Free School, Borough Band after contemporary engraving.
Note kites, hoops and bats'

Chapter 3
THE BOROUGH ROAD

*'A place for everything and everything in its place'. (Joseph
Lancaster) ('Improvements . . . 5th Edition')*

In what way did Joseph Lancaster's burgeoning school differ
from other London schools? Why did it begin to attract an
increasing number of curious, interested, and indeed eminent,
visitors? In 1803 Joseph Lancaster himself provided some of the
answers. He published the first of several editions of 'Improvements in Education as it respects the industrious classes of the
Community'.

In the introduction he set out two important ideas which had
moved him to action.

'The rich possess ample means to realise any theory they
may choose to adopt in the education of their children,
regardless of the cost: but it is not so with him whose
subsistence is derived from industry. Attention to this as

a primary object, ignorance, and incapacity, often prevent his having proper views on the important subject of
education, and when he has (such) slender resources as
often prevent their being reduced to practice. Yet,
among this class of men, are found many who are not
only useful members, but ornaments to society: and from
the labours of these it is, that the public derive the
convenience, and many of the comforts of life . . .'

'Therefore . . . education, as it respects those who are
unprovided with it, ought to become a national concern:
and . . . not (sic) doubt it would have become so had not
a mere pharasaical sectmaking spirit intervened to prevent it, and that in every party.'

'A system of education, which would not gratify this
disposition in any party, is requisite, in order to obviate
the difficulty . . . When I view the desolating effects
produced amongst the unprotected and unbefriended
orders of society, what shall I say? Alas! my brethren and
fellow Christians, of every denomination, you have been
contending whose influence shall be greatest in society,
while a national benefit has been lost, and the poor
objects of it become prey to vice, to an extent that all
your praiseworthy, but partial benevolence, can never
repair. A national evil requires a national remedy . . . let
your minds expand, free from narrow principle, and let
the public good become the sole object of your united
Christian efforts.'

'Above all things, education ought not to be made
subservient to the propagation of the peculiar tenets of
any sect, beyond its own number: it then becomes undue
influence, like the strong taking advantage of the weak;
and yet, a reverence for the sacred name of God and the
Scriptures of Truth, a detestation of vice, a love of
veracity, a due attention to duties to parents, relations
and to society; carefulness to avoid bad company, civility
without flattery, and a peaceable demeanour, may be
inculcated in every seminary of youth, without violating the sanctuary of private religious opinion in any
mind.'

'When obedience to the Divine precepts keep pace
with knowledge, in the mind of any man, that man is a

Christian; and when the fruits of Christianity are produced, that man is a disciple of our blessed Lord, let his profession of religion be what it may . . .'

'Impressed by these sentiments, I feel a wish, as every friend to mankind must, that names may perish, but truth prosper.'

The importance of regarding education as a national concern and the Christian, as opposed to sectarian, foundation for schooling, were to remain constant themes in Joseph Lancaster's thinking through all the vicissitudes that lay ahead. Historically they were inextricably intertwined. From very early times education had been focussed on the church: every settlement of ecclesiastics was a centre for learning, each cathedral, through sculpture, illumination or stained glass, a source of information.

In England, after 1604, teaching publicly or privately without the licence of the Ordinary was forbidden. School masters had to subscribe to the supremacy of the Crown and the orthodoxy of the Church of England. All children were to be instructed in the catechism. The rallying cry at the universities was 'Church and Crown'.

It has to be acknowledged that by the end of the eighteenth century the anglican parish clergy had been grossly neglectful of their exceptionally privileged position in English elementary education. It was philanthropic Christian laymen in the main who encouraged the growth of Charity Schools and Sunday Schools though, for all her apathy, the Church viewed with a jealous eye any attempt to encroach on her ancient rights. It is said that Robert Raikes, seeing the initial enthusiasm of dissenters for the Sunday School feared 'that if it became identified with a Non-conformist body, the Established Church, blinded by the mistaken prejudice of the age, would refuse to take it up'.

As the popularity of Joseph Lancaster's schooling grew, so inevitably did the seeds of conflict inherent in his insistence on a non-sectarian education.

Nor was the concern with a national education any more free from pitfalls. The right of parish clergy to undertake the catechism of their own children and the teaching which was implicit in this duty made the thought of any overall State intervention a matter which touched on questions of religious and individual liberty. Both the Charity School Movement and the Sunday School Society had led to loose national networks.

But these were voluntary movements, affording some stability with access to information, while making no effort to dictate patterns which might conflict with local circumstances. Both Parliament and people were openly suspicious of any suggestion of government interference with the jealously guarded liberties of the English. On this subject there was far less discussion in England than was to be found in some of the countries of continental Europe.

Joseph Lancaster was not interested in politics. When advocating that schooling became a national concern he was thinking of the formation of a voluntary Society.

Part 11 of 'Improvements' gave some hints for the formation of such a Society.

His first precept was that there should be no reformation through compulsion. 'A spirit, breathing the language of independence is natural to most Englishmen, few of whom are disposed to brook compulsion, or submit to the dictates of others when not softened by reason, or tempered by kindness'. Coercion was the most disgusting word in the British vocabulary.

Public aid and patronage would be essential for an undertaking of the magnitude he envisaged. It would only succeed if active and influential men, in a Society established for the purpose, met poor men as brethren and Christians.

The Society must be founded on general Christian principles. 'The grand basis of Christianity alone is broad enough for the whole bulk of mankind to stand on, and join hands as children of one family.' Thousands of young people had been lost to education, their morals ruined and their talents gone to waste, as a result of mortifying and degrading sectarian quarrels. Let the parties unite on the basis of common humanity, on what agreement was possible, 'that society at large may no longer suffer loss, by a set of the most valuable and useful men our nation can boast, employing themselves to little better purpose, than to declaim or make wry faces at one another'.

He went on to list the principal evils that such a Society would set out to remedy: improper and immoral persons having youth under their care – and the difficulties under which those who supported schools lay in assessing the characters of teachers: the poverty of teachers – and consequent lack of respect from parents: bad accommodation – 'in summer, may be compared to a baker's oven; in winter, to the peak of Derby: filthy': total want of system and stimulus to action: the diversity of methods used, so that when children changed schools – which happened very often – they lost much valuable time retracing their steps.

The first object of the new Society would be to provide suitable teachers and to bring those already in schools under its patronage; to set standards. This would give the teacher a degree of credit in his neighbourhood, and ensure that poor men had some certainty of finding good teachers for their children and not wasting their pittances: equally, that the scholar would not fritter away his time under an ignorant and unqualified master. The patronage of the Society would encourage worthy men to exert themselves: '. . . particular prospects of success not only present opportunity of action and advantage, but often animate the mind to embrace it'.

There was, however, one important caveat. The Society should not infringe individual rights by dictating to teachers in their own schools what they should teach. 'I conceive any person, whose moral chäracter and abilities were likely to make him serviceable to the rising generation, should be an object of the Society's protection, let his denomination of religion be what it may; and let him pursue whatever methods of religious or other instruction, his sincere and best intentions may dictate.' A Society had the right to expect a teacher to be honest, assiduous and careful, and to pay attention to health, cleanliness and morality; further than that it should not go.

A number of ideas were then put forward by which the work of teaching might be made more attractive and the status of 'the teachers of youth, many of whom are, naturally, men of amiable and liberal minds, but discouraged by the depressing circumstances of their employment' enhanced. The measures included a fund for deserving teachers in distress, and a teachers' friendly society which would provide financial help in sickness, with funerals, and even some support in old age.

A typical Lancaster suggestion, an idea which was to become one of the hallmarks of the Lancastrian schools, concerned the importance of rewards for pupils. With the maximum publicity the Society might give gold and silver medals for good work. There would be a public presentation, a list of prizes in the newspapers, handbills distributed in the neighbourhood of a teacher whose scholars had been so honoured, stating who the medal had been given to and for what and the Society's satisfaction in being able to recognise distinguished merit. Such a proclamation would have the effect of establishing a teacher's reputation, raising the number of his scholars and so his income.

Ways of increasing the master's remuneration were important. The Society could buy in bulk those items which schoolmasters traditionally provided for themselves, Bibles, Testaments, writing books, quills, etc., and retail them without profit to affiliated teachers. Joseph calculated that teachers might save ten guineas a year; a sum of consequence to those with families to maintain. In this way it would be possible to give help 'in a manner that would not hurt the feelings of any individual', as a ten guinea charity donation could well do. The Government might be persuaded to allow the Society 'a drawback of total duties on writing papers'.

A public library containing books which teachers could borrow, backed by information on the subject of tuition published by the Society, might be another measure for improving teaching standards.

The emphasis on bettering the teacher's conditions and developing his skills was striking and far ahead of its time. Though the content of the curriculum was to remain undisturbed, the manner in which it was taught would undergo a radical reconstruction, enabling schools to be widely, and uniformly, reorganised in a way that would promote a disciplined and attractive atmosphere for children to learn in. Lancaster himself said that his proposal 'goes not to establish a new order of schools, which would be attended with great expense, but to reform those we already have'.

Joseph Lancaster was a successful practicing teacher, not an educational philosopher. It is unlikely that in 1803 he had heard of Pestalozzi, also an advocate of popular education, whose writings were beginning to attract notice among thinkers; nor, in the circumstances of nineteenth century England, would he have found his ideas helpful. Pestalozzi was a generation older than the young Lancaster. He too was a man of his period who had written 'The poor must be educated for poverty'. Both men loved children and both sought for solutions to the problems with which they were confronted. Pestalozzi, faced with the rigidity and discipline of Swiss schooling, searched for ways of releasing the child from its stifling grip. In a rural country he dealt with small numbers and based his schools on the family group. Though he was concerned about education for the poor, his least successful practical experiments were with the poor. It was to be many years after his death before the power of his ideas penetrated deeply into educational thinking.

Joseph Lancaster, with warmth of heart, an understanding of the young and organisational rather than intellectual gifts, began to teach in an urban society where schools were chaotic and undisciplined, the numbers of children who received no schooling enormous, the rivalry of the factory and workshop very strong, the status of teachers non-existent and sectarian interests paramount. It was those shackles that he set out to shake off by means of the Lancastrian System.

Of what did this System consist? For it was not his ideas but his school that first brought Joseph Lancaster to the attention of the public.

Part III of 'Improvements' described the Plan. Joseph was proud of it and he recognised that pride might make him less than modest. He admitted that his account was biased. 'A degree of confidence in our own powers is a useful and necessary incentive to action: but that confidence heightened by unusual success, frequently degenerates into self-conceit . . .' If it seemed that he was in vain, he begged to be forgiven.

The school was based on the need to encourage and reward pupils, rather than simply to punish. An important ingredient was the active employment of every boy. 'The predominant feature in the youthful disposition is an almost irresistible propensity to action; this, if properly controlled by suitable employment, will become a valuable auxiliary to the master but, if neglected, will be apt to degenerate into rebellion. Active youths, when treated as cyphers, will generally show their consequence by exercising themselves in mischief; this is often the cause of that unpleasant riotous disposition evinced at our public schools, where the pupils brave everything but the censure of their friends, or the disgrace of expulsion.'

With this in mind the school was divided into smaller groups, a rare phenomenon at this date, each in the charge of a monitor who was responsible for its morals, improvement, good order and cleanliness and who made daily and monthly progress reports. But the use of monitors extended far beyond this disciplinary function. Every aspect of the school was controlled by boys. They ruled the writing books and cut the pens; work always undertaken, or neglected, by the master in other schools.

Boys were in charge of general cleanliness, gave out the slates, handed out the various tickets which led to a reward, made the decisions as to who qualified for such marks of merit. Boys examined the proficiency of new pupils and assigned them to the appropriate class. Boys checked the names each day for absentees, wrote the notes to parents, to be delivered by other boys, and conducted truancy round-ups two or three times a week. Above all, boys taught other boys, and it was boys who inspected the work of those who taught. '. . . liveliness should never be repressed, but directed to useful ends; and I have ever found the surest way to cure a mischevious boy was to make him a monitor. I never knew anything succeed much better, if so well'.

All this was made possible by minute attention to organisational detail and by a strong sense of confidence exuding from Joseph Lancaster and pervading the whole school that, given genuine opportunities, boys could be trusted to show themselves responsible.

Each action that went on within the school Joseph subjected to a close analysis, breaking it down into a number of simple automatic steps.

The basic curriculum consisted of reading, writing which included spelling, arithmetic and religious instruction. Each class in any subject had a specific task to master, from the first reading class tracing its ABC in sand, to the 6th, 7th and 8th studying Testament, Bible and Selected Readers respectively.

It was not, in fact, the duty of the teaching monitors to instruct, but to see that pupils taught each other. In groups of ten or twelve, boys would stand in a semi-circle round an alphabet card hung on the wall. Tickets, numbered one to twelve, hung from jacket buttons, the best boy in the first place. On the monitor pointing to a letter on the card this boy would name it. If he got it wrong it was not the monitor's job to correct him, but to ask the next boy if he knew what the right answer was. If he did, then number tickets were exchanged, a place gained or forfeited.

The same method was used when it came to simple two or three letter words, and with numbers, though the composition of the cyphering groups was not necessarily the same as the reading groups. Single school books were cannibalised and the individual pages pasted on to card so that they could be hung on the wall to serve a whole class.

A complicated series of movements and commands was devised to make the changes from class to class as orderly as possible. Once again Joseph Lancaster had systematised the giving of orders so that a limited number of words was used and only those words. There is an interesting variation between his defence of this method of keeping discipline as it appeared in the 1805 edition of 'Improvements', and the reasons given in his biography thirty years later. In the latter he made no effort to deny the martial connection and the influences of old 'Green Eyes'. In 1805, having been a full member of the Society of Friends for only five years and with a large portion of his support coming from the pacifist Quakers, including the newly married Elizabeth Fry, he was more circumspect. 'It is not a desirable thing to raise the love of war and false glory in the youthful mind', so 'Go on' took the place of 'March', and signs substituted for 'Right' and 'Left'. 'When new boys come in they enjoy the novelty of orderly movement. They are allured into obedience and where individually they might object to being ordered about by a monitor, collectively they never do.'

Spelling and writing went together, the monitor reading out a word, often broken up into syllables, his group repeating it to themselves while at the same time writing it on a slate, a development that took place when the price of sand in London proved prohibitive. This method, rather than the old one where pupils spelt one at a time to the master while all the others 'were looking at their books or about them, as they pleased,' had the merit of preventing idleness and 'procuring that great desideratum of schools, quietness . . . for, as it requires much writing, but few boys can talk and write at the same time'.

There were two sorts of boys in the school; those learning to read, and those who had learnt. To the latter reading was not a study but a medium of instruction. '. . . a boy who can read, can teach, although he knows nothing about it; and, in teaching, will imperceptibly acquire the knowledge that he is destitute of, when he begins to teach, by reading.'

On the master's platform, visible to all and with every section of the school room visible to him, Joseph Lancaster superintended. 'It is very important, that in all those modes of teaching, the monitor cannot do as the watermen do, look one way and row another. His business is before his eyes; if he omits the smallest part of his duty, the whole circle are idle or deranged: and detection, by the master, immediately follows his negligence. In society at large, few crimes are ever committed openly; because immediate detection and apprehension of the offender would follow. On the contrary, many are committeed in privacy and silence. It is the same, in performing the simple duties of monitors in my institution: their whole performances are so visible, that they dare not neglect them; and, consequently, attain the habit of performing the task easily and well'.

It was not, however, fear of detection that kept the boys at their tasks. It was the spirit of competition and the certainty of recognition if their work was good.

Emulation and reward played a very important part in Joseph Lancaster's System. He believed that superior merit, on however small a scale or of however lowly a kind, should always be honoured. A series of paper tickets, numbered from one to five, were given for rising a place in class and could be taken back the next moment for losing that place again, for good manners, for cleanliness, for being helpful and any one of a dozen other acts. The tickets carried a monetary value; three number ones equalled a halfpenny; twelve number fives sixpence and could be cashed in at certain times for a prize of similar value. Joseph was profligate with prizes; books, bats, balls, kites, tops, pictures if he could find prints suitable for his children, and so on.

When a boy moved from one class to the next he got a prize and the monitor who had taught him received a commendation ticket. If this happened six times the monitor got a special prize. A bookbinder was asked to make some leather tickets, gilt and lettered differently for varying degrees of merit. These hung from a coat button and were highly valued. There were even a number of silver medals, distributed afresh each morning and afternoon, and forfeited for bad behaviour. They were worn round the neck, as a special order of merit, patterned on the monarch and his nobility. This flight of fancy was later criticised as leading to ambition and vanity in Joseph as much as in his pupils. But Sydney Smith, who visited the school, wrote: 'When we saw these ragged and interesting little nobles, shining in their tin stars, we only thought it probable that the spirit of emulation would make them better ushers, tradesmen and mechanics. We did, in truth, imagine we had observed in some of their faces a bold project for procuring better breeches for keeping out the blasts of heaven, which howled through those garments in every direction, and of aspiring hereafter to greater strength of seam and more perfect continuity of cloth. But for the safety of the titled orders we had no fear!'

If a boy had done really well, a letter was written to his parents. If a whole class excelled, then it could change places with the class above it. At the end of the day, or the week, Joseph would make a tally of tickets and commendations and hand out prizes; sometimes as many as two hundred so generous was he with encouragement. Then a procession formed and the boys marched proudly round the school room, displaying to themselves and to each other the trophies they had acquired. 'Honour is as powerful a motive as material gain.'

If honour was the spur to endeavour, shame was its counterpart.

Lancaster's punishment, in an age when brutal punishment was normal, came in for a disproportionate amount of comment and considerable adverse criticism. He had thought carefully about them, starting from the premise that 'Lively active-tempered boys are the most frequent transgressors of good order, and the most difficult to reduce to reason; the best way to reform them is by making monitors of them'.

However, vice and immorality were punishable offences; so too was talking because it prevented children learning. If punishments had to exist, then those that he advocated were preferable to the more severe of common practice, though, 'I wish that they were never in sole practice, without anything of a more generous nature existing in schools where they are made use of'.

The Lancastrian punishments were based on a principle of placing the offender in a conspicuous situation of public shame. There was the pillory, a wooden log tied round the neck: wooden shackles tying the legs together, after which the offender was made to parade round the schoolroom: the left hand tied behind the back, or both hands tied elbow to elbow behind the back: frequent offenders might be yoked together by the neck and made to walk round backwards. Most dreaded, and used only in extreme cases, was the 'bird in a cage', when the offender was suspended from the roof in a basket.

Disobedience to parents, immorality or slovenliness, merited being labelled with the offence, or crowned with a tin crown and paraded with a crier in front shouting out the cause of this exhibition. If habitually dirty, a public washing of the face was performed, with a member of the opposite sex doing the washing. Variety was important so that no punishment lost its effect by being too frequently applied. Truants might be tied up in a blanket and left in the school overnight.

But Joseph Lancaster had other ways of dealing with truancy, a perpetual problem for any serious school master.

'Several boys belonging to my school were in the habit of playing truant continually. The habit was contracted, as it usually is, by frequenting bad, idle company. One boy seemed quite incorrigible: his father got a log and chain, chained it to his foot, and in that condition, beating him all the way, followed him to school repeatedly. Nothing was of any avail . . . At last he was reformed by a contest about an old rusty nail. I am not fond of laying wagers; but without any other design than the improvement of two classes, by raising a spirit of emulation among them, I betted with one of my subordinate monitors, a shilling against an old rusty nail, that another class would excel in writing on the slate, that in which he taught. In case it did, the rusty old nail was to be mine; and the oddity of the thing tickled the fancy of the boys, and served as well for the bone of contention as anything else. Both classes were disposed to exert all their powers on the occasion, determined not to be excelled. I lost the wager in the sequel; but if it had been fifty times the value, it could not have had a better effect than it had. The truants I have been mentioning were in the two contending classes. The interest they took in the honour of their classes was so great, that instead of playing truant, they came to school, to aid their companions in securing the honour, which was more than the prize . . . they became pleased with the school; and, above all, the most incorrigible boy became reformed, and one of the best proficients in learning . . . for the two years after which he remained with me, no more was heard of his playing truant!'

For those who wished to run successful schools Joseph Lancaster contended that the passions of the human heart must be their study. His own school, after many false starts and much hard work, now resembled nothing so much as an orderly beehive, humming with activity, each member of the swarm engaged in fulfilling a task which he understood and knew came within his capabilities. Even Lancaster himself, who believed in his children, was surprised at the sense of responsibility they displayed. Society, who only knew the children of the poor as apathetic little slaves or unruly infant criminals, was amazed.

By 1803, when the first and second editions of 'Improvements' were published, Joseph Lancaster's school just off the Borough Road was becoming well known. With some ambiguity, for paying pupils were still accepted, he called it the Free School. There were about three hundred boys being educated and, under the superintendence of his older sister Mary, a girls' school had been started. In the third edition of 'Improvements' Joseph added a section on 'Female Education' which, while admitting that he had not much experience in this field, made plain his conviction that what applied to boys applied also to girls. Needlework took an important place in this curriculum. The introduction of Schools of Industry was also discussed; an idea which had had adherents at the end of the previous century, but had failed, largely because the industry drove out the schooling.

By taking a number of older boys to live with him, as 'House Lads', Joseph Lancaster had started a primitive form of teacher training. He had begun to make the idea of becoming a school master a desirable possibility, instead of the last available option.

There was a school circulating library of three hundred volumes calculated to improve the morals of youth, which could be used gratis. The accounts for 1802 show an item for thirty additional books. For any day school this was an unprecedented extension of classroom reading matter, particularly at a time when the New Testament and the Bible were considered all sufficient as textbooks and very little else was written specially for children. Mrs Trimmer, herself the mother of twelve, had tried to fill this gap with her own pen. Her 'Introduction to the Knowledge of Nature' and 'The Reading of the Holy Scriptures' appeared in the Free School library alongside Turner's 'Introduction to Arts and Sciences', Watts 'Hymns for Children', and anything else that Joseph considered might interest or edify his pupils. No doubt Andrew Bell's 'Experiment' was also on the shelves, for in the first edition of his own publication Lancaster acknowledged that he had discovered it in 1800 and it had been useful to him. It was priced at one shilling from Cadell and Davies in the Strand and he 'begged leave to recommend it to the attentive perusal of the friends of education and of youth. . .'

The next year a different item found a place in the accounts, with a note of apology to subscribers for what they might feel an unnecessary expense. This was for three hundred loads of rubbish, at 4d a load, for creating a playground next to the school. Joseph thought it very necessary that the children should have somewhere, other than the streets, where they could spend their free time and pupils who came from a distance could eat their dinners. Such a playground of their own attached them to the school and kept them from the unsavoury life of the evil smelling courts and lanes.

Sometime in the winter of 1802/3 the Free School Borough Road had its first aristocratic visitor, Lord Somerville, a representative peer with agricultural interests. He was introduced by the Quaker Edward Wakefield whose mother, the author Priscilla Wakefield, Joseph Lancaster knew. Soon these two men brought a more influential supporter. On March 1st 1803 Edward Wakefield sent a note to Joseph Lancaster 'to inform him that the Duke of Bedford, Lord Somerville and self will be at the school next day at 2 o'clock. Hopes all the boys will be in school'.

It had been, as usual, a bad winter. Coals for one cauldron cost £2.13.4d. Freezing temperatures, inadequate clothing and poor food had pinched already sallow faces and filled the schoolroom with coughing. But what he saw impressed the Duke with its simplicity and utility. He instantly decided that this 'humble but industrious Quaker' should be supported and became a subscriber and patron.

When the august inspection ended Joseph, taking an open, voluble and most unquakerlike pleasure in its success, dismissed his pupils and ran all the way to his father's house to cheer his mother with the news. En route he told anyone who cared to listen. This included a pious Friend who, to Joseph's astonishment and mortification, received these stupendous tidings with a solemn face as though they were a stumbling block. For Joseph this visit opened vistas of achievement, for the idea of universal education as well as for his school, his boys and himself. He saw good reason to rejoice.

The two noblemen's subscriptions were put at the head of a new list dedicated to enlarging the schoolroom. At least Joseph entered a rather small percentage of them there, for the Duke had given £100, an unspecified amount of which was to be used at Joseph Lancaster's discretion. The two names, however, quite regardless of the sum involved, were of great importance. Raising money was a laborious chore: '. . . it cost me much time, fatigue and walking many scores of miles. I had to seek aid from

the haughty and powerful, as well as the amicable and benevolent . . . the time spent thus in obtaining aid was so much lost to
the institution.' Many people had good excuses, in the biblical
fashion. 'One friend did not like to take the responsibility of
standing first in a subscription, upon himself. Another, very
properly, did not like to stand before his father, who was out of
town; and a third was indisposed.' So Lord Somerville and the
Duke of Bedford, prepared to accept Joseph Lancaster's priorities and with no hesitations about appearing at the top of the list,
were valued patrons.

The visit was also of great importance to Joseph's morale. He
complained that most of his friends, though willing to give a
certain amount of financial help, never actually came near the
institution. 'In fact those who befriended it most, either never
came to visit it, or never entered into its detail when they did.'
The Duke of Bedford had not only come, he had been interested
in how the System actually worked.

This was an age of patronage. From candidate for an unre-
formed Parliament to potential parson in a remote rural parish,
author, artist, locksmith, lawyer, schoolmaster, soldier, each
man if he was to have some success in life, needed a patron. In
the intricate network of what was still in essence an eighteenth
century society, patronage, with the Royal Family at the peak of
the pyramid, was power and an essential element in the pattern
of living. Virtually all social experiment or public relief of human
distress was financed by voluntary subscription. Many, though
possessed of birth and talent, depended on patronage; large
numbers found themselves in debtors prisons when it failed.

In its practice patronage made no fine distinction between
public benefaction and private benefit. Political corruption was a
fact of life; adulation of the aristocracy, even for staunch, plain
living Quakers like the chemist William Allen, normal. Andrew
Bell made his fortune in India by patronage; the same source was
to provide him with a respected and cushioned old age. Joseph
Lancaster lacked personal resources, such school fees as he
collected amounted to a bare pittance. Without patrons his work
could not have survived. Patrons too sought channels through
which to exercise and enlarge their influence. The evolving
Borough Road school and its energetic, visionary master provided that opportunity.

Others besides those with patronage to dispense began to find their way to the Free School, or now showed themselves willing, when called upon by Joseph Lancaster, to add their names to an increasingly illustrious subscription list. Some came because the spectacle of hundreds of ragged urchins teaching each other was a new and fashionable titillation. More importantly, and in far greater numbers, were those visitors of non-conformist creeds, Quakers and dissenters, who saw in this experiment a release from the hold of the Established Church over education. There were the supporters, some of them eminent Whig politicians, of education for the poor; and those, inspired by radical French thought, who perceived here the seed of a national education system. The social disciplinarians and the philanthropic liberals came too, and many who were none of these things but simply saw in what Joseph Lancaster had done the chance, at last, of an education for their own children or those of their community.

As early as 1804 there was even an enquiry from America. Thomas Eddy of New York, a Quaker active in social reforms and prominent in the effort to provide more schooling for the city, wrote to say that he had procured, through an English friend Patrick Colquhoun, police magistrate in London, copies of 'Improvements', and was having one thousand printed in New York. He asked for any future editions to be sent him, and also a copy of the 'tract published by Bell' which was not available in America.

At first the personality of Joseph Lancaster overshadowed the very real advances and advantages of his educational experiment. Early supporters admitted his success but denied the System a legitimacy of its own. Conditioned to an acceptance of youthful irresponsibility, they found it impossible to believe that the disciplined ordering of the school, on which everything depended, could exist if the all-seeing eye of the master was removed. But as the Borough Road bandwagon gathered momentum Joseph Lancaster, a formidable propagandist for his own System, was frequently away travelling, visiting, talking; above all talking. William Wilberforce wrote, 'I too lightly asked him to come in . . .' At this moment when the tide of creative excitement ran high, visitors who arrived at the Borough Road when he was absent, in the months before the public was requested to come only at stated hours, were surprised to see the school running smoothly under the surveillance of the monitor-general and the monitors; living proof that constructive use of young energies and the appeal to adolescent pride were as important components in Joseph Lancaster's achievement as the imposition of a mechanical System.

It was a later generation that began to criticise the System precisely because it was mechanical. In the early years of the nineteenth century, when industrial processes had begun to show what miracles could be achieved by mass production, and factories, to those who did not have to labour in them, presented dazzling glimpses of the possibilities of technical invention, the very mechanisms of the System were in themselves cause for admiration. It was this that promised to bring within reach the schooling for large numbers which a rising population and an increasing public concern were beginning to demand. It was the use of pupils themselves, under the supervision of a solitary master, that held out the hope of providing such an education for many thousands at a reasonable financial outlay; an important consideration when every penny had to come from men and women of goodwill. Where, in the beginning, the Lancastrian System had put the rate for the education of one child at a guinea a year, Joseph Lancaster was now claiming, though with very little evidence for the justice of his claim, to educate three or four for that same amount.

'A degree of confidence in our own powers is a useful and necessary incentive to action; but that confidence heightened by unusual success, frequently degenerates into self-conceit . . .' Joseph Lancaster had written in the first edition of 'Improvements'. Perhaps he recognised a weakness in his own character more clearly than his friends gave him credit for, and had begun to feel the pull of the temptations that accompany success. In five years he had gone from being an awkward, unknown, peculiar young man, running a ramshackle school for a few illiterate urchins in a workshop belonging to his petty tradesman father, to a position of some public fame, master of a flourishing, well run institution whose rapid expansion showed few signs of slowing down, acquainted with men in the highest rank of society and acknowledged to hold the key to a problem of national concern. Not all his Quaker principles could prevent hubris from lurking close at hand.

'Reading — after engraving in Improvements, 5th ed.'

Chapter 4
FRIENDS AND SUPPORTERS

'My maxim has been to dwell on the bright side of things.'
(Joseph Lancaster) ('Report of J. Lancaster's Progress . . .
RFS Press 1811')

Increasing worldly esteem and exposure to a highly sophisticated society with customs and values very different to those of Newington Causeway and the Borough, intensified strains and revealed weaknesses. In everything concerned with the physical aspects of schools, from the composition of classes to the exact dimensions, lighting and heating of schoolrooms, Joseph Lancaster was capable of meticulous organisation: in his dealings with young people he had an inspired touch: but when it came to financial considerations he lacked all sense of how to order money. His naturally optimistic temperament led him always to overestimate the elasticity of present substance or future promise; just as the vision which constantly beckoned him forward left little room for the more mundane considerations of consolidating foundations already laid. His notions of numbers, whether of people or pence, were always suspect.

By 1805 the list of subscribers for copies of 'Improvements' and to the various financial appeals of the Borough Road school, which included a buildings fund, a fund for the training of schoolmasters, and presently a printing press and slate manufactory, was long and exceedingly distinguished. Lord Somerville and the Duke of Bedford had been joined by Dukes and Countesses, Earls, Lords and Ladies, Members of Parliament, Archbishops, Bishops, Clergy, distinguished Quakers, a Chief Justice, well-known philanthropists and a long list of concerned, or simply good-hearted, men and women from all over the United Kingdom. It had become acceptable, even fashionable, to support Joseph Lancaster and the Free School Borough Road.

A more prudent, or perhaps a less naive, man would have suspected that such a foundation might prove too insubstantial to bear the proliferating stuctures he began to build on it. Though a later Duke was to take a stern view of the way his money was used, there is no evidence that the Duke of Bedford questioned the disposition of his hundred pounds, or protested that the flamboyance, which success and a bouyant spirit nurtured in Joseph Lancaster, was fed by the generosity of benefactors. Patrons liked to see an appearance of prosperity.

The fact was that the man Lancaster, the Lancastrian System, a concern for national education for the poor, and the Borough Road school were so tightly bound together in Joseph's mind, and indeed in the public mind too, as to be indistinguishable. The long hours of work, the total immersion in the development of this child of his brain and hands, the personal efforts to raise money, the bonds which made of pupils and master 'The Family', and now recognition, made it impossible for Joseph Lancaster to differentiate between himself and his creation.

'The Family' consisted of boys who lived in Joseph's house and those senior monitors whom he already saw as potential future teachers. This group developed many of the characteristics of a natural family, deep loyalties and a close comradeship arising out of shared experience, alternating with moments when propinquity exaggerated tensions and a difference of opinion was seen as betrayal. Though the name applied to an inner core, there were times when the school as a whole took on the aspect of an extended family.

The accounts for 1804 contain items for excursions with 180 boys to Clapham; 450 to the Green Park; to Greenwich, Sydenham and Kew with select parties. Of course both he and they had to be dressed for such expeditions into the haunts of the beau monde. Queen Charlotte had a house at Kew. They no longer always went on foot, though when moving in large numbers it is likely that they continued to do so. Joseph now sought new subscribers in a carriage, with some of his lads in one or two post chaises behind him: or made more intimate excursions, to dine and perhaps stay the night, with a few of his senior monitors. There was even a journey to Scotland, to visit the radical philanthropist Robert Owen at his New Lanark Mills, when Joseph Lancaster travelled not by stage coach but with four horses to his hired post chaise. No wonder Quaker friends pursed their lips and preached heart-searching humility.

Then there were 'sundries, for encouragement of children'. 'Gingerbread, nuts, apples, oranges, cherries etc. for scrambles'; several thousand toys, bats and balls, kites and so on, cost £16.6.0d. John Pickton, whose name was to stand first on the earliest register of Borough Road trained masters, came to the school at this time.

'Improvements,' sold entirely by subscription, was doing well. This too confused the financial issue, for Lancaster was the author of 'Improvements'; that he put the money gained into the institution did not alter the fact that this was also almost his only source of personal income, that from fees being drastically reduced by the extension of the free school principle.

In the heady excitement of public acclaim Joseph made plans to enlarge the Borough Road school to seven hundred boys, 'at a very trifling expence above the estimate' which had been £180, and suggested to the Duke of Bedford that for a further £300 he could raise the numbers to one thousand, including the school for two hundred girls. So the magic number of 'One Thousand Children, taught and governed by one Master only', which was to ring triumphantly through the institution's broadsheets, came into being.

But even Joseph Lancaster, for all his euphoria, recognised that he was stretching his resources beyond their limits. In 1804 he got a mortgage on his premises, possibly from Samuel Rogers the poet, who was later bitterly to complain of non-repayment.

Sometime about this year too Lancaster met William Corston.

William Corston was a successful straw plait manufacturer from Fincham in Norfolk, now living in Ludgate Hill. He presented to George III the first Leghorn hat made in England, which Queen Charlotte wore, starting a fashion which greatly benefited the manufacturer and resulted in his being given a gold medal by the Society of Arts.

A simple, good-hearted man, William Corston was very interested in education. In 1779, walking from Deptford to Greenwich, he had noticed an inscription: 'To the Glory of God and the benefit of poor children this school was erected by Dean Stanhope', and had resolved to be connected with such an institution himself one day. Twenty-five years later, making sensible use of his own occupation, he started a school of industry and instruction in his native village. But when he met Joseph Lancaster for the first time, having heard of his work and written to him, he was overwhelmed.

The thing that surprised William Corston was Joseph's youth. He must himself have been about twenty years older and what he had heard of the Borough Road school and its founder had clearly impressed him as being the work of a contemporary. The discovery that here was a man who could have been his son added to his admiration, and when he visited the school he was captivated by it. He immediately put his name down for fifty copies of 'Improvements', at five shillings each, and over the next few months took another three hundred. He also made a most generous offer to 'stand in the gap' if funds at any time failed to meet needs. The offer was accepted. Over the next thirty years William Corston was to prove himself a faithful friend to Joseph Lancaster, and financial backer to an extent which he could never originally have imagined.

Another man, who was to be influential in Joseph Lancaster's life, also came to see the school about this time. Francis Place, though his family too was that of a small tradesman, was very different in character from William Corston, and in temperament from Joseph Lancaster.

Francis Place began his working life apprenticed to a leather-breeches maker. A boy, and then a young man, of exceptionally orderly mind and a hard, disciplined worker, he early decided that he would make enough money by the time he reached middle life to be able to give up his trade and devote his time to the intellectual pursuits that interested him. It was a ferocious struggle but by his mid-forties he had achieved his aim and through private study and active membership of several trades clubs and, notably, the London Corresponding Society, he had made himself known and greatly respected among political thinkers.

A man of reason, he was frightened of passion and emotionalism, perhaps because he himself had a fiery temper: a committee man, who loathed publicity and found public oratory distasteful, he nevertheless craved power. His intelligence, his meticulous observation, his appetite for the collection and recording of facts made him much sought after by politicians, whose strategy inside Parliament was often laid down and directed from Francis Place's small library just off the Strand. Possessed of a strong sense of his own probity, he found it difficult to accept that others might occasionally be right! The greatest virtue he thought to be perseverance. Anti-monarchist and an atheist, he had no hesitation in making those views known if the situation seemed to demand it, even in company where they would be condemned as heresies.

A friend of Jeremy Bentham and James Mill, known to Henry Brougham, later to become Lord Chancellor, and to the Members of Parliament Samuel Whitbread and Samuel Romilly, Francis Place was interested, as they were, in the education system.

Unlike more fashionable visitors, there is little doubt that Francis Place inspected the Borough Road and its master with a detached, critical eye. He did not record his first impressions of Lancaster's school, but they were certainly favourable for he became a contributor to the extent of half a guinea monthly, quite a considerable sum for a man who was never more than adequately comfortably off financially.

On June 5th 1804, Joseph Lancaster, Southwark Schoolmaster, married Elizabeth, daughter of Henry and Abigail Bonner, at Red Cross Street, Southwark. Mrs Trimmer, who did not care for Friends, called the bride 'a pretty Quaker'.

Joseph had first seen the girl who became his wife as a pupil at the school to which he had originally gone as assistant master. She was then about sixteen and had been recalled from a Friend's Boarding School because her father had gone bankrupt. Much later Joseph found her again in a shop where he had gone to buy pencils. She was warm-hearted, attractive and deeply in love.

Joseph was a natural family man, with memories of a happy parental home. He felt the need of a woman at the centre of his life, complementing his own role in dealings with his pupils. Elizabeth was no doubt dazzled by his fine physical presence, his energy and his growing fame, and lacked the perspicacity to arrive at a true estimate of the character of the man who by dedication and commitment, and a talent for public relations, had brought the Borough Road school into being. She certainly had little idea of the demands that would be made on her nervous system when she plunged into the realities of living with such a husband. She was admiring, compliant and literate. Joseph took it for granted that, as his mother had done, she could keep house, organise the daily routine, and feel as he did about the triumphs, and even the disasters, of educational pioneering. He gave up the Sunday School, which he had conducted for six years, perhaps to have the Sabbath at least with his wife. But he expected her to come into the centre of his ready-made 'Family', to live in the hurly-burly of boys and visitors, and uncertain domestic and financial arrangements. Even to stay with friends and relatives while he travelled round. Each married in good faith, but the union was to prove a tragedy for poor Elizabeth and a disaster for Joseph Lancaster.

The pace was quickening. The day after the wedding Joseph addressed a letter to the Duke and Duchess of York, soliciting a subscription. Two months later he was writing to Elizabeth, who was staying with relatives at Rochester, of having slept the night at Earl Stanhope's country seat at Chevening and being kindly received by Lady Donegal at Tunbridge Wells; of a fruitful Quaker Meeting at Maidstone and the way the boys cheered him when he arrived back at the school, 'till I was obliged to go aside to vent my tears which thou mayest think were not tears of sorrow'.

In November the crowning achievement took place. Joseph Lancaster met King George III. Through the most highly placed of his supporters he had been trying for some time to be presented. He dined at Leonard's Hill near Windsor with General Sir William Harcourt to whom he had a letter of introduction from Lord Somerville. Joseph mentioned his desire to see the King and the General took him into the Castle Yard to watch George III mount his horse when he came out to exercise.

Placed between General Harcourt and the Honourable Charles

Villiers, Joseph Lancaster was in a strategic position when the Royal Party came into the yard. The King moved round greeting some of those known to him, including General Harcourt. Noticing Joseph Lancaster he enquired who he was. On being told he turned to Joseph who, unabashed and continuing to wear his hat as was the Quaker custom, immediately addressed his Sovereign in words expressing a subject's loyalty and humble hopes for His Majesty's welfare and preservation. The King asked, 'Mr Lancaster how does your school go on?' To which Joseph replied, 'Under the blessing of Divine Providence it goes well'.

As he had hurried to tell his parents when first visited by Lord Somerville and the Duke of Bedford, so now Joseph hastened to let his old friend 'and father', Thomas Urwick of Clapham, know of this latest triumph. The King had been affected and shed a tear. 'This interview led to much enquiry and conversation in the Evening at the Castle respecting the institution, and one who honours thee as a friend of his unguarded youth. The King told the Queen of the event, and some of my friends are not without hopes that this event will lead to something of more importance'. A prodigious publicist and letter writer, it was not going to be Joseph's fault if it did not.

In December 1804 another meeting of significance took place. Joseph Lancaster met Andrew Bell in Swanage.

Hindsight and partisanship slanted all subsequent accounts of this encounter; even the principals themselves altered their own descriptions of it within a few months. In the winter of 1804, however, before too many outside influences had been brought to bear, it would seem that these two men came together without jealousies or animosities, on ground common to them both. In November Joseph had written to Andrew Bell, as befitted a young man of twenty-six to his elder of fifty-one, asking for information and advice. 'I had hoped and intended long before this, to have done myself the pleasure of coming down to Swanage, in order to take a lesson from thy superior experience . . .' He then set out the reasons why, although he had stumbled on a plan similar to Andrew Bell's he had not yet succeeded to the extent that he might have hoped.

'1st – mine being a day school, the children are much at their parents' command, are often absent, or attend late – an evil that could not possibly occur at the Madras Asylum, or in any well regulated boarding school, where all the scholars begin their lessons together, being assembled at one time.

'2nd – the price of sand in London, 9s, the load, and the room it takes to teach a great number of children by that method. This induced me to substitute slates with many of the classes.

'3rd – The poverty and bad principles of the children's parents often operated to hinder their learning, by removing their monitors to place (work) or other schools, by being prejudiced against the plan of a school taught by boys, and by their bad example and ignorance.

'4th – By having, when I opened it as a free school . . . not only the school, but the funds to establish, and no individual to assist me with advice, influence or capital . . . If thou wilt favour me with any original reports of the Asylum at Madras . . . I should be much obliged.'

On December 6th Andrew Bell replied:

'I had before heard of your fame, and the progress which you had made in a new mode of tuition, and have long expected the pleasure of seeing you at Swanage . . . I shall endeavour to find my original reports at Madras, that I may communicate them, but you will not meet with the details you expect . . . When I began this letter, I meant only to acknowledge your acceptable communication, to request the favour of a visit from a friend, with whom I can indulge and revive my old and favourite pursuits, almost forgotten, in this insulated situation in which I am placed: and to say that I would not fail to visit your Institution, as soon as I can make it convenient to be in London . . . your letter has revived and renovated old ideas and I have written as to an old friend.' He added that he had been strongly urged to republish 'Experiment' and asked Joseph Lancaster to do him the favour of drawing his pen through every line that he felt might be spared in it, 'taking care to efface whatever is not necessary to give an idea of the system of instruction'. In a second edition he might be able to recommend the Borough Road Institution, but to do this 'I must see everything with my own eyes . . . I am most anxious to see your book, and still more to see yourself'.

A week later Joseph Lancaster wrote:

'I have not answered thy most acceptable letter, because I intend being at Swanage within four or five days, to pass two or three days with thee, if, under the blessing of Providence my health and the roads admit of travelling'.

So the scene was set for an interesting and amicable meeting between colleagues each of whom, in a pattern constantly recurring in human affairs, had separately stumbled on an idea which promised to extend the limits of current social thinking.

The differences between the Lancastrian System and that of Andrew Bell were not very great. Joseph Lancaster did not dispute that the older man had first made use of pupils as assistants, nor did Andrew Bell withhold admiration of the way in which his junior had developed the application of this theory.

When Andrew Bell chose out John Friskin to help in the reorganisation of the Madras Asylum, he had also paired off the boys into tutors and pupils, couples sitting side by side, the abler boy assisting the younger. Assistant teachers, themselves pupils, had been appointed to instruct and help the tutors, above them the teacher in charge overlooked the work of the assistant teachers; then came the schoolmaster, always an adult and the Superintendent. The emphasis of the system was the same as Lancaster's, tuition by the scholars themselves.

Andrew Bell kept a register of Daily Tasks as an aid to discipline, and a Black Book in which all law breaking appeared. Offenders were tried by a jury of their peers. Andrew Bell too had directed his pupils' play, and taught them swimming; the latter sometimes through deliberate terror, if they were frightened he threw them into deep water. Reading, writing, cyphering and religion, conforming to the creed of the Anglican Church, had been the basis of the curriculum. His method of breaking down words into syllables to teach spelling had been taken over, with acknowledgments, by Lancaster.

Though one or two attempts had been made to transplant the Madras model, particularly into his own old school in Scotland, Andrew Bell himself had been uncertain of its more universal validity. It was Joseph Lancaster's success that brought home to him the wider possibilities.

Joseph Lancaster came to Swanage and stayed a night or two at the Rectory. It would have been unnatural if there had not been animated discussion or the flash of temper. Both were passionate and possessive men; each was certain of the value to others of his own ideas.

Andrew Bell was not too pleased by Joseph Lancaster's attempts to get him to subscribe to 'Improvements'. They discussed the training of teachers, upon which there were radical differences. Andrew Bell objected to Joseph Lancaster's advocacy of 'Forming his teachers by lectures on the passions', an interesting comment perhaps indicating a facet with which Lancaster is not often credited, a tentative search towards a form of educational psychology.

Andrew Bell preferred a more authoritarian and practical method, 'not by lectures and abstract instruction', though here there was a difference in objective, for Bell was thinking of his young tutors and assistants within his school while Lancaster was already concerned with teachers who would go out and set up schools of their own.

Nevertheless, Andrew Bell admitted that Joseph Lancaster had greatly contributed to the cause of the monitorial school. 'In his hands this beautiful system has the advantage of being conducted with admirable temper, ingenuity, and ability; and he discovers much contrivance and even wit, in the ramifications of its application'. Joseph, when he left, was still deferential. The 3rd edition of 'Improvements', published the next year, though lacking the generous tribute to Dr Bell in the first two, acknowledged his invention of the syllabic system.

Four months later, in April 1805, Andrew Bell came to London. He presented Joseph Lancaster with fifty copies of the revised Madras Report which had doubled in size since 1797. Joseph Lancaster, with some ceremony, sent a deputation of his scholars to thank him. Andrew Bell came to the Borough Road to see the school, presumably on a Monday, Wednesday, Thursday or Friday at three o'clock, which were the public hours, with prior notice in writing. He again refused a subscription, but said he would take four copies of the new edition of 'Improvements' due out in July. Joseph Lancaster, who hoped to make at least two hundred pounds from this venture, was disappointed. Already relations had begun to deteriorate.

Joseph Lancaster's confidence was in no danger of being undermined by this coolness. Royal patronage, the summit of philanthropic ambition, was within his grasp. Through aristocratic supporters he had sent papers, pamphlets, copies of 'Improvements', to the Royal Household, to keep warm the interest that he hoped had been kindled at the first meeting at Windsor. In August 1805, when he was at Weymouth, where the King and his family were taking the sea air, Joseph received a summons to the Royal presence.

This time it was a proper interview. He arrived at Royal Lodge at 2.30 pm, and was shown upstairs. There was a contretemps about his Quaker hat. '. . . my conductor finding that there was an adhesion between my hat and my head rather common among persons seriously professing with me, after eyeing the union of the said parties a little, laid soft hands on my hat and made per force an amicable separation, by taking the said hat off my head and carrying it down stairs not with a polite apology for this interference. As however my heart was in the right I did not care about my hat being in the wrong place and only returned his civility with a smile . . .'

After that everything went swimmingly. The King had Queen Charlotte and his five daughters with him and showed a genuine interest in the work of the school.

William Corston, writing in his eighties, when those halycon days were long gone, gave an account of this meeting which may owe something to dramatic reconstruction, but accords reasonably well with contemporary fragments.

The King said: 'Lancaster, I have sent for you to give me an account of your System of Education. One master teach five hundred children at the same time? How do you keep them in order, Lancaster?'

Joseph Lancaster: 'Please Thy Majesty, by the same principle Thy Majesty's army is kept in order – by word of command.'

The King said: 'Good, good; it does not require an aged general to give the command – one of younger years can do it'.

On Joseph then describing his System the King said: 'Lancaster I highly approve of your system, and it is my wish that every poor child in my domain should be taught to read the Bible; I will do anything you wish to promote this object'.

'Please Thy Majesty,' Joseph answered, 'If the System meets Thy Majesty's approbation, I can go through the country and lecture on the System, and have no doubt, but in a few months, I shall be able to give Thy Majesty an account where ten thousand poor children are being educated and some of my youths instructing them.'

'Lancaster,' said the King, 'I will subscribe £100 annually,' and to the Queen, 'you shall subscribe £50 Charlotte; and the Princesses £25 each. Lancaster you may have the money directly.'

In voicing his thanks Joseph Lancaster could not help adding:

'Please Thy Majesty, that will be setting thy nobles a good example.' According to William Corston, the Royal party smiled. The Duke of Kent, who was present added his own £10.

When shown downstairs afterwards 'a person paid the King's subscription directly'. The Queen sent hers and those of the five Princesses later. Joseph was introduced to the Duke of Cumberland and made much of by people of importance. He wrote to Elizabeth that the whole Family had subscribed 'for several schools I am going to establish at Royal Command' and sent her his dear love, and love to his Father, Mother, sisters and 'my boys'. In presenting his petition to the King that same day, August 19th, his message had been, 'Two thousand pounds and some waste land to build on would immediately enable thy petitioner to establish schools in the country, at Weymouth and elsewhere for Ten Thousand children'.

He was, as always, over-optimistic, but the Royal subscriptions were real enough. Joseph's feelings were much affected by the kindness of the King, who was a man without pretensions and no doubt gave him the impression that His Majesty could be treated like a valued personal friend. An anecdote of a later date, when opposition was steadily growing, related by another friend David Holt, seems to bear this out.

Visiting Windsor one day Joseph Lancaster, seeing the numbers of uncared for children running about the streets, called on one of the deans and, in a friendly way, mentioned this to him. He also told the dean that he, Joseph Lancaster, proposed to call a town meeting and deliver a lecture which would result in the opening of a school for these neglected urchins.

Affronted at being approached in this way the dean said: 'Pray Mr Lancaster, mind your own business. We are quite as well qualified to educate our own poor as you are.' To which Joseph Lancaster replied, 'I know you are, but you don't do it'.

'Sir,' answered the dean, 'the countenance you have received from the King and other exalted characters has given you a confidence which you do not know how discreetly to use. My friends, the archbishops and bishops, assure me that you will not much longer be favoured with His Majesty's support.'

'If I do lose the King's countenance,' replied Joseph Lancaster, 'I have no doubt that it will be occasioned by the interference of thy friends, the archbishops and bishops: but as the King is here, I will before I leave Windsor, ascertain whether he is with me or not.'

The dean was greatly alarmed at this bold assertion and attempted to prevent any such proceeding taking place. But, undeterred, Joseph Lancaster went up to the castle and asked to see the King. He was granted an audience and related what had passed.

'No Lancaster,' said the old King, 'you have not lost my countenance. You are a good man and have done much to benefit my poor subjects; you may therefore count on my support, but you must not tease these men; let them alone – never mind them – never mind them.'

Obtaining royal support and interest represented a major coup and it rang alarm bells in many Anglican vicarages.

The Royal hundred pounds was a handsome gesture, but the expectations of affluence and security which it aroused were by no means sustained by a parallel growth in the subscription list. The fact was that, after an initial surge, subscribers were beginning to fall off. Some complained that now there were so many great names their 'mites' would no longer be needed; others, no doubt, had found fresher ventures to encourage, new diversions to taste; many promised but never fulfilled. But Joseph Lancaster, royal patronage achieved, was launched on a pathway of expansion which took little account of financial constraints.

A printing press was set up in the Borough Road school, with the understandable aims of providing training in a trade and at the same time producing, with a minimum of expense, Lancaster's own writings, school books and other related materials, the profit from which could be ploughed back into the institution. The idea seemed sound, but somehow the profit failed to materialise. A slate manufactory was set up, to service the Borough Road school and also the other schools which it was hoped would be started with Borough Road teachers; the theory of simply influencing existing schools to use the Lancastrian System having already been superseded. From the beginning the endeavour lost money. But most expensive of all, while at the same time most vital to Joseph Lancaster's whole concept, was the centre for training schoolmasters.

In 1805 Joseph Lancaster had about eight lads and several young men in training. They lived with him, he fed them, saw that they were properly clothed and generally made himself responsible for their well-being. Most were senior pupils from his own school, some were sent by sponsors, anxious to start a school in their neighbourhood; only those who subscribed ten pounds or more could have a Lancaster-trained master for schools which they planned to set up.

Financially Joseph Lancaster was caught in a trap of his own making. Much of his publicity emphasised the cheapness of operating the System, but sponsors naturally wished this benefit to extend also to their part of the enterprise, and Joseph Lancaster himself was blinded to the real costs of the work, partly by his own financial incapacity and partly by the necessity of keeping his sponsors happy.

But the training of teachers, whatever the real cost, was of major importance. This was the tool that would spread the work over the United Kingdom and indeed much further afield. It was Lancaster trained teachers, who knew the System, who were going to raise the status of the schoolmaster and change the face of education for the poor. On them depended the future, for without them the Borough Road school, however well organised and publicised, might have turned out to be a nine days wonder. So, although extravagant optimism and possessive pride both resulted in Joseph greatly overestimating the potential of the institution for training teachers in those early years – 'it seems probable that when I have had a little more practice and experience in the art of training men to a knowledge of their duty as schoolmasters, hundreds of persons might be properly qualified, in an expeditious manner, and at a trifling expense' – the need for such training was indisputable and the thinking valid.

It was in 1805 too that Joseph Lancaster began to dwell on the idea of a rural school and training institution, to complement the urban Borough Road, on land belonging to the Duke of Somerset at Maiden Bradley.

It was mainly to the Duchess that Joseph Lancaster communicated his hopes and plans for this new project. On August 9th, because the Duchess was just recovering from her confinement, the Duke wrote to say that the schoolroom at Bradley was nearly finished, and that he would be willing to allow the master a salary and a house, though he recognised this would not be sufficient without extra means. He added his good wishes for the success of the venture, but he was not very hopeful. The common people were mostly ignorant and did not wish to learn. He doubted whether there was so much need for literacy in the country anyway. The Duchess had sent some of the estate children to a school in the village and after two years they still did not know their letters.

Joseph had much larger plans than this, which he confided in a letter to the Duchess when she had recovered. She and the Duke clearly thought they were attracting Joseph Lancaster himself to take up semi-permanent residence on their acres, and at this date, early September 1805, he concurred in this arrangement. He expressed himself gratified by the care they had taken about the place for his dwelling, certainly it was best that he should live near though he expressed surprise that they should have had the premises valued. The Duke, as it was to turn out, liked to know what was happening to his money.

Joseph Lancaster showed himself willing to accept a loan from the Duke for the rent of the 'house, college and garden and the fields adjoining', with the provision that he could give up part of them if things did not turn out as he hoped. He also wanted a clause in the lease entitling him to renewal in case they did.

'I mention this as if Maiden Bradley is to be the chief seat of my country operations, it is probable I may found there an Economy nearly similar to those established by the Moravians but with more emulation interwoven in its system. This will require more buildings which will be erected on plans laid down by myself as occasion may occur – and in this case I shall naturally desire a conditional interest in the land for a term of time in proportion to the improvements I may make on it, but which I am not prepared at present absolutely to promise I will.'

He also wanted a considerable acreage of waste land belonging to the Duke on which the children could grow food. Given the land a thousand children could be 'as easily boarded and maintained by their own exertions at Maiden Bradley as they could simply be educated in London'.

He had thoughts of bringing down with him a number of other people; a pious Friend who had a business that might employ about forty persons, a steady and accomplished old lady and her daughter to look after his household concerns, Mr Taylor, carpenter in Southwark, to live in the village and teach his trade. It was a colony of industry that he visualised, such as William Allen twenty years later established at Lindfield. Even had everything gone well it is unlikely that, given Joseph Lancaster's other commitments, such a grandiose scheme could ever have come into being. As it was it never stood a chance.

'I expect an addition to my family daily', Joseph had written in this same letter. He was delighted, but already there were portents of tragedy in his home life. Faced with the turmoil and uncertainties inherent in marriage to a man who spent much time travelling the country, alternating between the demands of aristocratic society to which he was quite unaccustomed and the close and affectionate company of his boys, living always at a fever pitch of emotional stimulation, Elizabeth Lancaster was already showing signs of an inability to cope. On September 8th her daughter, Elizabeth, to be known as Betsy, was born at James Street, Borough Road. She was destined to be Joseph Lancaster's only child, the light of his life and the apple of his eye. Her birth may have hastened the disintegration under stress which was shortly to overtake her mother, eventually resulting in Elizabeth Lancaster being pronounced incurably insane. His wife's incarcerations in the private care of various friends and medical men were to form a bitter counterpoint to the next fifteen years of Joseph Lancaster's life. As he wrote to the Duchess of Somerset, 'this seems such a damp on all my joys, on every prospect of domestic comfort . . . nothing but religion can help'.

'Mrs Sarah Trimmer — after portrait by Henry Howard'

Chapter 5
THE CHURCH MILITANT

'I heard he was very angry and said S. Trimmer was a bigot.'
(Mrs Trimmer to Andrew Bell)

It was Mrs Trimmer who rallied the cohorts of the Church Militant.

Sarah Trimmer was sixty-four in 1805, when she began to fear that Joseph Lancaster presented a real threat to 'Church and Crown'. Born Sarah Kirby, she was the daughter of Joseph Kirby, originally from Ipswich, friend of Gainsborough and Reynolds, Hogarth and Dr Johnson, who in 1759 had been appointed Clerk of Works to the Royal Household at Kew Palace. Both Joseph Kirby and his father wrote books; Sarah, who had some school education and was proficient in English and French, was to follow in their footsteps. She was a somewhat smug, pious girl who had once impressed Dr Johnson by producing a copy of 'Paradise Lost' from her pocket.

At the age of twenty-one Sarah Kirby met and married James Trimmer of Brentford who, with his father, owned a brick and tile works in Kew. The union resulted in twelve children, six sons and six daughters, in whose education their mother took a great interest; indeed much of it she conducted herself. This close involvement in teaching the young led to a concern with the wider question of schooling and, finding that very few suitable books existed for children, she began to write, setting down in simple language the great truths of Christianity and the Anglican creed as well as stories of birds and animals. Her first work was an 'Easy Introduction to the Knowledge of Nature'.

Once begun she proved a prodigious authoress. She extended her range and became known as an educational authority, printing a quarterly, 'The Guardian of Education', to act as a critical enquirer into the increasing number of publications for the use of children. She also originated and edited 'The Family Magazine' addressed to cottagers and servants. Her books were admitted to the SPCK list of material for Charity Schools. Some of her volumes were used at the Borough Road and appeared on Joseph Lancaster's library shelves. Their contents were simple and sensible, adhering without question to the custom and practice of the time. In 1797 her best known work appeared, 'The Oeconomy of Charity'. The first edition sought support for Sunday Schools; the second, dedicated to Queen Charlotte set out, by examples of things already happening, how 'ladies can involve themselves in assisting the poor; especially in the field of education'.

In 1786 Sarah Trimmer herself had opened Sunday Schools in Brentford, to which she later added a School of Industry. The latter was not a success. Business management was not her forte any more than it was Joseph Lancaster's.

By 1805 this plump, homely widow considered herself the arbiter of education for the poor and the defender of the Church of England. Simple both in her outlook and her intellect, the soft elderly face under the frilly white cap concealed stubbornness of purpose and an invincible conviction that what she knew and practiced was unquestionably right. For one who stirred up one of the major controversies of the first years of the nineteenth century, she was curiously averse to argument. She did not like to disturb her mind by conning disputatious books, so at no time did she read or consider opinions contrary to her own. Of the rightful supremacy of the Church of England, in both religious and civil matters, she had no doubt at all.

Certainly from the moment his school began to attract attention, Mrs Trimmer had her eye on Joseph Lancaster. She it was who, in her publications, pronounced on educational matters and her views were widely regarded. Her public looked to her for critical assessment of the young man beginning to make a stir in this field. The fact that he was a Quaker made watchfulness all the more imperative.

For his part Joseph Lancaster respected Mrs Trimmer's writings. Her volumes held a valued place on shelves where books addressed specifically to children were all too rare. He recognised the importance of her influence. In 1803 he sent her a copy of the first edition of 'Improvements'. She noticed it in the 'Guardian of Education', '(page 117 I think) . . . I heard he was very angry and said, S. Trimmer was a bigot . . .' she wrote to Andrew Bell.

Mrs Trimmer did not take this stricture lightly. She had a 'warm debate' with Mrs Priscilla Wakefield, also an authoress, when she was introduced to her in April 1804, on the dangers to the Church of mixing children of different religious professions, and the want of instruction in the forms of the establishment. Priscilla Wakefield urged her to visit the Borough Road school, and Mrs Trimmer admitted that her criticisms might have been too harsh. '. . . notwithstanding her bigotry I must allow her to be a good woman', Mrs Wakefield wrote to Joseph.

That was in April: Mrs Trimmer must have visited the school shortly after, for in June she wrote to Joseph Lancaster thanking him for the compliment he had paid her in adopting her books as part of his plan and suggesting she make another visit at the end of that week to see the use he actually made of the books in such a large school. The letter was dated June 4th, the day before his wedding. Elizabeth Lancaster was plunged into the centre of controversy before she was a week-old bride.

It is important to stress that it was not with the practice, but with the principle that Joseph Lancaster's early critics took issue. It was precisely because the practice was so successful that the principle became dangerous. Sarah Trimmer was 'highly gratified' with the orderly sight that greeted her at the institution. 'He sat upon his throne, I may call it, like a king ready to receive the homage of his subjects, and in speaking to me of his boys who are distinguished by the insignia of his 'Order of Merit', he actually said, 'These are my nobles'. But this was not what she admired. 'The quietness and diligence of the whole school were what pleased me; nor could I help being diverted with the military movements of his little soldiers . . .' She had, after all, a long experience of teaching both her own and Sunday School scholars and she knew how difficult it was to achieve a quiet atmosphere in which young people could learn.

Sarah Trimmer, however, did not mince words when it came to the all-embracing Christian basis of Joseph Lancaster's educational design. 'I took the freedom of telling him then, that I thought the plan altogether not favourable to the Established Church . . .' Perhaps she thought that a quiet word from one old enough to be his grandmother would bring the young man, Quaker though he was, to see the error of his ways.

He did not. That 'education ought not to be made subservient to the propagation of the peculiar tenets of any sect, beyond its own number' was a fundamental ground of belief for him. To abandon it would have been impossible. He did not mind denominations educating their own, but that the Established Church should claim the right to oversee the religious education of those who were dissenters, or create, through its own negligence, an educational vacuum for the children of the poor, he would never allow.

Though his mind was neither profound nor intellectual, Joseph Lancaster was curious about the world, an avid reader, interested in acquiring knowledge. A true teacher, it was these gifts that he wished to pass on to his children. Charity Schools, Schools of Industry, Sunday Schools, were all designed to educate children for certain primary purposes; to make them better servants or 'mechanics', as a social restraint, to bring them up within the fold of a particular creed. Joseph Lancaster's aims were, though perhaps unconsciously, very different. Under his influence the Borough Road school stressed the excitement and interest that came with learning to read and write. Books, other than the Bible, were available and prized. The only future occupation for his children that Joseph Lancaster cared to emphasise was schoolmastering; because through the Lancastrian System they would spread the message that literacy could unlock the doors of knowledge for every child whatever their eventual work or status.

All the same, optimistic as ever, Joseph Lancaster must have convinced himself that even Mrs Trimmer would come to see the essential sanity of his path. After his marriage he and his principal monitors, taking the bride with them, marched in procession to Brentford to pay their respects to the matriarch. It was an amicable meeting and they parted 'in a very friendly manner'.

Mrs Trimmer was not placated. All her instincts in defence of tradition and customs were alerted. Already contemplating a critical pamphlet, she went once more to see Joseph Lancaster to warn him that she was going to enter into public controversy. Somewhat light-heartedly, and as it happened quite falsely, he answered that he would not take offence. He reserved the right to reply.

Everything about him had begun to annoy her. He ordered some tiles for his new schoolroom from her son who ran the tile factory. 'His seal carried the impression of PEACE!' she commented indignantly. Some time later, ignoring her warning of the duel to come, Joseph wrote and asked if he could put her name on his list of subscribers. She refused. She had already convinced herself that his Quaker profession was not genuine and perhaps Joseph's flamboyant and extrovert behaviour gave her ground for this unfounded suspicion. The kindness of his reception by the Royal Family, the heart of the aristocratic establishment of which she and her connections were servants and admirers, must have deeply alarmed her.

It was Joseph Lancaster's 'Improvements' that first brought Andrew Bell's 'Experiments' to Mrs Trimmer's notice. When she read the latter she saw to her hand the instrument that she could use both to discredit Lancaster and to encourage the Church to take hold, on its own account, of this new educational plan. She set herself to revitalise that respectable cleric, Andrew Bell.

In September 1805 she wrote to tell him that a notice of his work would appear in the next 'Guardian of Education'. 'From the time, sir, that I read Mr Joseph Lancaster's 'Improvements in Education' in the first edition, I conceived an idea that there was something in his plan that was inimical to the interests of the Established Church, and, when I read your 'Experiment in Education', to which Mr Lancaster referred, I plainly perceived that he had been building on your foundation . . . Engaged as I long have been in striving to promote the interests of the Church by the exertions of my little talents for the instruction of the rising generation, and the prevention of mischief that is aimed against them in various ways, I cannot see this 'Goliath of Schismatics' bearing down all before him, and engrossing the instruction of the common people, without attempting to give him a little check.'

Andrew Bell did not immediately rise to Mrs Trimmer's challenge. He was susceptible to flattery, but he had already amassed his fortune and was well provided with the influential contacts that he valued. For himself he was looking to a comfortable benefice, preferably where he could be an absentee occupant and the possibility of a stall at Westminster, rather than the active promotion of an educational plan. He had come to a time of life when enjoyment of what he had was more important than the ardours of pioneering in fresh fields. Though influenced by Mrs Trimmer's view of Joseph Lancaster as a conceited upstart, he nevertheless was not dissatisfied to leave the hard work of propagating the monitorial system in his hands.

In his reply to her letter Andrew Bell described the Lancaster visit to Swanage in terms clearly coloured by her opinion of his visitor. 'I observed his consummate front, his importunate solicitation of subscriptions in any and every shape, his plausible and ostentatious guise . . .'; but he added, 'The monitorial plan appears to me, who am an enthusiast, so simple, so natural, so beautiful and true, that it must sooner or later have obtained a footing; and all I ever expected by my humble essay, printed rather than published, was that it might fall into hands that would bring the system forward sooner than might otherwise happen in the course of things. Joseph Lancaster has certainly contributed to this consummation . . .' A month later, in October 1805, he wrote again. 'I cannot dismiss this subject without observing, that though Mr Lancaster does not, and cannot claim the palm of originality for his system of tuition, yet he has displayed much originality, both in its application and in his individual improvements.'

In answer to a second letter from Mrs Trimmer saying that, 'Of all the plans that have appeared in this kingdom likely to supplant the Church, Mr Lancaster's seems to me the most formidable . . .', and giving notice that she intended to attack Joseph Lancaster both on religious grounds and on the ground that he had stolen the good parts of his System from Dr Bell, the latter stated that he had no intention of entering into controversy.

Undeterred by the reluctance of her major protagonist, Sarah Trimmer published her blast in November 1805. Its title was 'A Comparative View of the New Plan of Education promulgated by Mr Joseph Lancaster . . .' It was dedicated to Members of the Society for Promoting Christian Knowledge.

She gave as her credentials authorship of the 'Oeconomy of Charity', the enlarged edition of which had appeared in 1802. In this book she had set out a proposal for religious and moral instruction of the children of the poor, 'which was consonant with the system of our pious forefathers'.

The plan advocated in the 'Oeconomy of Charity' took as its basis the existing Charity Schools and proposed to multiply them. It contained many sensible, practical suggestions and indicated much common ground between herself and Joseph Lancaster. She acknowledged that the education in the Charity Schools was in general very defective and left to the discretion of ill-qualified teachers. Children learned by rote lessons above their capacity and read without reflection. The religious books used in Charity Schools were written by men of deep erudition, who had no idea what was needed by the young and illiterate. Children should have books in which amusement blended with instruction, and it would contribute greatly to the general improvement if the head scholars were permitted to read aloud every day.

She thought, 'The generality of Charity Boys in London . . . may be more advantageously occupied in helping to teach the younger ones, and in committing different things to memory; and I cannot see why they might not be taught to mend their own shoes and stockings'. This would furnish not only schoolmasters for the poor superior to those of the present day, but good Parish Clerks. She had herself produced a 'Teacher's Assistant' which could be used for this purpose; indeed she had confined the first volume to general instructions suitable also for dissenting schools, which were not to be condemned. Many were good and many dissenters were ready to work with Church members in educa- tion. 'Whatever blame may be attached to Methodistical teachers . . . they can scarcely be accused of instructing the children to doubt the divine authority of the Scriptures or prefer books of infidelity to their Bibles'. She also admitted that dissenters sang better than the Established Church, where psalmody was left to ill-taught Charity children and a set of 'illiterate men, who sing for their own amusement'.

Her principal recommendation for improving the existing state of affairs in Charity Schools was the much greater use of ladies as teachers. Those who had taught their own children had some experience; unmarried ladies could use talents otherwise lost in their single fate, and young ladies could, with propriety, assist in the instruction of their contemporaries. With the increased feminine presence in the schools she anticipated an influx of practical action and common sense. 'Men do not want ladies on the board, but they need them. Ladies see things that men do not, or have not time to'.

There was much in the Lancastrian System that Sarah Trimmer admired. Had Joseph Lancaster not been a Quaker and taken his stand on a non-sectarian, Christian foundation she might well have placed her considerable influence at his disposal. Indeed, 'A Comparative View . . .' opened with a complimentary description of the institution in the Borough Road.

'A school consisting of seven or eight hundred boys, chiefly collected from the purlieus of St George's Fields, trained in habits of diligence and order, and taught with surprising expedition, and at moderate expense, the useful arts of Reading, Writing and Accounts under the conduct of one master, is an interesting spectacle, which affords a striking contrast to the schools wherein the children of common people generally receive their education; and it is impossible to view such an Institution without earnestly wishing to see the real benefits of it extended to all the children of the lower classes in this nation.' Her assessment of two of the Lancastrian monitors was that they were 'clever and indefatigable . . . their cheerfulness and steadiness is really surprising;' and she was astonished at the silence in the school when Joseph Lancaster took up a book to read to them.

Commenting on the division of the institution into classes, she called them a series of 'small schools', in which the master could only bring his influence to bear on the monitors and had to trust them in turn to convince their groups. Surely this meant the inculcation of 'habits', and not, as Lancaster claimed, of 'principles'. She approved of the emphasis on emulation and reward, unless this led to ambition and vanity. Competition was all right on a small scale. But what if several hundred boys, full of the honour of their school, met another hundred similarly fired. To kindle and blow on such a flame in the heart of youth could end in fatal mischief. If Joseph Lancaster condemned party spirit in religion, then equally he should discourage partisanship in schools.

For his punishments she reserved harsher strictures. They were disproportionate to the offences; though she made no comparisons with the much more brutal penances practised in some Charity Schools, even Robert Raikes was known to beat his Sunday scholars when they irritated him more than he could bear and flogging was an accepted part of Quaker schools. The use of ridicule as a basis for reprimand seemed to Mrs Trimmer quite wrong; especially as in everyday worldly matters ridicule was fashionable and she thought young people should be taught to stand against it, rather than being made party to its infliction.

On the training of school masters she expressed contradictory views. For a teacher going out to spread the ideas of a national system, a year's probation was not enough: but as the Lancastrian ideas were all mechanical, what need was there to train school masters at all.

She disapproved of educating boys and girls together; and took issue with the use in school of 'Turner's Easy Introduction to the Arts and Sciences', which she considered unsuitable for the labouring community. What had they to do with Philosophy, Logic, Physics, Metaphysics, and so on. She recognised that this opinion might lay her open to the charge of being illiberal, but her own experience told her that the poor were far happier being taught useful things. On the other hand she contended publicly that it was oppressive to deny the poor the advantages of reading in an age when the rich cultivated literature.

So much for the practice of the Lancastrian System. Of a great deal of it she approved, for it was not here that the root of her quarrel lay. She even went so far as to admit that Andrew Bell had 'left the field open to whoever should be disposed to follow his example. No one has done so, on an extensive scale at least, but Mr Lancaster; who has shown in a manner that surprised every spectator, what the Plan is capable of and it is to him that England must look for actual experiment'.

But the heart of the matter lay in the teaching of religion. Though Sarah Trimmer would have found such a stance equally, if not more, dangerous, she nevertheless wrote that if Joseph

Lancaster's System had been totally secular all Christians might have agreed to support it.

But it was not secular. Indeed it was impossible that it should be so. There were no secular schools in England. From earliest time religion and schools had gone together. It had been religious communities that had pioneered each new development. However worldly, apathetic, or frankly antagonistic, groups within the kingdom might be, the nation was based on religious ideas and ideals, and the hearts and minds of men were passionately engaged in them.

Joseph Lancaster contended that the cause of education had been stifled by sectarian disputes and that a national evil should be answered by a national concern. Mrs Trimmer reminded him that education had been a national concern since the Act of Uniformity in 1662 established the Protestant Church and laid down that every school master or teacher instructing youth must conform to the liturgy of the Church of England. Had the parish priests carried out their obligation to educate adequately there would have been no need for schools to be in a condition which made reform necessary. History showed that there should be a State religion, and that children should be educated in its doctrines. This preserved cohesion. British society was a tolerant one. Groups were able to dissent, but if they tried to supersede the national church that would be 'undue influence', in Lancaster's own words. However, she hastily added, this term could not be applied to the Established Church, which tried to keep baptised children in her fold, or bring back those who had strayed from it. It was not enough to hold God's name sacred; doctrine was essential to form Christian character.

To Joseph Lancaster's argument that parents could teach their own children doctrine and send them to Sunday Schools, Mrs Trimmer retorted that poor parents did not know how to teach their children, and Sunday Schools were not enough. She saw his assertion that the spirit of sect exalted a particular creed as a direct attack on the Church of England, for she did not accept that there were any dissenting creeds. The question was not one of sects, she admitted that the Lancastrian System did not create Quakers, but whether the Church of England, consistent with its principles, could depart from the established system of education with day to day instruction in the catechism. Joseph Lancaster would have replied that for the poor there was no established system of education giving day to day instruction in the catechism, or in anything else.

Sarah Trimmer credited Joseph Lancaster with genuine Christian feeling, but considered him infinitely too idealistic in supposing that Christians could ever unite in this world. The Established Church was the bulwark against more than the machinations of the Devil, it was also the defender of the Constitution. Should the Church fail, it would take with it the State.

So the great argument of the indivisability of Church and State, recently and vividly illuminated by the drama of the French Revolution, took fire once again, this time focussed on the growth of schooling for the poor. Mrs Trimmer had blown upon a flame which was to spread into a conflagration and over the next forty years highlight, or retard, the struggle to develop a national system of education.

In 1806 Andrew Bell, somewhat reluctantly, roused himself at Sarah Trimmer's urging and came up to London to assist in introducing the Madras system into Whitechapel Charity Schools. In June that year Archdeacon Charles Daubeny preached a sermon in the cathedral at Salisbury thundering against the Lancastrian System and the 'deistical' principles of its founder. Though the national reaction was mild, it was the first blast in a war that was presently to rage over the whole of England. Meanwhile Joseph Lancaster was assuring the Archbishop of Canterbury, by mail, that nothing would be done to the detriment of the establishment, and his school was receiving admiring visits from a number of Anglican Bishops among them the Bishop of Durham who was presently to become the patron of Andrew Bell.

Archdeacon Daubeny stimulated Joseph Lancaster to public retort. 'An appeal for justice in the cause of ten thousand poor and orphan children . . .' and a 'Vindication of some truths contained in the Scriptures by the exercise of reason only. . .' appeared in pamphlet form in 1806 and 1807. Restraint was not their chief characteristic. It was not in Joseph Lancaster's temperament to remain silent in the face of misjudgement or calumny; as it was not in the nature of the times to use words mincingly or to indulge in euphemisms. His supporters may have been mellifluous aristrocrats, but Joseph Lancaster was a blunt man of the common people. Pressures, some self-generated, some beyond his control, were beginning to make him feel persecuted. His personal religion was the basis of life. He profoundly resented the charge that he was a deist who did not believe in the divinity of Christ; a charge moreover that he considered could, and might, be stretched to cover jacobinism and sedition. He also strongly refuted the denigration of the Bible implicit in the accusation that religious teaching based on the Bible alone was inadequate.

Had his reply rested with the religious arguments all might have been well, but his pride, strengthened by spectacular success, was stung by criticism of his System. Now, and on many future occasions, he was to defend it hotly, not scrupling to justify himself and lay about his critics, notably Sarah Trimmer, in extreme and often excessive language.

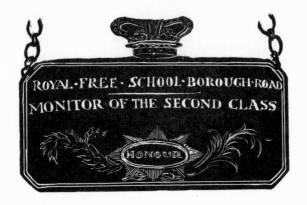

'Design for silver medallion — original in possession of West London Institute'

Chapter 6
SPREADING THE GOSPEL

'Proper teachers cannot be expected to spring up like mushrooms, completely formed in a night' (Joseph Lancaster, Letter to John Foster Esq. Chancellor of the Exchequer for Ireland)

Some time in 1804 or 1805 James George Penney found his way to the Royal Free School, as the Borough Road Institution now came to be called. He was an orphan, aged about twelve, dull and listless and, as it turned out, starving. Joseph Lancaster, hearing that some of his schoolfellows were sharing their own food with James Penney, took him into the 'Family'. Among those contemporary samaritans may have been John Pickton, Thomas Harrod, or John Veevers, all of whom were to become, as was James Penney himself, respected Lancastrian school masters. By 1809 Thomas Harrod was taking responsibility at the Royal Free School, John Pickton was in Bristol, James Penney had a school in Shropshire for two hundred and fifty children whose progress was considered by some local people to be due to the powers of witchcraft, and John Veevers was being offered an educational establishment in Birmingham at a starting salary of £120 a year. The two latter young men had both spent some time at Maiden Bradley where the rural training institution was supposed to be taking shape.

By December 1805 Joseph Lancaster was based at Bradley, waiting for the return of the Duke and Duchess of Somerset from town before actually starting work. As usual he was making full use of both his families. Sarah Lancaster, his mother, was keeping house at Bradley and helping to look after the baby and Elizabeth, whose instability precluded her from giving much help in day to day matters. There were also some of the lads, for Joseph took members of his extended Family with him wherever he went. Back in the Borough Road Richard Lancaster, anxious but devoted, kept an eye on various extraneous activities, including printing, while the sisters, Sarah and Mary, ran the girls' school. It is not clear who was in charge of the Royal Free School itself. No doubt the senior monitors, imbued with Joseph Lancaster's spirit and inspired by occasional visits from him, contrived to keep the System going.

John Pickton was eighteen this year and Thomas Harrod seventeen.

Transferring the System to an agricultural setting, an example intended to spread over the west and other parts of England, was to prove more difficult than Joseph Lancaster anticipated. Ever optimistic, however, he wrote of its beginnings in glowing terms.

'It is a curious circumstance that boys from London, who scarce ever handled a spade before, should teach boys in the country, brought up to agriculture, a new method and how to use it: but this is the fact: and they do it to very good purpose. The boys who break up the land, are classed according to their strength, a monitor being appointed to each class: all the classes are under one general monitor; they keep their spades, hoes, etc in a place for that purpose; every implement is numbered; and each boy knows which belongs to him by that number; and is required to keep it clean and bright: when they go to work, they uniformly take their spades, etc, at the word of command, and whatever movements they have to make, before they begin to work, are effected the same way . . . When they arrive on the ground, from which the dwelling house is some distance, they divide into two classes; one, the senior and most industrious boys, have square perches of land measured out for them and they work, after receiving the order to begin, without any other command till they have done their work; the only question being which shall get done first. The other class do nothing without a new command for every motion; they consist of boys who are able to work, but either not so habitually active as the others, or more idle. The commands generally given are, 'Prepare to dig'; in which case the spade is grounded, and the foot placed on it by the boy whose it is. When the monitor has seen each boy ready, he gives the word 'Dig', and each spade is immediately pressed the full depth into the ground: when the monitor has seen every spade properly in the ground, they are ordered to 'turn', and each boy, with one motion, turns the spade, and breaks the earth he turns over with it . . . The suspense between each command, prevents their being overworked, and the monitor is occasionally relieved in giving commands by others'.

The stones dug out were sold at one shilling a load for building cottages or mending turnpike roads. Half the money went to the boys.

Joseph gave his own services freely, but he hoped for reasonable remuneration from the Duke for a specially recommended school master. It is not clear whether the school was intended to be a wholly free school but, in the circumstances of it being on the Somerset estate, it is likely that Joseph saw it as such.

The question of salaries was a vexed and confused one, with the school master commonly making what kind of living he could out of the pittances that parents could muster. At the end of the eighteenth century London Charity School masters could earn £50–£65 a year. Ducal supporters were not always eager to take on financial responsibility, though they were very ready to accept any prestige or perks that went with having a school on their land. In 1809 George Howell, from Woburn, complained to his old master, Joseph Lancaster, that he could not manage on his salary of £60 per annum and the Duke of Bedford declined to raise it. At the same time the Duchess expected him to tutor her own children privately at considerable inconvenience and no extra charge.

Meanwhile Joseph, forwarding money to his father who seemed by now to be giving the greater part of his time to his son's affairs, putting his hand in the Lancastrian pocket for housekeeping, travel, the needs of his two families and to pay the bills that never ceased to be presented, had no income of his own that was not inextricably mixed with subscriptions for schools, buildings, training masters, or publications.

Though Lancastrian schools were to spread over the nation, and beyond, it was in urban rather than in rural conditions that they flourished, where their ability to deal with large numbers was a positive asset and social and industrial conditions stimulated parental and community pressure for some education for the children of the poor. In the countryside populations were smaller, parents saw less need for their offspring to be literate, and the natural rhythm of the seasons did not lend itself to digging by numbers.

It is difficult to say whether Maiden Bradley would have been any more successful if Joseph Lancaster had settled down and concentrated all his considerable powers on making it so. But the fact was that he had other calls upon his time and was very often absent. He went up and down to London to keep an eye on the Royal Free School. He travelled many miles seeking subscriptions from the great and the influential. He wrote tracts, revised 'Improvements' and brought both to the attention of anyone who might help to patronise schools and spread the idea of universal education. He cast his net wide and indiscriminately, being no respecter of political persuasion or religious affiliation, delighted to have the name of the Princess of Wales on his list alongside that of her husband the Prince, though most public men were careful to ally themselves with one or the other of those bitter opponents. In February 1806 he was in Windsor, soliciting advice from Colonel Disbrowe, Queen Charlotte's Secretary, on the advisibility of convening a Town Meeting to interest the inhabitants in setting up a school. About the same time he was suggesting to Lord Somerville that he might take the children to the palace gardens at any time for the Queen to see the System in action.

His correspondence was prodigious. Postage was a continuing source of worry. In order to avoid expense Joseph was constantly requesting 'the favour of a few franks' from his wealthy supporters. He told the Duchess of Somerset, when asking her to approach her husband on his behalf, that Lord Somerville had decently franked twenty-five letters and General Calvert thirty-five; if the Duke would do the same Joseph, with the help of

another nobleman or two, would easily get the number he
needed. To the Marquis of Blandford he wrote that he wanted
several hundred letters franked to spread the news of the
subscription list. 'It being a Royal subscription thy Uncle
Spencer who is at the head of the Post Office might be disposed
to let a considerable number pass post free'; perhaps the Marquis
might care to introduce the matter to his uncle.

There is no doubt that money was short; rather the management of money which made sure that outgoings were balanced
against incoming finances was entirely absent. Everything paid
out was for the cause and to keep Joseph Lancaster and his
families in health and strength was essential to that cause.
Somehow the subscription to raise 'a fund to establish schools in
the country for 10,000 poor children'; of which Maiden Bradley
was the first, slipped away. Bills not considered urgent were
ignored. Those who could afford to support the great work were
openly and frequently asked to do so. If Joseph Lancaster was
prepared to pour out his life in the cause of education, he saw no
reason why others should not give as freely of their treasure.

He was dogged by minor illnesses and the problem of Elizabeth
was continually with him. She loved him, but she could not
stand the strain and she was jealous of the warmth of his affection
for others, perhaps especially his lads. Seeing him made much of
by society ladies was not the future she had necessarily anticipated when she married him. By August 1807 three physicians
had pronounced her incurably and constitutionally deranged and
the first of a series of removals from her family began. The
tragedy was that Joseph needed a wife prepared both to support
him and to let him go, while Elizabeth wanted a husband the
centre of whose world was his home.

He had trouble too with his co-religionists. At New Year 1806
he continued a long letter to Thomas Sturge, from Bradley.
During November and December Joseph had several times
visited Bristol and Bath. The reasons given were practical; in
quest of slates 'in order to furnish the Boys with employment in
winter evenings' and to find materials for the basket maker, but
it was more likely because he felt the need of contact with
Friends, such as Priscilla Gurney, Richard Reynolds and George
Cumberland, and of the kind of conversation and discussion of
which he was deprived at Bradley. Yet the meetings had not been
altogether happy ones. Joseph was low in his spirits, conscious

that he was disapproved of by many Quakers and feeling sore because at that time so few had joined the 'King's subscription list'. With kindness, for his own good, in each house he visited Friends preached humility. Joseph found it hard to bear. 'I hope I shall always value what comes from the openings of truth but common advice as well as common proverbs grow tiresome if out of their places and this I meet in every house'. Another Friend had described him as 'heady, high-minded, set up and that nothing but a miracle of Grace could preserve me'. Joseph said he was mistaken, that he had even contemplated suicide and, his mercurial temperament buffeted by such a hostile reception, was reduced to tears.

Consciousness of criticism, however, did not stop him being moved to speak in Meeting. He was not a Quaker minister and it is clear that he felt hurt that his Meeting had not seen fit to accept him as one. Though there was no reason why he should not hold forth if the Lord so inspired him, no doubt the fact that he did so often, at length, and powerfully, added to his offences in the eyes of Friends. A parents meeting at the Borough Road, for which one thousand tickets had been issued, had turned into a religious gathering with Joseph preaching. Poor, but decent and sober people, they listened with reverend attention.

But when he got back to his Family, either in London or Bradley, optimism reasserted itself. The cheerfulness of his spirits, and a natural jolliness in the company of young people, made for an atmosphere of warmth which many of his lads remembered long afterwards with nostalgic affection and tried to emulate when they themselves were out struggling with the harsh realities of schools, committees, parents and pupils.

Robert Ould, writing from Swansea in 1809, described for 'his dear master' the grand feast that the boys in his school had had on Jubilee Day; roast beef, potatoes, biscuits and strong beer. Two hundred and twenty boys and seventy-five girls seated under one roof 'making faces as it were by instinct, to above 100 Ladies and Gentlemen assembled to view our large and happy Family'. After church, following Joseph Lancaster's custom, they marched round the town behind drums and fifes.

A jolly boy called William Gatward wrote back to a contemporary, Richard Holland, who was still working in the printing offices at the Royal Free School. Young Gatward had just arrived in Wales, at Melin Griffith school near Cardiff, in February 1808 and was homesick for them all at the Borough Road. In an effort to recreate the high spirits of the Family he addressed his letter to 'Sir Richard Holland, Commander in Chief of the left handed squad at the Borough Road, London, from a true Welchman', and added a 'PS How I love to laugh. Grimaldi'. He signed it W. Drawtag.

He did not have much to laugh at. In March he was saying that he would do better at cheesemongering in London. He was 169 miles from his friends and only earning sixteen shillings a week. Still, he was glad he had tried it, and he had seen beautiful country. In August he wrote directly to Joseph Lancaster, saying that he would like to leave at the end of his year. He could not manage on the salary. 'I am not an extravagant young man yet I think decency becomes everyone.' But he wanted his old Master's approval. He would not have it said that Joseph Lancaster had sent down a young man who behaved ill.

There were only thirty boys in the school and the committee had no spirit to keep it afloat. The following November William had moved on to another Welsh school, but was still in touch with Joseph. 'The lad who is now at Melin Griffith is but 12 years of age and if I may use the expression is left as a 'Lamb among Lions'. A nice boy, sharp and industrious and almost as steady as a man . . .' But how William Gatward wished that Joseph Lancaster would come down and set Wales in a blaze.

With equal affection and concern Joseph Lancaster corresponded with his lads. In September 1807 he was writing to Richard Holland about proofs. 'I long to see you again as much as you do to see me – tell Harrod to be careful of the money I send him and not let the girls in the house have too much at once.' He was grieved at the lack of letters from London. There had been only one from his boys 'which gives me no information about my child. Love to the whole family'. To another he wrote, 'Dear Boy . . . my wish my prayers and hearts desire to God is that his heavenly blessing may rest on thee – and all my beloved lads – and in my habitation . . . As with tender love I conclude to thyself and all my family thy affectionate friend and master Joseph Lancaster'.

Not all of those first young teachers had been boys at the Royal Free School. A number, whose experience of the Family was necessarily shorter, came specially to be trained there; usually sponsored by some philanthropically minded gentleman. In May

1808 Joseph Lancaster signed a reference for one such.

'This is to certify that the bearer Joseph Brignall Junr has attended my institution in the Borough Road Georges Fields Southwark in a diligent and attentive manner for the space of five weeks, to acquire a practical knowledge of the new system of education, which he has done to my very great satisfaction.'

It was not only boys who went out to preach the Lancastrian gospel. In September 1808 Jane Thomson was given £6 for wearing apparel and set off from the Borough Road to take charge of a girls school at Maiden Bradley, for sixteen shillings weekly boarding herself. From there, for the next year, she was to write highly practical and increasingly disillusioned letters. Then there was Harriet Howell.

It is not certain what age Harriet was, but when she was in a boarding school at Milverton in Somerset, probably as a teacher, her twelve-year-old brother Joseph came to the Royal Free School. Harriet was a managing young woman, given to writing letters in the third person with many underlinings, and she clearly thought Joseph Lancaster had need of a female to bring order into his somewhat chaotic arrangements. Though born into the Church of England, Harriet was, like Joseph himself, a Quaker by convincement. In her Joseph found someone with whom he could share his enthusiasm and who was interested in the voluminous details of his day to day efforts to promote the System.

Some time in 1806 there had begun to be whispers in Quaker circles that Joseph Lancaster was too fond of Harriet Howell. No doubt he found her practical concern for his welfare and interest in his work attractive, in contrast to the depression and despair of his poor wife. At any rate he wrote to her at great length and frequently. On January 1st 1807, in a letter which may have been addressed to Thomas Sturge, Joseph said that he hoped his friend had seen the most important of his missives to Harriet for then, if slander reared its head, he could bear witness that no improper correspondence had passed between them. On the contrary Joseph felt himself blessed in having her as a sympathetic friend to whom he could write under religious freedom. With her too franking letters was a worry. In October of that year he wrote to her that 'our union of mind and labours is still in his sanctified fear and I hope will enable me to assist thee so, with money as to cover every unavoidable expense of that kind incurred by my letters', the postage of which was paid by the recipient.

By July 1808 their relationship had grown cooler. On the 7th Harriet was writing from London to Joseph at Woburn. She had been looking after his affairs and did not hesitate to tell him that he should be at home instead of gadding round the country. 'Of course I would not have taken the liberty (of opening his letters), considering that we now stand on very different terms from the time when my interest in, and attention to them, and every other part of thy concerns were acceptable.' But his rooms were comfortable, as far as she could make them and she just wished he were there to occupy them.

In October she went to Bradley, where the situation had deteriorated, and was shocked at what she found. She wished she had been sent earlier to see to things. Joseph trusted people too indiscriminately. 'Sorry to observe the usual unmethodical untrade-like way in which orders are still attended to.' All the bricks and most of the lime and mortar had been stolen. There were thirty-four females in the girls seminary. She thanked him for the offer of a chaise, but preferred to walk and save the expense.

Shortly after there was a breach between them, which Joseph Lancaster tried to patch up in 1809. But Harriet had had enough. She continued to write from East Anglia, where she set up schools at Fincham, Lynn, Norwich, Yarmouth and in other small towns. She was still devoted to the System and, she hastened to tell him, loved by rich and poor alike but her devotion to the person of Joseph Lancaster had definitely waned.

In the autumn of 1806, when prospects at Maiden Bradley still appeared bright; though Joseph, becoming restive, confessed to feeling 'kidnapped' by the Duke of Somerset and finding himself 'committed but not supported', he decided to visit Ireland. Though he had been for over a year in correspondence with a number of important personages in that country, notably John Foster, Chancellor of the Exchequer for Ireland, his actual departure was very sudden. Maybe the decision to go in 1806 was influenced by the appointment of his patron the Duke of Bedford to the position of Lord Lieutenant in Dublin. Harriet, in her usual knowing way, said, 'This will be a preaching journey'. Joseph laughed at her. As so often, however, she turned out to be right.

In 1806 the state of education in Ireland was abysmal, with the added complication of a largely Catholic population ruled by an anti-Catholic establishment in Dublin and among the big land-owners of the Protestant Ascendancy. In the eighteenth century Charity Schools had been set up, as in England, to provide for both Protestant and Catholic children to be decently educated in the English language, the three Rs and the Principles of the Christian Religion; Anglican of course. They were openly intended to proselytise, a positive reinforcement to the penal laws against Popery.

These schools, and spinning and agricultural schools, were a failure. There was no Irish middle class to support them, parish clergy were too poor, and the penal laws had no effect in discouraging a strong Roman Catholic reaction, and the determination of Catholic priests and school masters, in the face of punitive legislation, to teach in their own faith.

In 1780 John Howard, the prison reformer, made a journey through Ireland visiting remote Protestant schools. He found an appalling situation, filthy, half-starved children criminally neglected. Both public and legislative opinion were unaffected by his report and well into the next century conditons remained virtually unchanged.

The successful rivals to this fragmented imposed schooling were the illicit Hedge Schools, run by proscribed teachers in fields and under hedgerows, financed by parents and filled with peasant children without distinction of sex or religion. Many of the Hedge School masters were men of learning and the curriculum could range from spelling and English to Hebrew, Latin, Greek and mathematics. It is not hard to see why such open air, illegal academies were attractive to children and, by the beginning of the nineteenth century, they were the common schools of the Irish people.

This was fruitful ground for the promotion of the Lancastrian System.

Where proselytising had failed, men of more liberal views could see the advantages of bringing together children of both denominations within the framework of Joseph Lancaster's non-sectarian teaching on a broad basis of Christianity. In 1798 Ireland had had an uprising, when it had been confidently expected that the French would land and sweep the English into the sea. In the event the French did not come in the necessary strength and the rebellion was easily put down but, as had happened in England, voices began to be heard in support of popular education as a method of social control. 'It seems no small danger that Ireland will be lost to this country, or at least be perpetually liable to internal discord unless something is done to train the rising generation in habits of peace, loyalty and religion,' Joseph had written to Lady Harcourt.

Ireland was the only part of the United Kingdom in 1806 where the possibility of State intervention in education was viewed with equanimity, and that year the Commission on Irish Education Enquiry, which had been appointed by the Lord Lieutenant in 1788, was revived to sit again for the next six years with R. L. Edgeworth, father of Maria, as one of its members. In 1805 John Foster, the Archbishop of Dublin and the Irish Lord Chief Justice had all subscribed to Lancaster's fund for training schoolmasters.

In January 1805 Joseph Lancaster published an open letter to the Chancellor of the Exchequer for Ireland in the form of a tract 'on the best means of employing and educating the poor of that country'. In acknowledging it John Foster wrote that he was proud to be so addressed.

In this letter Joseph Lancaster, while once more setting out the mechanics of his System and its virtues, laid emphasis on the training of schoolmasters, which experience had shown him to be of great importance. In fact he now gave such training top priority among his aims.

'It is surprising,' he wrote, 'that among the great number of volumes written on education, not one should be found that will lay down a general plan, founded on experiment, which may tend to make youth more useful and more intelligent, without educating them above the station in life for which they may be designed. It is more surprising still, that nothing should have been written on a method of training young men as good schoolmasters'. . .

In a series of notes he laid down some guidelines for such training. Aspirants should be from sixteen to twenty years of age and not already fixed in bad habits. He added that students should be of poor circumstances and dependent on their own industry, so that they would be content with homely fare and small salaries. There was to be a central school of large numbers surrounded by subsidiary practice schools. At this stage he suggested locating such an institution in London, clearly with the Royal Free School in mind. Trainee teachers would live in and return to the main school at night, where an eye could be kept on their conduct and morals. Every evening a conference would take place on the day's work, and each transaction was to be 'journalised'. Occasionally students would change practice schools. The training was to last twelve months, after which teachers would be ready to take sole charge of schools catering for fifty to three hundred children.

Students should be trained to develop the principles and passions of the juvenile mind. 'God gave us passions and does not require the depression of them but rather that they should be channelled to good purpose.' It is interesting that the founder of a System later to the stigmatised as being unduly mechanistic, should have laid such stress on the recognition of principles and passions in education. Joseph Lancaster, himself a man of passions and principles, saw his System as releasing the teacher from the repetitive drudgery to which he had so often been subjected, to allow him to concern himself with wider and profounder educational implications.

Each master was to keep a register of the temper and conduct of the children under him to be passed on to his successor. Instruction should be simple and definite. Force of habit was often more powerful than principle, and the spirit of emulation should not be overlooked. Aspiring teachers should know the theory of education and be taught to reduce it to practice. All controversial points of religion were to be kept out of sight. Proselytising should not be for a creed; only for good as against evil. Girls ought to be taught by women, and the importance of female education thoroughly understood.

This letter set the stage for Joseph Lancaster's first visit to Ireland, during which he intended to encourage patrons to send intending schoolmasters for training.

The Irish expedition was to last two months. This time Joseph does not seem to have taken any of his lads with him. He journeyed in more bizarre company.

On October 9th 1806, having landed ten days earlier at Waterford, he reported his arrival in Dublin to John Foster and requested him to mention this event to the Lord Lieutenant the Duke of Bedford. 'We are three of us travelling together through this divided land – we have come to show you the cementing influence of real religion – a Clergyman, a Friend and a Turk and we may truly say we three are brethren.' The clergyman was the Reverend Archibald Douglas of Clonmell, who was said to have raised thousands of pounds for charities by preaching in Dublin. He occupied a living in the gift of Lord Hardwicke, the Duke of Bedford's predecessor as Lord Lieutenant, whose Countess had expressed herself delighted with the Royal Free School. The Friend was Joseph Lancaster. The name of the 'gentleman in Turkish costume' who accompanied them was Ombark Boubay (Anbark Baubi), 'a native of Morocco and Arabic interpreter to Elfi Bey when in these kingdoms'. This gentleman's motive for being in Britain was to improve his mind, 'a trait highly honourable to the good sense of his character, the reverse of the prejudices of his education, which among his barbarous country-men teaches them to despise European learning, and to account Christians as a species of Devils living on pigs milk'. He had been mentioned in a letter by Joseph the previous April and almost certainly travelled with him at Lancaster's expense.

Joseph's fascination with this colourful character was clear from the descriptions he wrote to the Duke of Bedford, to whom he hoped to introduce Boubay. He admired his clothes, particularly the turban which set off his handsome features, his way with fine ladies, and his eagerness to acquire knowledge; all to a greater or lesser degree traits which Joseph himself cultivated.

'He is a master of twelve languages and has gone through many sufferings in travelling. He once went to Timbuctoo with a caravan – ninety days without seeing anything but sand, sky and his fellow travellers in a Great Desert. Once a lion wanted to make a breakfast of him but was disappointed. Another time an enormous serpent coiled itself deliberately up and lay down to sleep upon him – at which he moved, and the serpent was frightened away by the motion. He said to the Bishop of Limerick the other night (the Bishop pledged him and said you won't drink a glass of wine with me) 'No my Lord, it is against our religion to drink wine, wine make the head ache, and when men's heads ache, they are not fit to say their prayers, but lay down quite. We think it not right to take anything which will hinder our prayers'. The Bishop replied, 'I wish you could give some of our Christians a lecture'. He is very diffident at times in company but soon recovers himself and I never yet saw a company in which his interesting and fascinating manners did not draw round him a circle of the most intelligent part of the company among whom he shone by his knowledge of men and things, his polished manners and the strength of his intellect'.

The visit was full of Bishops. Indeed it was important that the Church should be placated and won over if Lancastrian schooling was to spread. It is doubtful, however, if the singularity of Joseph's travelling companions helped towards this end. Nor did the clergy necessarily accept with a good grace the moral example of religious brotherhood so strikingly held up before them. The Bishop of Limerick admired Boubay; the Bishop of Ossory was wary, 'there were evident marks of surprise in his countenance, when he saw the celebrated Parson Douglas along with a heretic schismatic Quaker . . .' It was the Bishop of Meath who roused the passions in Joseph Lancaster. He went with Boubay to see him, without an appointment, and met the Bishop, who was living in the house of a friend, just going out. The Bishop attempted to excuse himself by saying that there was nowhere they could talk. Unfortunately for him a gentleman at that moment came out of a front room and gestured that it was empty.

Cornered, the Bishop engaged in trifling conversation, but Joseph Lancaster had not come to exchange social gossip. At a previous meeting he had extracted a promise from the Bishop; probably of a measure of support, which he now wished to redeem. In the meantime the Bishop had thought better of it. Tempers rose. The Bishop retracted. Joseph Lancaster insisted that a 'solemn voluntary promise' had been given and must be kept. 'He said he felt his own dignity and would not be talked to in this way – He said – did I put myself on a level with him – I told him I was under the patronage of my sovereign. He said the King was very sorry for it; in fact throughout the whole, he behaved in the most illiberal insulting manner possible.' Of the 'virtuous, pious enlightened Anbark . . . "He goes with fine ladies," said the Bishop in a way that shewed the influence of envy', so Joseph wrote to the Duke of Bedford adding that he saw the hand of Sarah Trimmer in all this.

The suggestion that His Majesty might withdraw his patronage touched Joseph on the raw. He must by now have been well aware of the fickle nature of much aristocratic support; though a number of the nobility made generous contributions. The King's favour was the solid foundation on which Lancaster's claim to represent a national interest rested. Had there been truth in the rumours, now beginning to be put about, that George III had withdrawn his patronage many of those with money and influence to bestow might have followed his example.

Although, as so often, Joseph's expectations for this visit proved over-optimistic, yet he made many good friends in Ireland. The Irish subscription list issued for a proposed 'Abridgement of Improvements' contained distinguished names, headed by that of the Lord Lieutenant, the Duke of Bedford. The Duke had also handed Joseph Lancaster personally £160 to help defray expenses on this visit.

Travelling from Waterford to Dublin Joseph Lancaster stayed in several great houses, including that of Henry Grattan MP, where his eloquence in elucidating the simple truths of Christianity perhaps struck a warmer response than was now the case in his own country. With his Quaker brethren relations were less smooth. Staying in Clonmell, while Pastor Douglas arranged his affairs, Joseph attended weekday Meeting and 'opened his mouth'. Afterwards, questioned as to his own affiliations, he described the Southwark Friends and their opposition to his preaching in derogatory terms, to the surprise of local Quakers.

In Dublin, on his birthday November 25th, he again stood up in testimony. This time Meeting did not go with him. When he flung himself on his knees in prayer, Meeting remained seated. Insulted, he asked if this was common practice or a personal affront. The reply, that it was usual unless the person praying was an acknowledged minister, opened old wounds. An ancient Friend admonished him on the dangers of his fondness for the company of the great. Upset Joseph wept. He could never admit that his connections with those in high places had any motive other than the good of the cause. To cheer himself he bought a pair of new stockings on his way to an interview with the Duke of Bedford, and then, with his usual temperamental resilience, spent the evening cordially with the same ancient Friend.

In spite of criticisms, especially among Friends, Joseph Lancaster felt close to the Irish and was hopeful that a new era in his life had been opened by his coming among them. More importantly, certain respectable persons had asked him to furnish them with schoolmasters.

By December 11th he was writing from Liverpool to a member of the Latouche family, who were influential in Ireland, enclosing a copy of 'An Appeal for justice in the cause of ten thousand poor and orphan children' and asking whether she could alter her subscription from ten copies to twenty or thirty. He wrote optimistically to William Corston that one hundred and thirty copies were already subscribed for in Liverpool alone, during the four days that he had been in that city. He hoped to get to Scotland, where he already had correspondence, to recruit prospective schoolmasters; and certainly he spoke on both sacred and secular subjects in Liverpool, Manchester and Warrington.

At the beginning of February 1807 Joseph Lancaster returned to London. Though it was to be another two years before Jane Thomson reported that there were only nine children in the school, whose parents said they must make hay, and that she was getting a salary for doing nothing, Joseph Lancaster virtually never went back to Maiden Bradley again.

'William Allen — after early portrait, artist unknown'

Chapter 7
FINANCIAL CLOUDS

'Experiments are seldom made without expense'. (Improvements, 3rd edition)

1804 was the last year in which Joseph Lancaster had no debts. The harsh fact was that from very early in its life the Borough Road school's financial position had been a precarious one. All the funds on which it relied for success had come from the benevolence of friends and well-wishers.

Very little of this income was spontaneously generated. For the greater part it was brought in by Joseph Lancaster's own efforts. He talked and wrote letters, he visited everyone who might have money to spare, he produced publications for sale by subscription. Each new development; and some that owed their freshness to semantic sleight of hand, was put before the public as worthy of support. The work was prodigious, the energy consumed incalculable, the miles covered in pursuit of patrons enormous. It was surprising that Joseph had any time left to teach in the school. Indeed by now he was being seen comparatively rarely in either of the schoolrooms for which he was responsible, the Royal Free School or Maiden Bradley. Inexorably, with widening horizons and increasing reputation, he was seduced from his original allegiance to the physical act of teaching children, though he retained close contact with his boys, rarely travelling without one or two in attendance.

By 1807 the burden of debt could no longer be ignored, even if Joseph did his best to do so. He recognised that it was impossible to put plans into practice without money, but he had little feeling for gold as a desirable end in itself, and unbounded confidence in Divine assistance. He was perpetually optimistic as to the results of any fresh appeal. More damagingly he expected those whose own livelihood depended on serving others to take the same sanguine view of unpaid bills as himself. Naturally they did not. The butcher, the candlemaker, the bricklayer and many others, seeing Joseph Lancaster well dressed and calling at the houses of the great, began to get restive for the monies owed them that were vital to keep their families from starvation. All in all, he now had debts of upwards of £3000 and in the spring of 1807 his creditors 'were clamorous in the extreme'.

Although among the Quaker community, to whom business ethics were of very great importance, debts were a matter of the utmost seriousness and bankruptcy occasion for separation if misconduct were suspected, in the circles of the wealthy and aristocratic with which Joseph Lancaster was now familiar unpaid bills were a normal fact of life and carried little stigma. Many men, including the Prince of Wales, lived openly beyond their means and thought nothing of it. Joseph Lancaster, on his return to London, had received a gift of £500 from a donor he had never seen before and was certain that now all was going to be well. Unfortunately such windfalls were not put to the more mundane purposes of keeping the books straight, but poured out prodigally to finance fresh endeavours.

Richard Lancaster, keenly aware of the prudence essential to small tradesmen like himself if they and their families were to survive, was distressed by his 'firebrand-like conduct' and remonstrated with his son. But he too was not certain that the rules by which he himself lived necessarily applied to the world in which Joseph moved. Joseph for his part was writing to his father, at that moment staying in Liverpool with his elder son William, urging him not to be afraid to use his small stock of money as it would soon receive additions. He was anxious that Richard should return to London via Warwick, which had been his birthplace. Any extra expense incurred by this diversion was far outweighed in Joseph's mind by the pleasure that such a visit would give to his father.

He also had another Royal conquest to report. George III's fifth son, the Duke of Cumberland, had asked Joseph Lancaster to wait on him at St James's Palace to discuss the establishment of a naval school. Joseph, hat firmly on his head, was received with great affability and given a ten pound note into his hand. He complained about the slow progress of the subscription, which was suffering from the damaging rumour of the King's withdrawal, and the Duke promised to visit the school 'and that speedily'. The Duke then compelled the Earl of Scarborough, who was present at the interview, to fix a time when Joseph could call on him for a subscription. 'Is this not a cause for admiration', Joseph wrote triumphantly. 'The King's son soliciting subscriptions for thy son . . .'

In March, however, Joseph was writing to William Corston that he was ill, poor and penniless, adding characteristically that he nevertheless put his confidence in the Rock of Ages.

A month before this, on February 19th 1807, Samuel Whitbread, Whig MP for Bedford, made a speech in the House of Commons on the Poor Laws and was given permission to bring in a Bill including a proposal to set up a general system of national education by the establishment of rate-aided voluntary parochial schools. Whitbread advocated raising the sights and standards of the poor and encouraging them to sturdy indpendence. One of the ways of doing this was by schooling. He mentioned the cheap, simple and effective Lancastrian System and praised its founder. The Bill failed but the educational debate initiated by the speech did not.

On February 21st the Archbishop of Canterbury Dr Manners-Sutton wrote to Sam Whitbread enclosing a copy of Andrew Bell's 'Experiment', and setting out his fears that Mr Lancaster was directing a powerful instrument to mischevious ends. When Whitbread's speech was published a note at the end gave the actual credit for the discovery of this method of schooling to Dr Bell. Andrew Bell himself sent a letter to Mr Whitbread on

February 26th, admitting that 'to the zeal, perseverance, and address of Mr Lancaster, the mechanical parts of the system are under the greatest obligation'.

On March 2nd Joseph joined the fray with a letter to the MP. He had been pleased to see the dawn of any system of education in England, believing any to be better than none, but it hurt him to find the actual invention attributed to Dr Bell. He described, at some length, the origins of his own school and denied that he had seen 'Experiment' until two years after he had started it. The anger of a man who had toiled unremittingly to bring a dream into focus burst out against this usurping of the ultimate accolade. He gave warning of his intention to appeal to the public with a tract; adding however, in a postscript, that his opinion of Samuel Whitbread remained high and he would write nothing disrespectful of him or Andrew Bell. It was to be a resolution that he would find impossible to keep.

The public debate was well launched. In the autumn the 'Edinburgh Review' entered the battle on the Lancastrian side; to be countered by the 'Quarterly Review' supporting Dr Bell. Acrimony was to grow during the next four years. In the meantime, in May 1807, a third, greatly expanded, edition of 'Experiment' was published and Andrew Bell was given two years leave of absence from his benefice to propagate the Madras system. In the same month Joseph Lancaster was arrested for debt.

In mid-May William Corston had received a letter from his friend. The address was a spunging house near Rowland Hill's chapel. William Corston, who had spent his own money freely to keep the man he admired, must have opened the missive with considerable trepidation. At the very least a spunging house, a preliminary step to the debtors prison for those who were thought to possess assets, would charge exorbitant prices for the board and lodging of their occupants, a charge which Joseph would probably take for granted that William would defray. The note itself was couched in optimistic terms.

'My beloved Friend, Wm Corston,

I am in watch and ward; but I bless God, the best of all is, I am as happy as Joseph was in the King's Prison in Egypt – the Lord is with me, as he was with him. I have wrote to several friends, but no one have I seen. I have been here three days – wilt thou come and see me. Joseph Lancaster.'

William Corston answered this call immediately. On the way, however, he was overcome by doubts. It was no light thing to become financially involved with a debtor and Corston knew very well Joseph Lancaster's continuing and precarious pecuniary position. Crossing Blackfriars Bridge he became so agitated that he collapsed on to one of the stone seats. If he put up bail for a man who was liable to be rearrested for other debts the moment he was released it might bring ruin on the whole Corston family. He did not know whether to return home or to go on.

'If I had had the money in my pocket, I could not have bailed him. To go and tell him this, I thought would only increase his distress; while the refusal to visit him, I knew, would bring certain misery into my mind. I resolved to go forward and tell him the truth. At this thought, though with fear and trembling, I arose and went. As soon as the bailiff unlocked the door, Joseph saw the state I was in. He took me by the hand, and said, "my beloved friend, tell me all that is in thy heart now". I replied, "I will, Joseph". and then related all I had experienced on my way. "My dear friend," he replied, "I see thou art not to assist me at this time, compose thyself; this will never made a breach of friendship between me and thee."'

When William Corston left Joseph asked the Sheriff's officer to take him to the King's Bench which lay just off the Borough Road. On the way he was permitted to call in at his home where he found both his families grief stricken at seeing their master on his way to prison. The turnkey allowed Joseph some time alone with them, but after a while he was invited into the parlour to join in the reading of the Scriptures.

According to William Corston this glimpse of Joseph Lancaster's personal life deeply affected the turnkey who said, 'Sir, have you got no friend to be bound for you then this debt?' 'No', Joseph replied – not entirely truthfully for, in fact, two unnamed gentlemen appear to have been of financial assistance. The turnkey then offered himself as a guarantor. He surrendered Joseph Lancaster to the King's Bench where, on the officer saying he would secure the debt, he was released. 'About ten o'clock the next morning,' William Corston related, 'he came jumping into my warehouse, Ludgate Hill, saying "Ah, friend William, did I not tell thee thou wast not to assist me this time".'

Writing nine years later Joseph stated that he was allowed his liberty during the day, but slept in the prison at night, and that it was during this time that he founded a school at Deptford. Thanks either to the turnkey, or to his anonymous friends, by September he was in the west country recovering from a bout of ill health, but also safely out of reach of the rest of his creditors. Except among the Quakers, little stigma seems to have attached to his temporary incarceration for on August 6th the Duke of Somerset sent a note with his compliments saying that he had franked most of Mr Lancaster's letters and was glad to see the new building at Bradley go on so prosperously and the new school master so attentive.

It was during this, partly enforced, foray into the country that Joseph Lancaster first began to lecture seriously on education. And it was on a visit to the ageing Robert Raikes that the suggestion was made that he should charge for this service. He accepted it instantly. The time was to come when his ability to attract an audience was to be all that lay between his family and starvation; all that is except the generosity of his friends.

Ill health there may have been, there should have been a measure of financial anxiety, certainly there was real pain caused by the worsening state of Elizabeth's derangement, but the exhilaration of travelling and exercising his undoubted gifts as a speaker overrode those afflictions. He sat outside on the coach because he could not afford the fifteen shillings fare inside, to Bradley and Bristol, then on to Swansea and Carmarthen. In the latter place, said to be the most corrupt town in Wales, a school committee was formed in the morning, announced in the evening to a public meeting in the Town Hall and thereby pledged to do something effective for local boys and girls. Back again to Bristol, where Joseph had many good friends, to lecture to a respectable assembly of about eight hundred. He was 'put into a pickle' and given a 'fit of the bile' by a deputation of Quakers who fearing a hostile reception, waited on him beforehand to try to dissuade him from a public appearance. Agitated by this unexpected circumstance Joseph went out without shaving and in a dirty necktie. Borrowing a clean stock from a friend he put the soiled one in his pocket, only to draw it out in mistake for a handkerchief at a moment of tension during the lecture. 'However no one smiled'.

Next day, unable to resist the riposte, he went to see the Friends, pointing out to them that the predicted riot had not taken place. He considered that they had overstretched their ecclesiastical authority and, moreover, had been responsible for his bile; 'now I had a great work and the bile was only an impediment which I wished to get rid of . .' As they had given it to him he hoped they would take it back. Among so many it would not be a great affliction. They did not accept the proposition, but laughed and parted in good humour.

From Bristol Joseph Lancaster returned to London, but once again bankruptcy or ruin threatened. William Corston, harassed by his friend's financial improvidence and beginning to fear that Joseph might end up permanently in prison to the detriment of the work, had decided to call a meeting of the creditors and fling himself on their mercy, pleading that the value and importance of the Lancastrian System must mean that they would eventually be paid in full. The unpredictable Joseph, however, in high spirits after a successful tour, appeared one morning at Ludgate Hill and asked William why he was so 'low and pensive'. No doubt somewhat annoyed, William Corston, who had lost many hours tranquillity attempting to sort out the Lancaster transactions, replied that he was despondent '. . . not upon my own concerns, Joseph but upon yours'.

Brushing aside this personal solicitude, Joseph then announced that he had had a dream which had impressed on his mind that he must not follow the advice of friends in resolving his affairs. William Corston was extremely sceptical about Joseph's dream. He knew his friend, and kept interjecting during the telling of it that he saw Joseph was still determined to go on in the same old way. When he revealed that he had struck a docket against him and proposed to call a creditors meeting, dream or no dream, Joseph Lancaster erupted into anger, shouting that there was no need. All his creditors would have twenty shillings in the pound. 'Ah Joseph,' replied William Corston, 'these are great words from an empty stomach.'

Nothing that he could say, however, would persuade Joseph to take his advice. The latter was full of plans for raising a £2000 loan with the help of the Duke of Bedford and Sam Whitbread; '. . . their names will carry us through; then we shall go on swimmingly'. Though the straw plait merchant's own prudent nature was appalled at such a light-hearted approach to a situation of extreme financial urgency, nevertheless he could not help admiring the faith and optimism of his friend's temperament.

All the same, he was left to deal with the results of Joseph's decision. Joseph himself took the stage for Dover, taking with him two lads, Charles Bowyer who had been in training at the Borough Road and George Howell the master in charge of the Duke of Bedford's school at Woburn.

On the way they stopped at Canterbury because Joseph had violent toothache, '. . . where dear George saw dinner come on the table, and seemed to regret our stay on account of the expence'. Well he might! But the Master assured him that there must be some wise purpose in such a delay. Almost immediately Sir John Jackson, Director of the East India Company, MP for the Borough of Dover and an admirer of Lancaster, arrived to stay the night. In the morning he paid their bills and took them on to Dover with him in a post chaise, thus assuring Joseph Lancaster of an arrival which would establish him as a person of consequence and confirming his belief that Providence, if sufficiently trusted, could be relied upon to take a hand in human affairs.

John Jackson was to prove a good friend; during one of the public lectures Joseph delivered in Dover he was to find another, Joseph Fox.

Joseph Fox was a surgeon dentist of Lombard Street who taught at Guy's Hospital in London. He was a founder member and gold medallist of the Jenner Society for promoting vaccination and was interested in the art of making porcelain teeth, about which he was later to correspond with Josiah Wedgwood II. A wealthy bachelor, two years older than Joseph Lancaster, he was also the possessor of an unstable temperament.

Fox had been involved in a dispute with Jenner, from which he emerged defeated. On recovering he vowed that he would devote his property to good works. But hard work and theological gloom had begun to upset his mental balance and friends had insisted on a period of recuperation at Dover, where he had indeed considered suicide. The confrontation with Joseph Lancaster had the effect of a blinding revelation on Joseph Fox. The fervour and faith that flowed through the founder of the Lancastrian System galvanised him. The attraction of a passionate conviction combined with pulsating optimism was too much for him. His was an instant conversion. Without hesitation Joseph Fox put both his new found confidence and his fortune at Lancaster's disposal.

He was not the only person in Dover to be impressed. There

had been an earlier attempt to set up a school which had met with little success. Someone remarked, 'Mr L, if you can tame Dover boys (they are the sons of pilots and seafaring men) you can do anything'. After Mr L's lectures a committee was formed, with John Jackson as the moving spirit, and a school for three hundred boys set up '. . . and brought into order in two weeks by a boy of 17'. This was almost certainly Charles Bowyer, who remained master at Dover for the next twelve years.

Flushed by this success plans were made to introduce a Trojan Horse into the very heart of enemy country at Canterbury. Joseph Fox left to prepare the way and also to initiate business of his own. On December 8th 1807 a notice appeared in the Kentish Gazette informing the gentry and inhabitants of Canterbury that Mr Fox, Surgeon-Dentist of Lombard Street, London proposed to visit that town in his professional capacity every Saturday until the spring. It also advertised his book, 'The Natural History and Diseases of the Teeth' in two vols. quarto, price Two Guineas.

Although there is some confusion as to dates Joseph certainly spent his twenty-ninth birthday, November 25th, at Woburn, from where he wrote with cheerful insouciance to William Corston.

'I wish all my children to have a plumb pudding and roast beef; do order it for them, and spend an happy hour in the evening with them, as thou didst this time last year in my absence in Ireland, furnish them with money, and when the Good Samaritan comes again, he will repay thee . . . Farewell; my love to Thomas Sturge and thyself and thy family; perhaps thou wilt have a plumb cake or tart for my little unprotected infant on my birthday.'

No doubt he was buoyed up by his conviction that the Duke of Bedford now home from Ireland, would help to float his £2000 loan. Nothing less would seem to excuse the extravagance of a journey from Dover to Woburn only to return a few days later to Canterbury.

Indeed his optimism seemed based on a solid foundation. The Duke received him very cordially. He dined with the ducal couple and the Duke of Manchester, and gave a public lecture to which Bedford came. On this occasion an incident occurred which tickled Joseph's ready sense of humour. His platform was two or three squares of oil cake.

There was some 'fear of my pulpit melting under my feet, but I did not much dread that . . . However, when speaking, and the whole audience as well as myself deeply attentive to the subject, out came the (black) dog and began to nibble the corners of the pulpit, and certainly would have devoured some part of it, if a gentleman had not driven him away'.

Joseph managed not to laugh; nor he noted, did the audience. Though not all agreed, there seems no doubt that he was an inspired speaker. One after another, during the next few years, towns and cities all over the United Kingdom fell under his spell, and committees of worthy, but often cautious and canny, citizens found themselves formed on the spot, and within a remarkably short time responsible for fully operational Lancastrian schools. In Sheffield in 1809 Hannah Kilham, a sober Quaker, reported that Joseph Lancaster's enthusiasm produced a powerful effect. Three weeks after a public meeting at which he spoke a committee had been formed, subscriptions of £627 4s taken and a building rented at sixty guineas a year. At Dover Joseph himself said:

'I care not where I go, or what I do: any sacrifice on my part, so the Lord goes with me and makes my way by the might of his invisible power, which sometimes goes through me far more sensibly than the circulation of the blood through my veins.'

When he returned to Canterbury, early in December 1807, the effect was the same. A former Archbishop's palace had been rented for a school and dwelling house, probably by Joseph Fox. The irony was not lost on Lancaster.

'Believe thine eyes, Wm Carston! Joseph Lancaster at Canterbury: five hundred children to be educated in the Archbishop's palace: and where many Lollards were tortured for reading and having bibles, there is the bible to be read and taught . . .'

He wrote this on December 6th. At a meeting of subscribers on December 14th, at which Joseph Fox was present, a committee was set up and it was decided that every endeavour would be made to open the school on January 1st 1808.

By this time Joseph Lancaster was again on his way to Bristol, where he had already made certain of advance publicity by instructing friends that resolutions should be inserted in the Bath and Bristol papers; 'tell him (Richard Cumberland) I mind no expence that is proper'. He had many supporters in this city which had seen his early naval adventures, particularly the

Cumberlands, father and son, who were to remain faithful through all Joseph's future vicissitudes.

The Bristol lecture was a triumphant success.

'On this occasion,' the Bristol Mercury commented, 'the powers of mind of this extraordinary man were most happily evinced: while he explained the admirable economy and method of his school, he exposed the puerility of those prejudices by which some well meaning people are led to doat on ignorance and barbarism . . .'

On January 2nd 1808 the Bristol Journal, the Mirror, reported:

'The citizens of Bristol will hear with pleasure that they may now congratulate themselves on being likely, in a very short time, to rank with the metropolis, in that useful and necessary establishment, a public school on the economical plan of Joseph Lancaster . . .'

A room for three hundred was already hired, twenty-six respectable inhabitants had put their names on a committee, Joseph Lancaster had generously refused all compensation and advanced £60 from what he called 'the Royal Fund' for teaching materials. He recommended John Pickton as master at a salary of £52 per annum. On December 27th William Corston received a triumphant letter.

'All here is Victory . . . Every child, male and female, is to be educated, no piece work, no retail business, no local charity, but general education in Bristol for all, now, henceforth and for ever! The enemies are amazed and confounded . . .'

Back in London, however, it was the friends who were beginning to find their tolerance wearing thin.

In the curious balancing act that Joseph Lancaster's life had now become increasing recognition abroad was counterpointed by a perilous struggle against debt at home in the Royal Free School, Borough Road. The influential Whig journal, the 'Edinburgh Review', with whose editor Archibald Constable Joseph corresponded, came out strongly on the side of the Lancastrian schools. It set the pace for a steadily growing controversy in print which helped to bring the cause of education for the poor and the name of Lancaster before the nation. Meanwhile, in January 1808, one of the two gentlemen who had assisted in bailing Joseph out of the King's Bench prison was complaining of the latter journeying abroad instead of staying at home to attend to affairs that sorely needed his presence. The letter making this accusation was forwarded to Joseph who indignantly scribbled on it, 'This unnecessary letter came after I had actually taken my place in the coach to return to London'.

He arrived back from Bristol on January 19th in excellent spirits, his travelling expenses and a new suit of clothes having been paid for by another affluent friend. En route he had a meeting with Sam Whitbread in Hitchin, who remarked that Lancaster had been making a fine blaze in the country and asked him to call at Dover Street. Never able to refrain from a joking reference where he felt it to be particularly apposite, Joseph added in a letter to William Corston, '. . . shall be truly glad, if my dear Fox has come to London, to eat a bit of goose with him . . .'

His dear Fox had come to London. No less than William Corston, Joseph Fox was increasingly concerned about the finances of the school cause. Both men saw themselves as backers of a remarkable genius, and founders of a movement that would change the face of the United Kingdom. But, being business men, accustomed to handling money, they naturally wished their patronage to be properly disbursed and sensibly accounted for.

They met for the first time on January 22nd 1808, at William Corston's premises 30 Ludgate Hill. Joseph Lancaster was also present. The occasion was an initial meeting to set up a society to manage Lancaster's affairs. Minutes were kept. William Corston was to be Secretary, Joseph Fox Treasurer, Joseph Lancaster Superintendent of Education and to direct the printing office. The resolution setting out the aims of the society covered the interests of each individual man. It indicated how little recognition they had of the magnitude of the task which, if successful, they faced. For Joseph Lancaster, a man whose decisions often involved an instant emotional commitment to what he perceived to be a necessary course of action, it was the first faltering step in the painful process of the institutionalisation of his vision that was to wreck his life.

'It was unanimously resolved, "That, with a humble reliance on the blessing of Lord God Almighty and with a single eye to his glory: and with a view to benefit the British Empire: the persons present do constitute themselves a Society for the purpose of affording education, procuring employment, and, as far as possible, to furnish clothing to the children of the poorer subjects to George III: and also to diffuse the providential discovery of the vaccine inoculation in order that at the same time they may be instruments in the hands of Providence to preserve life from loathsome disease: and also, by furnishing objects for the exercise of industry, to render life useful.'

'That in order to prevent any impediment to the prosecution of this grand design, the persons present do constitute themselves Managers of this Society, to plan, prepare, and direct all its future operations; and that no business shall be brought before any meeting of subscribers who may probably come forward in aid of this Society but what has been recommended by this Committee of Managers'.

Joseph Lancaster was to be relieved of pecuniary difficulties and his private affairs were to come under the Committee. Joseph Fox was to advance certain monies. He handed over instantly £315 to deal with bills at the Royal Free School.

Two days later, on January 24th, Joseph Fox wrote to his colleagues. 'Yesterday, having spent some shillings in coach hire, in order to see a man worth £300,000 . . . and today having also spent some shillings in coach hire and walked seven miles in great uneasiness to see another worth perhaps £80,000 in order to gain their name to a loan: but without effect: I cannot but be of the opinion that this measure is not the direction of Providence. For, in the first place, supposing the whole were to be filled, the subscribers would be continually desiring to pry into our secret movements, and might impede our progress. In the second place the debt would constantly hang upon the Society, like a weight on the mainspring of a machine. And in the third place it will cost many weary steps, and much expense of money, time and lungs; and perhaps some irritation of temper, before the whole would be completed.'

It would be far better to trust in God and for Joseph to bend all his efforts to revive the Borough Road school, increase the numbers 'and make the house clean and neat for the approaching spring'. He should also ready the printing office, finish his abridgement of 'Improvements', complete the 1/– book and lessons and prepare to take orders, sit down quietly to write his life, progress in schools, receipts and expenditures. Joseph Fox had better be the sole loan holder. A subscription could be raised and an advertised appeal made.

The financial discussion with Lancaster was difficult and alarming. William Corston described it.

'After dinner our first subject was of debt. "Well Joseph," said Mr Fox, "What do you owe now? Do you owe a thousand pounds?" He only replied "Yes!" After a little time he asked, "Do you owe *two* thousand pounds?" A significant pause ensued. Joseph again replied "Yes". The third time he enquired, with increasing earnestness, affectionately tapping him on the shoulder, "Do you owe *three* thousand pounds?" Joseph burst into tears. "You must ask William Corston. He knows better what I owe than I do myself."' Joseph Fox then asked William Corston, who replied near four thousand.

After some moments meditation Joseph Fox said to William Corston, 'Sir I can do it with your assistance'. He indicated that he could lay his hands on £2000. Would William Corston be prepared to accept bills drawn on him by Joseph Fox. William Corston agreed. Joseph Fox turned to him and said, 'The cause is saved'.

A week later the Committee met again and Joseph Lancaster presented a statement of debts which came, in fact, to more than £5000 'in liquidation of a part of which bills . . . amounting to £2698. 13. 4d have been drawn by Mr J. Fox and accepted by Mr W. Corston'.

It was also resolved to engage a clerk to keep the cash and accounts, a matron for the Family, and someone skilled in the work of a printing office. A list of those who constituted the Family and dependents of the Royal Free School was attached to the minutes. It included Ann Springman, who was to be offered the post of matron and went on to become responsible for opening a number of noted Lancastrian schools for girls; Thomas Harrod, who acted as Joseph Lancaster's deputy when the latter travelled; John Veevers, known as 'Dr Sixfoot', a 'fine youth' who was to make a success of Birmingham; Richard Holland, in the printing office; Charles Bowyer at Canterbury and John Pickton at Bristol, both of whom still seem to have been on the Borough Road register; a washerwoman, a bricklayer and a labourer; Kenneth McRae, school master, and five employees at Bradley. Altogether there were twenty-eight souls, and Joseph Lancaster was asked to diminish this establishment in the most convenient manner possible.

So the Managers entered upon their responsibilities, little realising how severe was to be the drain on substance and nervous energy to which, for the forseeable future, they had committed themselves.

On February 1st Isaac Walters was appointed clerk at the Royal Free School. A few days later Joseph Fox was married.

Though his situation was desperate, Joseph Lancaster was made uneasy by the amount of control even these good friends now had over his affairs. Later he insisted that management of his financial concerns had been 'delegated' to Corston and Fox, and that 'This power was of course subject to legal revocation, at any period of Joseph Lancaster's choice'. Certainly it is true that in the minutes of the Committee for June 15th 1808 a resolution appeared, 'That once a month a statement shall be presented of all receipts in aid of J. Lancaster's Institution, together with all expenditure on account of Housekeeping, and other concerns connected therewith, and that whenever a balance be struck on the general account that all interference with the pecuniary concerns shall cease on the part of this Committee'. The trouble was that there was never any prospect of such a balance being struck.

It was in June also that the first reference to Joseph Lancaster appeared in William Allen's diary.

William Allen was a greatly respected member of the Society of Friends, a scientist and philanthropist associated, like Joseph Fox, with Guy's Hospital. A friend of William Wilberforce, Thomas Clarkson and James Mill, he ran a flourishing chemist's business in Plough Court, London, but was constantly called upon to undertake responsibilities in the promotion of causes connected with social reform. He was a man of wide sympathies and the utmost integrity, sober, unassuming and kind.

Like many others William Allen had visited the Royal Free School. He recorded his first reactions to it.

'I can never forget the impression which the scene made upon me. Here I beheld a thousand children collected from the streets, where they were learning nothing but mischief, one bad boy corrupting another, all reduced to the most perfect order, and training to habits of subordination and usefulness, and learning the great truths of the gospel from the Bible. The feelings of the spectator while contemplating the results which might take place in this country, and the world in general, by the extension of the system thus brought into practice by this meritorious young man, were overpowering and found vent in tears of joy.'

William Corston and Joseph Fox, alarmed no doubt by the

web of liabilities into which they now found themselves drawn, had already begun to enlarge the Committee. John Jackson, another committed supporter, was also a member when, on July 29th, William Allen and Joseph Foster, a merchant related to the banking Lloyds, were added to the number. In August Thomas Sturge, shopkeeper of Southwark and old friend of Lancaster, was to make up the complement.

Once again the minutes of the July 29th meeting showed a resolution.

'Upon an investigation of Joseph Lancaster's affairs, it appears that in bringing his System of Education for poor children to its present state of perfection he has had, through a long course of years to struggle with considerable difficulties for want of a capital: that these difficulties have produced a degree of embarrassment which not only tends to cramp his useful exertions, but is in danger of suspending them entirely if not speedily removed.

'It appears that although the whole amount of his debts is £6449 and his property taken at a low estimate only £3500, yet if liberally supported, there is a fair prospect of his being able to retrieve his affairs, in no very long period, from the profit of his Printing Office and other sources: he appears to have the material for producing a considerable profit from his establishment, but they will be wholly useless without a sufficient capital.

'It appears that the care necessary to the keeping up, perfecting and diffusing the benefits of Joseph Lancaster's system will for some time require his undivided attention. The following persons therefore, under a full conviction of the incalculable benefits which not only this country but the civilised world may derive from the measures in question, agree to act as a Committee for managing Joseph Lancaster's financial concerns so far as relates to loan of capital proposed to be raised by subscription in shares of £100 each.

viz John Jackson M.P.

Joseph Fox

William Corston

William Allen

Joseph Foster'

The money was to be put into the hands of a banker, and payments made only over three signatures.

'The Committee shall not interfere with Joseph Lancaster's Plans or System but shall leave him at full liberty to prosecute them in his own way, except where expence is to be incurred. And Joseph Lancaster shall not incur any new debts, on account of his Plans for educating poor children, without the sanction of the Committee in writing.'

This agreement Joseph Lancaster signed.

Like beavers attempting to dam a particularly turbulent stream with inadequate materials, the Committee settled down to control Joseph Lancaster's passionate instincts, financial mutualism, and large-hearted benevolence. Each of them paid £100 into the loan fund, but, for William Allen especially, this sum was soon swamped in the constant regular payments with which, week after week, Joseph Lancaster's personal and professional debts had to be subsidised. It was not just that the school at Maiden Bradley had become an expensive incubus, repairs and rent at Deptford and a third school at Camberwell had to be paid, the printing office, which never fulfilled its promise, to be supported, wages, housekeeping, building alterations at the Borough Road looked after; there were also Joseph's personal expenses, including board for his child and lodging and care for poor unhappy Elizabeth.

Most of the Borough Road debts were to small tradesmen; bricklayer, timber merchant, carpenter, typefounder, stationer, furniture maker, candle maker and those who sold food. Many were clamourous for payment, but not all.

'To the honour of a baker in the neighbourhood to whom there was a considerable debt owing, it must be mentioned, that when a degree of surprise was manifested at his having given so large a credit, he replied, "The good which Mr Lancaster has done to the poor of this neighbourhood is such, that as long as I have a loaf left, I will give half of it to enable him to continue such a beneficial exertion".' William Allen wrote in his diary.

Into the bargain the subscription list was showing signs of a steady decline. Only those of the King and the Royal Family, amounting to about £300, could be absolutely relied on.

William Allen, who rapidly took over the office of treasurer and in whose neat hand so many of the minutes of Committee meetings were written, had no illusions as to priorities. He saw 'that the prudent management of Joseph Lancaster was the first and great object', and recognised that 'We have a delicate subject to handle . . .' Admitting that Joseph's intentions were always honest and honourable, it was nevertheless obvious 'that although the man has a peculiar talent for this work, he is deficient in some of those minuter qualifications which are . . . essential to the final success of any measure in which property is concerned.'

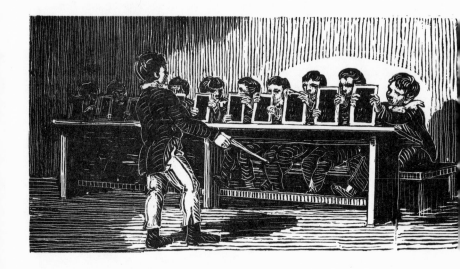

'Writing — after engraving in Improvements 5th ed.'

Chapter 8
A NATIONAL EDUCATION

'The treasures of Britain are her youth . . . the real wealth of a nation consists in the number of its intelligent good men.' (Joseph Lancaster. An Address to Friends and Superintendents of Sunday Schools . . .)

Eighteen hundred and nine was George III's Jubilee year. The old King, who had once expressed it as his wish that every poor child in his dominions should be taught to read the Bible, was entering his final madness. Joseph Lancaster, who had taken the Royal desire as a personal command, was poised to become a figure of national importance. He wrote a filial report to his Royal patron in June telling him of his successes and expressing his loyalty, affection and gratitude. He did not mention his debts; which seemed to him anyway to be of trivial moment when set alongside the great work.

For many, not least the Society of Friends, Joseph Lancaster was increasingly being seen as a dangerous man. Friends perceived his personality, with its unquakerlike exuberance and love of jollity and display, as being prejudicial both to the work, with which they were becoming responsibly identified, and to the whole Quaker image with its emphasis on integrity, sobriety and inconspicuous goodness. The Church Establishment also felt profoundly threatened because, like William Tyndale and others before him, Joseph Lancaster by-passed the teachings of the Church within his schools and took his pupils directly to a basic Christianity. Neither of those points of view made any appeal to Joseph's understanding. Though admiring individual Friends, he thought Quakers in general dry and narrow; worse, he was beginning to say so publicly. And the proposition that the Bible contained the basis of all Christian truth seemed to him so self-evident, particularly when combined with denominational ability to use the Sabbath to put what gloss they pleased on this foundation, that he came to believe that only a campaign of personal persecution could account for the virulence of the opposition he now encountered.

For all its difficulties the Royal Free School in the Borough Road, which held out the possibility of solving the problem of popular education in a way that Pestalozzi's Yverdon with its one hundred and forty mostly fee-paying pupils did not, was now almost the most important educational establishment in the world. Within the nation the sectarian battle, mounting towards a climax in 1811, engendered civic energy as well as public interest, resulting in the setting up of committees and the building of schools all over the kingdom. The Royal Free School's role within this spreading network was to provide teachers for the Lancastrian System, which in its turn made possible an enormous expansion in the normally tiny numbers of children at school. The Borough Road press supplied the tools for those teachers; printed lessons and the text of 'Improvements', in which the practical running of a school was minutely described. But the initiative for the actual development of schools was, and was to remain, a local affair, locally based.

In 1808 Joseph Fox had sprung to his friend's defence in print with the first edition, produced on the press at the Royal Free School, of 'A Comparative View of the plans of education as detailed in the publications of Dr Bell and Mr Lancaster'. Much of this pamphlet was taken up by quotations from 'Improvements';

the rest by illustrations from the writings of both Lancaster and Bell designed to prove the originality of the Lancastrian System.

Though it somehow failed to make the profit that was so eagerly expected, the Borough Road printing press was continually at work turning out tracts, broadsheets, school books, Church catechisms, etc., and in particular new editions of 'Improvements'. The third impression of the latter had doubled in size since 1803 and included sections on female and religious education without adding much of value to the basic content. The 4th and 5th editions in 1808 and 1810, though smaller, were marred by the bitter tone of the autobiographical observations which increasingly Lancaster found it impossible to exclude. But the fruits of experience still lightened the text:

'The less a master's voice is heard among his scholars the more he will be obeyed. The noise of a school is generally in proportion to the noise a master makes in it himself. The punishment of the scholars, and the fatigue of the master, is nearly in like proportion.'

Practical ideas continued to flow; the 5th edition had suggestions for heating by underground flues, rounding off the corners of desks and forms so that pupils did not hurt themselves, and instructions for operating a school circulating library.

During the years 1808-1811 Joseph Lancaster produced 'An Account of the Progress of Joseph Lancaster's Plan for the education of poor children and the training of masters for country schools', 'An Address to the Friends and Superintendents of Sunday Schools . . .', 'Hints and Directions for Building Schoolrooms', 'Instructions for forming and conducting a society', 'A Report of J. Lancaster's Progress from the year 1798 . . .', 'Sketch of an Economical Plan for Providing the Public with Good Schoolmasters', 'Fruits of Christian love . . .' and numerous other treaties and monographs as well as countless letters and appeals. He wrote as he spoke, with immediacy, passion and fluency, with little sifting of thought and even less diplomatic caution. He did not come from a world where words were carefully weighed. He said openly what he thought, felt and believed, seemingly unaware of the effect that his brashness and self-regard might have on others.

The battle lines had been laid down in 1805 by Sarah Trimmer. In the autumn of 1807, after Samuel Whitbread introduced his Bill on the Poor Law, the influential 'Edinburgh

Review', with Henry Brougham as a major contributor, entered the fray supporting Lancaster. In November 1810 it carried an article on Joseph Fox's 'Comparative View . . .' giving Lancaster the credit for establishing the System in England, and drawing attention to the energy of his efforts to promote it as compared with Dr Bell's lethargy. Some said that no good could come from educating the whole community; such a measure would result in anarchy and tumult. In countering this opinion the 'Edinburgh' quoted from Andrew Bell himself, that talent was no respecter of classes and might be buried anywhere. On the great religious issue the 'Edinburgh' considered that the fear was not of fidelity, but of dissent.

The Tory 'Quarterly Review' was established in 1809 to oppose the Whig 'Edinburgh Review'. In autumn 1811, also under the guise of a notice of Joseph Fox's pamphlet, the 'Quarterly' replied. They took their stand behind Dr Bell and that 'good old lady' Mrs Trimmer, who had died in December 1810, and repeated the argument of the ill consequences to the national Church of 'deistic' education. There was an admission that both clergy and government had neglected schooling in the kingdom, and attention was drawn to Andrew Bell's suggestion in the 2nd edition of 'Experiment' of the formation of a Board of Education. 'Sectarians', the 'Quarterly' proclaimed, almost as if it were an accusation, 'have more zeal than the members of an established church'. Especially among the Quakers Joseph Lancaster had been able to calculate on liberal and efficient aid. On the matter of fund-raising they added a revealing comment. 'His own peculiar character contributed not a little to his success. There was nothing in his education, temper or previous habits of life, which rendered it unpleasant for him to travel about soliciting subscriptions; a thing to which, however meritorious and urgent the motive, men of finer minds usually feel repugnant, even when it becomes an act of duty'. Joseph Fox too was stigmatised as 'violent and vulgar'.

The involvement of the 'Edinburgh Review' brought men of national importance into the forefront of the battle. Henry Brougham, later to be Lord Chancellor, took up the cause of popular education. In 1812 James Mill, utilitarian philosopher with his own ideas on educating his son John Stuart, contributed a pamphlet on the Lancastrian side to the controversy. 'Schools for all in preference to schools for churchmen only . . .' argued that even if Andrew Bell had first invented 'cheap' education, it was Joseph Lancaster's improvements that made its spread possible. However, should all credit be given to Bell, the great division still remained between exclusive or inclusive schools on a religious basis. The Church was no part of the British Constitution and to argue that there would be good in the separation of Church and State was not to argue against the Constitution, as so many of Lancaster's opponents averred.

With Jeremy Bentham and other educational theorists, James Mill hoped to set up a school for superior education on Lancastrian lines. So, by a gradually widening network of contacts, Joseph Lancaster, who did not mind travelling around soliciting subscriptions, was drawn into association not only with those who had money and patronage to give him but with the men of 'finer minds' who hoped, on his practical contribution, to build social and educational theories that would change the face of the United Kingdom.

In 1809 Joseph Lancaster, no doubt feeling that he had secured his financial rear by the creation of a managing Committee, set out to conquer the nation.

Leaving Thomas Harrod to head the Family in the Borough Road; with Ann Springman to look after the girls and the elderly Isaac Walters to deal with the daily accounts Joseph, accompanied by a demonstration team of his boys, took to the road. He had become very stout, which may have contributed to his often indifferent health. Above what he himself called 'his enormous load of flesh', the rubicund optimistic face gave little sign of the stresses through which he had already passed. The conviction that he was the standard bearer for an issue of national importance, gave him a sense of his own pre-eminence which to many seemed arrogance. Though he dressed soberly, as a Quaker should, he liked to travel in style and to make a splash. For some this was a man of humble origins with overweening pretensions to the society of those in stations far above his own; others found in him a man of vision, touched by greatness. His own enjoyment of his fame, combined with extreme sensitivity when he thought himself traduced, made him enemies; his lack of financial acumen, which went with a genuine, unworldly belief that Providence intended what faith produced to be used without thought for the morrow, made him the despair of many who liked and admired him. But his warmth of heart, his devotion to an educational ideal and his brilliance as a teacher and an inspirational speaker continued to bring him faithful and patient friends. His two families, who knew him best and were to suffer most at his hands, loved him to the end. In the next two years Joseph Lancaster was to lecture in over fifty places, many of which excited by his burning enthusiasm, would instantly set up committees and prepare to found schools.

The boys were an essential part of his method. In April 1810 he described the party's journey to Bath.

'. . . all the Boys happy, well and as merry as they could be – at the sight of Windsor Castle they burst out into singing God Save the King – and closed the day with singing the evening hymn – They were all inside (the coach) but one and slept very sound and happy – they made curious faces as boys do when they are asleep some frowning, some smiling others snoring and sleeping with their mouths open . . . we got in about nine o'clock yesterday morning thoroughly tired and fatigued . . . they came into Bath literally sleeping on . . .'

Kenneth Macrae and Maurice Cross were two of the lads who played an active part. Maurice Cross, 'an interesting boy of fourteen, conducts himself so as to make himself much beloved every way and gives great effect to the lectures by drilling in rows boys who have never known the plan before'.

Kenneth Macrae, who was older, acted as agent and scout going on ahead of Joseph Lancaster to find accommodation, see that handbills were printed and generally prepare for the coming of the Master. In Nottingham, not being able to get to the theatre because the owners were away, he waited on the Mayor and secured a large room. At Leeds the solution was not so easy. Joseph had written ahead to engage the theatre, whose proprietor, at that moment in Hull, agreed to let it at five guineas a night. When Kenneth Macrae arrived however the proprietor's agent, a man called Wright, had different ideas. Though Kenneth managed to secure the theatre key, when Wright saw the handbills announcing Mr Lancaster's lecture he came to the theatre and began to bully the caretaker for the five guineas, which Joseph probably expected to pay later out of the proceeds. The caretaker hurried to Kenneth, in consternation for fear the 'enemy' both could, and would, shut the doors. Kenneth produced the proprietor's letter of consent and, in spite of advice to let the matter rest, determined to confront the agent.

He arrived in Mr Wright's office where the latter greeted him 'making many congees and shewing him all the attention he would to a person of quality, for which he doubtless took him by his gold seals and long whiskers'. If his boys travelled with him Joseph Lancaster was determined that they should do so with equal panache.

With some haughtiness Kenneth Macrae said, 'Sir I have been to the theatre and the Doorkeeper informs me you have been enquiring for the money'. The agent retorted that he had been instructed never to let the doors be opened without either money or a written order from the proprietor.

'I have that written order in my pocket,' said Kenneth. 'To whom should I shew it.'

The agent replied, 'To the doorkeeper, or more properly to me'. But Kenneth Macrae, reflecting his master's often tactless and brash behaviour, preferred, on the excuse that negotiations with the proprietor had not included Mr Wright, to show the authority only to the doorkeeper, thus securing a point, and making an enemy.

The size of audiences varied, though it seems never to have been as large as Lancaster anticipated. In the spring of 1809, in Manchester, he 'lectured last night to above 1500, for 3 hours', and expected that the next evening the gathering would be three or four thousand. It is more likely that several hundreds attended those meetings, and certainly the money they brought in rarely exceeded board and travelling expenses. In Leicester, 'in inclement weather', there were one hundred and fifty of great respectability; in Derby a hundred and fifty, in Loughborough 'a poor few'; in Nottingham his talk was 'well attended and well received – (but expensive and unproductive)'. What mattered, however, were the resolutions taken at the Town meetings which followed, when committees were set up and subscriptions collected in order to bring a school into being.

Sometimes schools were already in existence, often struggling to follow a plan which was not properly understood. 'From Northampton in a very snowy day I proceeded to Leicester where I found a little school of one hundred children going on well and I think the master capable of managing 300 (or at least he might be made so in a short time . . .' In Sheffield, on the contrary, there was a 'stupid overgrown cabbage of a thing' – the master not the school. Nottingham had a young Scotchman who had started a 'Book School' with the help of a Church of England patron and a copy of 'Improvements'. Joseph found him a candid clever man with '220 children in a most excellent state of order'. When, however, at the Town meeting he suggested that this master come to the Royal Free School for instruction and then take over an enlarged school there was strong opposition from the clergy because this man happened to be a minister in the Church of Scotland and this made him a dissenter. Joseph Lancaster was infuriated by this move, 'to cast a useful man out of a situation of which he was worthy because after doing his duty on six days he chose to follow the dictates of his own conscience on the 7th . . .' He won the victory, but the spectre of Andrew Bell had been raised to persecute him.

As Joseph Lancaster travelled round, and schools began to proliferate, he saw more clearly than ever the need for a stock of good schoolmasters trained in the essentials of the Lancastrian System, and everywhere he went he was on the look out for likely lads. 'All these things prove the necessity of a prompt and active choice of a set of young men as schoolmasters who may have their mind imbued with a love of the cause and make the schools in practice correspond with the theory of the lectures'. In 1810 there were sixteen masters in training at the Borough Road and demand was rapidly increasing.

It was also considered important that these young men should be attached to the person of Joseph Lancaster. It was this that made for discipline and kept them in their proper orbit. 'My young people confide in my honour to make all arrangments for them and to alter or change as I see best'. The Lancastrian System was not just a plan; it possessed a spirit which was the result of highly personal relationships, a band of brothers supporting each other in a crusade, and owing allegiance to the creator. Joseph Lancaster was at the centre of a complicated jigsaw puzzle, doing his best to see that schools in major towns got his most trusted young lieutenants to start them off in the right direction.

Already, however, when the managing Committee had been in existence only a few months, this concept was threatened. Joseph was in Liverpool, staying with his older brother William. It is not clear who had started the school in Liverpool, but in March 1809 it was masterless and Joseph himself took it over, with the help of his niece Mary Ann. He then sent down an urgent message to the Royal Free School for John Veevers, aged nineteen, one of the Family, to come and take responsibility in Liverpool. The letter that came back told him that Veevers had been designated for Southampton by Joseph Fox. Lancaster was amazed and affronted that such a decision should have been taken without consultation. It also involved him in embarrassment with the Liverpool Committee to whom he had promised John Veevers.

Writing, as always before his indignation had time to cool, he accused Joseph Fox and William Allen of opening his personal letters, one of which contained the request from Southampton, and flouting his wishes. A few days later, when the Southampton decision had been reversed, he had to apologise for his haste. Thomas Harrod, who had been left with instructions to open all Lancaster's mail and forward copies to Joseph before he showed them to the Committee, had not done so. He had been reprimanded. In the meantime Joseph Fox's silence, on that and other matters, had been explained by news of the birth of his son.

Nine months later William Lancaster's wife in Liverpool was still trying to get a settlement of her bill for boarding and lodging John Veevers. By that time John had been offered the mastership of the Severn Street School, Birmingham at a salary of £120 per annum. He wrote to Joseph Lancaster asking if he could accept. Joseph at first had objections, wishing to ask the Birmingham Committee for a higher salary and a handsome commission for the Royal Free School. Nevertheless John Veevers got the job and made an outstanding success of it.

Patron of the Severn Street school was Charles Lloyd, Quaker philanthropist and banker. In November 1810, when John Veevers had been teaching in Birmingham for a year, Joseph Lancaster stayed with Charles Lloyd.

'. . . one day I went into school intending to make Veevers a present of a watch as a reward for his merit (which certainly highly deserves the honor it has) I found he was absent and had the happiness of remaining in school and seeing everything go on like clockwork. 400 boys governed by a little fellow not fourteen – Indeed the delight afforded me from seeing so perfect a specimen of my plan carried on (in) the master's absence – I could do nothing but think of him and it for many hours after, and I told my Friends that if my whole life had spent for no other

purpose but to make one schoolmaster and that one J. Veevers –
I should from what I had that day seen, have thought my time
and talents well employed'.

There had been a similar incident in Bristol when Joseph
Lancaster was very ill in the spring of 1809. He was taken into
the home of a local friend, who happened to be a doctor. The
master of the Bristol school, an ex-Borough Road boy, handed
over his responsibilities to his monitor-general in order to devote
himself to nursing Joseph Lancaster. This time it was the Bristol
Committee who, having visited the schol while he was in charge,
subscribed for a silver watch for the thirteen-year-old monitor.

In Manchester that year Joseph Lancaster stayed with David
Holt, a Quaker, owner of Chorlton spinning mill which employed several hundred people. David Holt, who devoted one
evening a week to general schooling in his mill, was to become a
close friend and supporter of Joseph Lancaster. The situation in
the city, as in many other manufacturing towns, was one of great
distress through an embargo on the American trade and the
disastrous effects of continental war and speculation in wool.

On that first visit lecture placards were printed and information circulated. The meeting was held in a large room at the
Bull's Head in the Market Place. David Holt, Joseph Lancaster
and some friends, who included the chief men of the town,
attended. They then waited several hours but no one else came.
David Holt put this down to High Church influence. Undaunted
the meeting appointed a chairman and proceeded to business. A
resolution was passed that 'The Manchester Lancastrian School'
should be opened, and so it was, in an old dissenting meeting
house in Lever Street. It went on to prove very successful.

Joseph had promised the Manchester Ladies Society eighteen
pennies out of every half crown ticket sold for his lectures, to
help create employment for poor females. There must have been
others, better attended, for the Society profited by £21.

'. . . now I believe the completion of the fall of a man was
accomplished fully in the degradation and vassalage of women in
society', he wrote to Joseph Fox, 'and much as the female
character is exalted in Britain compared with what it is in other
places – I believe it is much below what it ought to be as (to)
employment. Every man has a business etc by which to obtain
his livelihood – every woman has not and the consequence is that
women once reduced have often no choice but starvation, or

misery and infamy left to them . . .'

In the same letter he was suggesting that John Jackson send him £10 to buy Birmingham toys for rewards in the Dover school.

In Chesterfield there was a depot for French officer prisoners, fifty of whom were to be given free tickets for Lancaster's lecture in the evening in the hope that they would spread the message on their return to France. Unfortunately, to Joseph's great disappointment, on that day an order had arrived that they were not to be allowed out after 5 pm.

In 1810 there had begun to be an interest in the British Army in the possibilities of Lancastrian schools. Joseph Lancaster, son of a soldier, who though a pacifist Quaker could never forget that he owed his own education to his father's Army pension, welcomed this development. The Duke of Kent, George III's fourth son, a friend of William Allen who was later to take charge of His Royal Highness's own tangled financial affairs, had now become closely involved with the Royal Lancastrian System and had instigated a school for young recruits and the children of soldiers in the 4th Battalion the Royals, of which regiment he was Commander in Chief. In July 1810, at the suggestion of Joseph Fox, a Memorial went to the Duke of Richmond, Lord Lieutenant of Ireland, asking for his patronage for schools in general on the Lancastrian plan, and in particular for a model school in the vicinity of Dublin barracks. Quoting the experience of the Duke of Kent's school, the Memorial noted, '. . . and to such a degree of simplicity has the system been reduced that young drummers are converted into schoolmasters and in the change of quarters from Malden to Dunbar, the desk and necessaries for the school are conveyed with the baggage of the regiment'. When Joseph Lancaster went to Edinburgh a number of those young men came from Dunbar to act as living illustrations to his lecture.

In December a Colonel Borthwick and two officers from Woolwich visited the Royal Free School and asked if Mr Lancaster could lecture at Woolwich to 'get up a school for young soldiers and soldiers' children'. In the same month there was an application from the Cavalry depot at Maidstone and from Chelmsford barracks. The Duke of Wellington's 'scum' were reaching out just as eagerly as their ragamuffin civilian counterparts to learn to read and write.

During the various journeys undertaken in 1809 and 1810, when over three thousand miles were covered and fifty new schools founded, Joseph Lancaster wrote back constantly to the Committee. Sometimes there were two, or even three, letters with the same date; often they ended with a request for money, which William Allen unfailingly provided. 'Thence I went again to Derby and was obliged to draw on thee again – for £25 at one month after sight – of all the many I have drawn since I left London £30 only has been for private and personal use', he wrote in December 1810. 'It is with regret I draw for so much but it is unavoidable – and if I do not travel I shall not be able to do the good that I am doing to the cause . . . nor you be able to make the report you will at the year's end'. Despite harsh conditions – 'our way through the break neck roads in the ruts of which the chaise was tossed like a vessel in a storm . . . arrived 3am. Glad to get to bed' – and occasional confrontations with hostile audiences, Joseph's letters remained invariably optimistic. 'My lectures are most wonderfully received . . . you can hardly conceive what I am about,' he reported to his father; and to William Allen, 'The Victory at Nottingham has been complete and triumphant'. But back in the Borough Road life did not assume such a rosy hue.

The establishment of a managing Committee did not pay the creditors who were still clamouring at the doors. Nor, in fact, did it bring in as much extra money in the way of subscriptions as the Trustees perhaps expected. And fresh debts continued to accumulate.

In June 1809 William Allen had a poorish night worrying about Lancaster's affairs. They were by no means easy to disentangle. Joseph had opened three schools before the pattern of local committees became normal, Deptford, Camberwell and Maiden Bradley. All were costing the Committee more than could be afforded, and Maiden Bradley was ruinously expensive. The Royal Free School itself was the personal property of Joseph Lancaster, though Samuel Rogers had a mortgage on the premises. Joseph Fox had visited Rogers to persuade him to give it up so that a Deed of Security could be made out to safeguard the real estate for the creditors. In January the furniture had been valued at £199.18.6d and both premises and stock insured for £3000. While Joseph Lancaster continued to buy prizes for country schools, to promise to print a poem written at his request by a young woman in York, and to give her the profits, and to incur bills for inns and travel, William Allen was subsidising the Committee to pay for Elizabeth Lancaster's board, first with R. Carter and then with J. Withers at Thatcham, and for fourteen shillings for her mantua maker's bill, and was making himself responsible for a host of other public and private accounts.

In March 1809 there had been a blaze at Maiden Bradley which the Duke of Somerset blamed on Joseph Lancaster's workman Clements. It was said that he set fire to the furze so carelessly that twenty acres and a wood fence had been consumed and it was only because the Duke's men were turned out that a forest was saved. Relations with the Duke, already going sour, were further damaged. Jane Thomson reported that the school was failing; Joseph himself had lost all interest in it. There was rent due of £52.17.6d. In December Joseph Fox announced that the Duke had asked King of Frome to make a valuation of the premises, and Thomas Sturge was requested to write to young Sturge of Bristol to act for Joseph Lancaster. It took another six months, and some acrimonious discussion, before the Duke of Somerset agreed to release Joseph Lancaster from his obligations if he, the Duke, had his arrears of rent paid and got the land and buildings back.

In October 1809, after a visit and a lecture from Lancaster, Deptford formed a committee and took over their school, but for the Camberwell premises, put up for sale in May 1810, there were no bidders.

In an effort to keep up with the tide which threatened to engulf them, the Committee met every week at William Allen's chemist's establishment in Plough Court. Also in October a minute recorded that the subscription list had raised £3500 plus advances from William Allen, William Corston and Joseph Fox of £1353.19.11d, as well as loans from Joseph Foster, Samuel Rogers, Sir George Mackenzie, Sam Whitbread, John Jackson and Thomas Sturge which amounted to £2307.2.0d – in all £8162 was due from Joseph Lancaster 'for capital advanced, not including the Duke of Somerset's business and independent of Tradesman's Bills and other claims'. No wonder that on July 16th 1810 there was a minute:

'The present state of J. Lancaster's concerns being fully considered at this Committee it is deemed essentially necessary to procure a more extensive co-operation from benevolent Persons, whose situation in Life, may give them an influence, in order that a sufficient sum, may be raised, to relieve the members of this Committee from the unequal pressure which they have so long sustained, in supporting this great public work and to place the establishment upon a permanent footing: and also that Joseph Lancaster should take prompt and effectual measures to qualify a sufficient number of teachers upon his Plan, to answer the increasing demands of the country'.

Though Joseph Lancaster gave William Allen and his fellow Trustees many uneasy nights, the Royal Lancastrian System itself did not. Each of these men had complete faith in the Plan. Their vision of the future, if only the financial impasse could somehow be resolved, was as grandiose as Lancaster's own. Their thinking embraced dimensions which were not national only, nor even European, but global. William Allen was an active member of the African Institution, which interested itself in the new colony for freed slaves at Sierra Leone, and in 1811 the Institution had two young Africans training at the Borough Road to return as teachers to that country. Among their companions were an African from the West Indies, in danger of being taken back and sold as a slave, who unfortunately died of an abcess in the lung; Tapeoe a native of Otaheite; and Joseph Pen Selling, aged 16, a Danish prisoner of war released to train as a teacher in the hope that the Danish Government would set up a Lancastrian school for him in Copenhagen. Four schools were being set up in Glasgow; the schoolroom in Belfast was already built. America had been interestd since Thomas Eddy, who founded the Free School Society in New York City in 1805, had written to Joseph Lancaster the year before asking for information. In June 1811, in the District of Columbia, the cornerstone of the first Lancastrian school was laid in Georgetown. Joseph Lancaster answered an enquiry by highly recommending the Ould brothers, Robert, who had been a master at Swansea, and Henry. Robert had looked after Henry since their mother's death and was unwilling to leave England without him. Both had been Joseph's pupils in the Borough Road. In the event Robert Ould was to serve the Georgetown school for nearly thirty years. Distinguished visitors from other countries also frequently came to the school in Southwark. In 1810 they included Simon Bolivar, a young man still to make his name in Venezuela as Liberator; in 1812 William Allen showed the school to the Tsar of Russia.

But tension was growing between the Founder of the Royal Lancastrian System and those into whose hands, however unwillingly, he had entrusted its financial affairs. In 1811 they still needed each other, though the thought may already have occurred to one or two members of the Committee that life would be simpler without Lancaster. They had begun to feel that scandal might at any moment overwhelm them. William Allen's attempts at 'prudent management' of 'this delicate subject' did not seem to be meeting with any great success. But not only did the schools carry his name, he was the life-blood which flowed through the veins of the System. Known far and wide, it was Joseph Lancaster who stirred up local communities, loosened the purse strings of patrons, inspired children to undertake daunting responsibilities and poured a lively enquiring spirit into a mechanical plan. Lancaster might produce horrendous liabilities, but as an asset he remained of incalculable value. With all its careful, patient devotion to the cause, the Committee still needed the inexhaustible energy and passionate commitment that Joseph Lancaster brought to the publication of his vision and the spreading of his ideas.

The decision to enlarge the Committee was taken late in 1810, at a moment when Joseph Lancaster was travelling in the country. On November 23rd Henry Brougham and Joseph Fox dined with William Allen to discuss this matter. It had been considered 'essentially necessary to procure a more extensive co-operation from benevolent persons . . . in order . . . to place the establishment upon a permanent footing'. A number of people were contacted and on December 7th the enlarged Committee met at six o'clock in the evening. Fourteen attended; John Jackson was in the chair. A week later the Committee met again at the Thatched House Tavern. John Walker of Southgate took the chair, Brougham stated the business; about twenty or thirty persons were present. 'I hope this committee will be able to take off some of the pecuniary burden which has lain too heavily on a few,' William Allen wrote in his diary that night. On December 17th the finance sub-committee set up by the Trustees to lay before them a statement of Joseph Lancaster's affairs met. The Committee put its mind to drawing up a Constitution.

The pressure on Joseph was steadily mounting. He was conscious of the slow erosion of the independence which he considered vital to his life and work. The Trustees, whom he had called into being as a temporary measure, were now not only entrenched, but had greatly added to their number. On returning to the Borough Road he insisted that no one was eligible to serve on the finance sub-committee unless personally nominated by himself. It was already too late, and for all his optimism he must have known it, though during the next three years he was to fight a strenuous and increasingly rancorous battle to retain his own position. In January 1811 he wrote to William Allen about the appointment of vice-presidents. He wanted to give first refusal to Lord Somerville and the Duke of Bedford, who had been his earliest influential supporters. He saw no wisdom in changing proven friends for those who might be in with the 'gay licentious crowd' but would not 'stir over the threshold to follow the example of their Royal master'.

The connection with the King was another important area in which Joseph Lancaster did not trust the Committee. From the beginning he had felt that the King's patronage was personal to himself, and only through him to the System. At a period when the patrons of a man making his own way in the world meant everything to his success or failure, and gave him his public standing as well as his private backing, Joseph's debt to the Royal interest was undoubtedly enormous. But he had also come to have a filial feeling for old mad George III, and, in the most respectful way possible, the Royal household had grown to seem like his own third family. The rumour, which had been current in 1807, that the King had withdrawn his subscription, had hurt Joseph more deeply because it seemed to call in question the bond between himself and his Sovereign than because it might damage his financial prospects. Now William Allen and Joseph Fox, no less susceptible to the Royal favour, were suggesting that the Patronage, which carried with it the Royal subscription, should be shifted from the man to the institution and, in its major manifestation, from the father to the son, about to be sworn in as Prince Regent.

With these proposals Joseph Lancaster felt the foundations move under him. The old King, mad or not, had come to symbolise the conscientious paterfamilias, respected if not loved; the Prince Regent, flamboyant and factional, was quite a different kettle of fish. Joseph wrote to William Allen that he saw no reason to endanger or shock the present Royal patronage or make 'my Institution' the tool of any political party.

More difficult to refute was the personal argument. Here he felt himself to be fighting for something more precious even than the reputation of his school. What he saw as being threatened was the umbilical cord between himself and his System, reinforced yearly by the gift of One Hundred Pounds from the hand of the Monarch to Joseph Lancaster personally, for the education of the children of the poor. He saw what the shift in emphasis could mean to his own position. 'The King cannot be patron in any way than he has always been and nothing can be considered under his patronage without his sanction,' he wrote to William Allen. 'The Prince Regent cannot be a substitute for him.' Any attempts to divert Royal patronage from its present channel into that of the Committee would be dangerous, and if successful 'injurious to my plans as far as their success depends on my exertions as an individual patronised as such by them. Much of my success has hinged on this very thing and so productive of thorns has the honor been to me, that for the honor's sake any man may have it who will do my work, but seeing no one to stand in my place and take the toil and labour I do I am afraid for my work's sake of injuring the work and by my own movements achieving that for my enemies which they have never been able to accomplish'.

During the first half of 1811 Joseph Lancaster was at the Royal Free School, labouring day and night with his 'little troop' to make the institution, whose master had gone to take charge at Chichester, a model of perfection. He suggested that the schoolroom be enlarged, from 520/30, to take eleven or twelve hundred boys; though there were actually only four hundred pupils at the time. 'Would it not be good, as a stimulus to public benevolence, to increase holding out to view our great school with our little Generalisimo conducting it,' he wrote to William Allen. For much of January and February Joseph was, in fact, ill with a violent cough and racked by rheumatic pain and Maurice Cross took charge. The doctor and his wife called. He doubled the pills. She left a guinea. The good boys would get a halfpenny and were already sharpening their teeth to make war on the gingerbread that sum would buy. Could William Allen send him a 'phial full of patience'.

But it was William Allen who needed the patience. Hurrying from place to place with the books, trying to involve those whom he knew, Wilberforce on January 12th, Sir Samuel Romilly on

January 19th, he was often 'uneasy at the pecuniary advances I have made in the school concern'. That, however, did not prevent him, with the cooperation of Joseph Fox, from encouraging a school in Spitalfields, which was attacked in The Times, and promoting a school for several hundreds in Westminster.

'Indeed the work goes on in all directions exactly as we could wish, or more properly far beyond what we could have expected. Nothing discourages us but the unavoidable heavy expenses we are obliged to encounter,' he wrote to Richard Reynolds, the Quaker philanthropist. 'The average of our expenditure is sixty pounds per week: our income from subscriptions about twenty pounds; if we could make the annual subscriptions three thousand pounds we should be quite at ease, and able gradually to pay off the advances.'

The sums of money involved were very large, and all the Committee's management had not succeeded in reducing them. There were nearly forty lads in training as schoolmasters, being boarded and clothed at the Royal Free School. The half yearly accounts showed £1119.6.1d for this item alone.

From his sickbed, having been unable to keep a breakfast engagement with the Duke of Kent, Joseph Lancaster wrote to encourage his Trustees. Publicly, at any rate, he still paid glowing tributes to their management of his affairs. He went so far as to congratulate them on being led to advance money to himself and the cause, for he saw this as producing wider confidence. If only his friends would believe in him. Under praise or frowns, domestic infelicity and trials, debts, embarrassment, imprisonment, he had never lost his integrity. He needed their spirits to hold up his hands. The prospects before him were glorious 'but I must act on my own responsibility only and your business will be to investigate inquire and confirm . . .'

An attempt was made to draw up a Deed of Trust, which would clarify the legal position between Joseph Lancaster and the Committee. On February 18th, in a letter to William Allen, Joseph set out what he saw as the principal requirements.

To prevent Joseph Lancaster being dispossessed he should have a life interest in the use of the buildings at the Borough Road.

Profits from the printing office and the slate manufactory to be Joseph Lancaster's independent support. In future all his books or pamphlets to be sold for his own benefit.

The domestic economy of the household and the power to change or remove servants to be in Joseph Lancaster's hands.

Joseph Lancaster to be in sole charge of the admission of schoolmasters and the selection of boys to board; as well as the admission of every description of person to learn the plan.

Public and private accounts to be kept separate.

Contraction of debts or loans by the Committee not to exceed an extra £5000, with Joseph Lancaster's consent. The Committee to cease to exist when all debts were paid.

Any improvements that Joseph Lancaster might make in the 'commercial education of youth' to be solely under his own management, for his own gain.

The 'Department of Education' (in other words Joseph Lancaster) to be wholly without interference.

He knew his own weakness; 'I believe if I had thousands they would freely fly in the spread of the work', but his attempts to confine the Committee strictly to financial matters were doomed to failure. He was not himself capable of keeping his side of the bargain. The original Trustees, seized by the excitement of social change and aware that competition from the Bellites was growing in an alarming manner, could not dissociate themselves from decisions which affected policy as well as the daily purse. The Royal Lancastrian System was launched as a national concern and had drawn into its orbit men who were no longer content to remain on the sidelines. It was in vain for Joseph to complain that too much stress was being laid on addresses and reports. 'The fashionable never read them or if they do merely say well this is a good thing and go to the play and forget it directly. Many give orders never to take in two penny post letters or letters without a seal. Thousands of circulars have been delivered to West End houses without effect'. Once he had canvassed for every subscription himself. Now the momentum of circumstances was taking the personal initiative out of his hands. On May 11th at an anniversary meeting at the Freemason's Tavern, attended by the Duke of Kent a new name was suggested, the Royal British System of Education. Joseph was to regard this as a monstrous betrayal by his friends.

In July 1811, Sarah Lancaster, Joseph's mother died. Though closer to his father, Joseph had remained a loving son, sending news frequently when away, visiting constantly when at home. Acquaintance with circles far removed from the meaner streets of

Southwark had not loosened his ties with the humble origins to which both he and his pupils belonged. Travelling in 1810 he had stayed in Warwick with Enoch cousins, 'worthy interesting people', and gone to see the castle, which he regretted Richard Lancaster had not been able to visit. 'I saw an old man of the name of Smart a Friend, who knew thy Father but could give little information about him than that he was a splint maker and worked with his Father,' he wrote. He had tried to follow up the family ancestors in Quaker records but with little success. He hoped however that Richard Lancaster would be preserved to go on a journey with him 'and go over all we can fish out together.

Though he was the youngest child Joseph felt himself to have responsibilities; and because he had become famous his brothers felt so too. 'January 5th 1811. I wish not to be wanting in feeling or duty for Richard's children and *hope* the way will open soon for me to do something for them. In the meantime they must not starve and any little matter thou chose to do in feeding them as far as five pounds go I will make it up to thee again,' he wrote to his father. 'I will send a pound in a day or two to go on with – and the other when I can.' The irony was that he was less able to command ready cash than Richard Lancaster himself, and it is doubtful whether the debt incurred through brotherly duty was ever repaid.

The cruel fate of his wife's derangement meant that Joseph's parents continued to constitute his domestic family, looking after the baby Betsy and giving what help they could when asked. For Joseph Lancaster the family was an important stabilising factor in his life. That he used the word for the inner circle of those young people who boarded at the Borough Road indicated his feeling for and need of such a background. 'I cannot pass a quarter of a mile in any part of Southwark without meeting many lads, who address me in accents of the most cordial welcome . . . I feel among them the glow of paternal affection . . .' The failure of his marriage was a major tragedy. It is impossible to guess how his life might have been changed if his strong domestic affections had been centred on an active, supportive person, and some of his possessive energy been channelled towards caring for a growing brood of children of his own. For Betsy he felt the tenderest attachment and never failed to send her loving messages; 'embrace my dear little girl for me'. Writing to his parents after a quarrel with his brother William, which had taken place in their house, he begged that this unpleasant incident might not disturb the harmony of their own relations; 'It is enough for me to have no home as to wife without our love being weakened'.

Of his two sisters Mary, the elder, was in very poor health. Sarah, two years Joseph's senior, was to take over the household; but at a moment when he was coming under increasing public stress an older sibling was not the confidante Joseph needed. With the death of his mother a central female presence was removed from Joseph Lancaster's life.

'Lancastrian School Birmingham — after contemporary engraving, 1811'

Chapter 9
TRIUMPH AND DISASTER

'Most prophets whose passion is education are careless about money.' (J. W. Adamson. A Short History of Education)

In November 1811 Joseph Lancaster again left the Borough Road for Ireland. He was to be away for five months during which time much was to change. Before he left he had, unknown to his Trustees or any of his colleagues, taken the lease of a large house in Tooting at £200 per annum. In his requirements for a Deed of Trust he had stipulated to William Allen that any fresh improvements for the 'commercial' education of youth which he undertook were to be under his own management and for his own gain. He saw the Royal Free School slipping away from him and was preparing to safeguard his future.

Joseph Lancaster's personal education battle was not the only one that was building towards a crisis. The Church establishment had not been quiescent. Schools under the auspices of Andrew

Bell's Madras system were beginning to spring up in places where the clergy were active. Occasionally, to the alarm of the Lancastrian Committee, small towns had recognised the expensive folly of accommodating two schools in an area that could barely support one and had amalgamated.

On June 13th 1811 Dr Herbert Marsh, Margaret Professor of Divinity at Cambridge, took as his subject for the annual charity sermon at St Paul's 'The National Religion the Foundation of National Education'. He ushered in a period of intense public debate in the press, notably the 'Morning Post', the 'Quarterly Review', and a number of pamphlets. Joseph Fox, under the pseudonym Phythias, played his part in this exchange. So too did Joseph Lancaster, whose verbosity, self pity and vilification of Andrew Bell can have done him little good, though he at least wrote under his own name which many of his equally verbose and violent detractors did not.

In August the Archbishop of Canterbury began to make approaches to the Prince Regent through the Prime Minister, Spencer Perceval. It was a delicate task. The Royal Family, including the Prince Regent, had been long-term subscribers to the Royal Lancastrian System. His Grace had to tread carefully lest his attack on that System should be misunderstood. The Prime Minister was more willing to come to his assistance. He wrote to the Prince Regent enclosing the Archbishop's letter.

'It is indeed to be lamented that Dr Bell's system, which contains all the same mechanical advantages as Mr Lancaster's, with the additional recommendation of being applied to the education of children in the principles of the Church of England, had not been brought forward to notice with as much industry as Mr Lancaster's. In that case it cannot be doubted that many persons who have given their countenance to the Lancastrian system, principally if not entirely from the great mechanical advantages which belong to it, would, at least as gladly, have patronised that of Dr Bell. If however the Clergy of the Church of England feel it to be their duty at present to exert themselves in favour of the latter, it appears, as Mr Perceval humbly submits, a favourable opportunity for introducing it with every advantage to the public notice.'

On October 23rd Dr Manners-Sutton himself addressed Colonel McMahon, Keeper of the Privy Purse, requesting an audience of the Prince Regent, to lay at his feet 'ye proceedings and resolutions of a meeting convened for ye purpose of establishing a Society entitled the National Society for promoting ye education of ye Poor in ye principles of the Established Church throughout England and Wales'.

He got his interview, and the Prince Regent approved the foundation of the new Society. There was then some confusion because the Prince said that he would describe the same sum as he did to the Royal Lancastrian System and nobody was quite certain how much that actually was. Curiously, the Archbishop did not go directly to the Royal Comptroller but asked the Prime Minister, who then wrote to Joseph Lancaster himself for information. Lancaster was in Ireland, but the answer a day or two later, from the Royal Household, was: For the building £210; For payment of debts contracted by Mr Lancaster £105. The Comptroller added that he considered the first sum the subscription, the second in the nature of private relief. It was not to be the last embarrassment connected with His Royal Highness's subscription.

By January 1812 the National Society was organised under the auspices of the Society for Promoting Christian Knowledge, and in its offices. The SPCK had a century old interest in education through the Charity Schools. Andrew Bell was appointed Superintendent of Schools and an Honorary Member of the General Committee.

Joseph Lancaster went to Ireland accompanied as usual by a group of his lads. Since his last visit five years before not a great deal had happened in the educational field, though Joseph had kept up a correspondence with John Foster. This time he hoped to involve the Chief Secretary, William Wellesley Pole older brother of the Duke of Wellington, in his plans. Directly on arrival Lancaster wrote to acquaint him with the programme and express the hope that Wellesley Pole would, by his patronage, greatly increase the value of Joseph's own contribution. He intended to lecture extensively and expected the net proceeds to amount to £1000, which 'I fully mean to apply the whole to the board clothing and education of a number of Irish lads as schoolmasters – and in proportion as the fund is considerable to select the lads – Escort them to England myself and train them under my own eyes . . .'

That well trained masters were the heart of the matter he now had no doubt; 'a theorist will always be inadequate to the duty of tuition. It is only young men practically educated in the system, that have proved themselves capable of instructing others . . .' There was now a group in Dublin eager to co-operate with him. The Protestant Kildare Place Society had been founded in July 1811 by men of all religious denominations, to promote schools in which the Bible should be read without note or comment. The Society was already responsible for one school in the city and was pleased to work with Joseph Lancaster. In this country at any rate he was free of the shadow of Andrew Bell.

Even within a week of landing Joseph Lancaster had gone to work organising a school, or indeed schools, in Dublin; no doubt with the help of his lads. On November 9th he wrote again to William Wellesley Pole to say that in eight or ten days the schools would be in perfect readiness 'for I have reason to believe that no boys are quicker, than Irish lads in taking their learning aptly', and asking again for his patronage at public lectures. Then he left for Belfast, where Thomas Harrod, one of Lancaster's 'missionary' teachers, had set up a school of five hundred boys in beautiful order.

The lectures in Belfast were well received, but back in Dublin the Chief Secretary proved a disappointment, neither attending himself nor letting the Lord Lieutenant do so because the Government did not want to interfere 'one way or another'. There were, nevertheless, plenty of illustrious sponsors in Dublin itself, in Limerick, Cork, Waterford and other places.

Once again the powerful compulsion of publishing abroad his message about schools took hold of Joseph Lancaster. He had come to Ireland with some reluctance; now that he was there the excitement of his creative vision overwhelmed him. In February 1812 he was still travelling, writing to William Allen from Cork, 'Schools are springing up like shamrock . . . National education will probably be paramount in Ireland as a result of this journey. The openings among Catholics have been marvellous . . . Bellites can raise money, but they cannot command education or zeal'. The latter comment may have been put in to remind his Trustees of the real priorities.

Money, as always, had been the cause of some disagreeable communications between Dublin and London. On this journey Joseph Lancaster was wildly, perhaps wilfully, extravagant. It was as though his inability to comprehend financial values induced in him a perverse and fanatic disregard of any pecuniary prudence at all. There was not net profit from the lectures. They produced about £600, all of which was used to cover expenses. An equal sum was drawn in bills on the Committee. As these began to fall due they caused the maximum alarm and bitterness in the Borough Road.

But this Irish venture also brought gains. A Dublin Society for the Education of the Poor in Ireland was formed. At the next anniversary meeting it was to be formally invited to join with the Royal Lancastrian Society. Public opinion in Ireland, among the Protestant section, had been aroused; many committees were convened and a number of schools started; a move to find trained masters for Irish schools was set in motion. Always optimistic, however uneasy his personal circumstances might be, Joseph Lancaster urged William Allen to keep all these things secret until he, Lancaster, could make a speech at the next meeting which would electrify the subscribers.

But still he did not come back to England. It may be that he was unwilling to return to face the fearful financial liabilities, the family cares, the burden of his wife's madness and his father's loneliness, above all the uneasy sense that his life's work was being betrayed. From the moment that the Trustees had been appointed the two strands of management in the Royal Lancastrian Society were on a collision course. There was no way in which the Committee, prudent men of substance and station, could have come to an accommodation with the Founder, a man of extravagant passions and habits, a fiercely independent genius. Or vice versa. In Ireland, and in Scotland where he now went, Joseph Lancaster could feel comfortable, without major rivals, with still untarnished image, and above all with freedom to go where he wished, to develop his ideas as he pleased and to imagine all was yet well.

On April 12th 1812 he was writing from Edinburgh to William Allen, 'I am neither wanting sympathy or affection or unity with my friends'. He would be home in due time. He needed a period in Scotland to revive him after the horrors of some parts of Ireland. 'We got an easy passage with a direct wind to Portpatrick and the boys were very happy in going without seasickness. Balm in Scotland.' There was a chance of a Glasgow and West of Scotland Lancastrian Society, and a similar one in Edinburgh. 'I shall come home to propose the union of the three kingdoms in education.' He wanted to visit Newcastle and Alnwick on the way back. Could easily be home by the 25th, but if they would give him till the 30th he would like to go to Perth, Dundee and Aberdeen.

On the 24th he was still in Edinburgh, but leaving that afternoon for Newcastle and London. He had spent some time with Robert Owen, seeing his educational work at the mills at New Lanark, and had intended to go to Aberdeen on April 23rd but had at least listened to the entreaties of his agitated friends.

The Royal Lancastrian Society's anniversary meeting was scheduled for May 9th at Freemason's Hall. Since the establishment of the National Society the whole subject of education for the poor had taken on a far-reaching, if not yet political, significance. New subscriptions were more badly needed than ever. It was imperative that a united front should be presented and that Joseph Lancaster be there. 'I do not mourn to hear that your finances are low . . . We must have Faith,' he had written to William Allen from Edinburgh. He himself believed this implicitly. William Allen, whose health was suffering from the burdens imposed by the school concern, must have found his own forbearance sorely tried. It was to be the last anniversary meeting at which Joseph Lancaster's presence would be considered indispensable.

The Duke of Kent took the Chair. The fourth son of George III, he had been a strong Lancastrian supporter for some years. He had a high regard for William Allen and considerable admiration for Joseph Lancaster, and was willing to take more than a ceremonial interest in the day to day affairs of the Committee. Ironically, two years later, His Royal Highness was to engage William Allen to sort out his own debts. With the Duke of Kent was his brother the Duke of Sussex. The cachet lent to the business of the Society by this Royal condescension could not be overestimated, and William Allen, ardent royalist as well as egalitarian Quaker, was delighted with their presence and their 'able conduct'.

He also had to admit that Joseph Lancaster, whose speech he must have dreaded, gave a good account of himself. He 'gave some particulars of his Irish journey. There was too much bombast, but it was nevertheless an impressive account, and he made some remarkably good hits', he confided to his journal. Cordial thanks were extended to Mr Lancaster for his indefatigable zeal. He was warmly spoken of as founder and initiator. The

Societies for the Education of the Poor started in Ireland and in Scotland were invited to join the parent body. It was agreed that benefits could only be extended to qualified school masters, and that there should be a constant supply of young men in training. There were one hundred and thirty-seven known Lancastrian schools in the United Kingdom, with more than fifty percent of the pupils belonging to the Established Church. Schools were also attached to the Regiment of Royals, and to militia regiments in Stafford, West Kent, Lancaster, West Meath and Londonderry, as well as the Maidstone Military Depot. On the surface at least all was well with the Royal Lancastrian Society.

But the veneer was very thin. The original Trustees had made enormous financial advances which there seemed little chance of ever recouping; Joseph Fox nearly two thousand pounds, William Allen £1300, Joseph Foster £1217, William Corston £524, John Jackson £521. Subscriptions were falling off, helped no doubt by rumours of Lancaster's wild extravagance. Indeed Joseph himself provided valid evidence of their truth by his flamboyant living. He travelled in a post-chaise and four, was said to keep two carriages and to drink champagne at a guinea a bottle. No wonder the Trustees, struggling to tighten the net around him, must have felt that they had snared a phoenix.

At this moment, without a word to friends or enemies, Joseph Lancaster opened his commercial boarding school at Tooting, intending to make himself a private income quite separated from any claims that the Committee might bring forward. John Pickton, who was now in charge of the Royal Free School, said that Lancaster moved quite suddenly into Salvador House and then went to great expense to fit it up; having about this time been given five or six hundred pounds by a benevolent gentleman. He intended to take fifty boarders at £42 per annum, half yearly fees to be paid in advance. He engaged a clever young man, a classical scholar who had studied under Dr Valpy of Reading, and meant to adapt the Lancastrian System to the teaching of the classics and the higher branches of mathematics.

As soon as this news reached William Allen and Joseph Fox they hastened to meet Lancaster. While exasperated at not being consulted, both men felt that this departure might give them the opportunity to detach the Borough Road school altogether from Joseph Lancaster's grasp. 'On considering all these circumstances.' William Allen wrote to Richard Reynolds, 'Fox and I were clearly of the mind that the time was now come for drawing a close and strong line between Joseph Lancaster and the great public work, for however feasible his private scheme might be, it was still possible that it might fail, and if this should, unhappily, be the case, it would be a great reproach to him, and to us as guardians of the subscriptions, if these should be laid hold of to pay his private debts.'

Joseph himself agreed with this view of the matter; provided he was exonerated from all claims upon him up to this time.

Finding him in such a mood William Allen was anxious to press on. He drew up a document setting out certain conditions.

'The public work hitherto carried on in the name of Joseph Lancaster, was in future to be conducted solely by the committee.

'Joseph Lancaster to do his utmost to promote the public work, by superintending the training of masters and mistresses, at the Borough Road, and in every other way which shall not incur expense.

'The Committee will not be responsible for any expenses which they have not expressly warranted.

'The family, and everything at the Borough Road, to be solely under the direction of the committee.

'Everything to be ordered, and all bills made out in the name of the Committee or the Royal British, or Lancastrian System of Education.

'J. Lancaster to make over the premises at the Borough Road, and all the property there (an inventory of which shall be taken) to the trustees as security for their advances etc.'

On December 7th 1812 the Deed was signed, and after this the weekly committee meetings were removed from Plough Court to the Borough Road 'in order that the family might come more immediately under notice'. At this time they numbered forty-eight, six of them, including Ann Springman and Jane Thomson, girls. Of the boys one was Richard Jones, aged fourteen years and nine months, of whom much more was to be heard; there were also two Africans, George and William, one fifteen the other ten, and Joseph Pen Selling the Dane, as well as sixteen Irish boys, in age ranging between eight and fourteen, sent to train as masters by the Society of the Benevolent Sons of St Patrick.

In spite of the signing of the Deed, the whole situation had reached a state of such confusion that the nerves of all concerned were at breaking point. Matters were not helped by the failure of the Committee's bankers, Kensington and Co. William Allen, having had a 'very uneasy feeling about my heart', retired to the South Coast with his family. Joseph Lancaster, whose own heart was close to breaking point, was commuting between the Borough Road and Tooting, neglecting both while he continued to lecture and attempted frantically to raise private subscriptions. He also started a small periodical 'The Friend of Man'. An Enoch cousin was summoned to keep house at Tooting, due to be opened as a boarding school on September 30th. She was anxious and inexperienced, and feared that when Joseph was away she might do things of which he did not approve.

But such was the Lancaster reputation that pupils began to converge on Salvador House from all over the United Kingdom. A gentleman from Banchory in Aberdeenshire saw an advertisement in the 'Statesman' and proposed to send his son. The Vicar of Killigan in Ireland recommended his brother to entrust his offspring to Joseph Lancaster. Mr Davison from Reading wrote enquiring whether the forty guineas per annum, with only one vacation, included every expense, drawing had not been mentioned. The Paymaster of the 43rd Regiment sent his boy and twenty-three guineas entrance plus half a year's charge; and G. Langton Spilsby also sent a sum in advance and a son 'tolerably versed in the elementary parts of Latin' otherwise backward due to a family visitation that had carried off six children. One of those many sons committed to Joseph's care lost his trunk before he arrived at Tooting. Writing of this misfortune the father noted that extra was charged for a single bed – but he still thought that boys should lie separate. In December the Duke of Kent recommended a boy, and Francis Place, who was soon to be very closely drawn into Lancastrian affairs, sent his own son.

A more complicated aspect of the situation was the persuasion of a number of the apprentice schoolmasters at the Royal Free School to switch their allegiance and their physical presence to Salvador House. This was to cause further acrimonious disputes when Joseph sent the bill for their board and lodging to the Committee, who not unnaturally felt under no obligation to pay it.

In the meantime communication with Ireland, where Joseph Lancaster's reputation remained high, continued. For the right to publish and use his books of instruction Joseph asked the Irish

Society for one hundred guineas. Writing to Samuel Bewley about this Lancaster expressed the view that 'those who love elegant Theory should pay elegantly for it . . .' The Society agreed and forwarded a bill on Paget Bainbridge and Co for £105.

Then there was the request by the Kildare Place Society for a master for the Dublin school. A boy, Joseph Dunn, had come over to the Borough Road to train in July 1812. He was very satisfactory, Joseph Lancaster reported to Sam Bewley, 'Affectionate and faithful, steady and intelligent, interested and energetic.' A Roman Catholic but not a bigot. There was nothing against him but his youth. In September, however, by which time a good deal of correspondence on this matter had crossed the Irish Sea, Joseph had to report that Joseph Dunn, in fact, objected to returning to Dublin. Once more the hunt for a good school master was on.

In October the London Committee minuted a resolution noting an approach from Dublin about a master and suggesting that Joseph Lancaster be requested to write to John Veevers offering him the post of General Superintendent of Schools in Ireland at a salary of £100 per annum 'determined at the pleasure of this Committee with the liberty of receiving in addition whatever salary he can obtain . . .' It was also to be a condition of his acceptance that he retain a regular correspondence with London.

In November, with no reference to the Committee, Lancaster wrote to Sam Bewley that he now had a young man in view – John Veevers. He was the Field Marshall among all the 'young Generals who have been my armour-bearers and aid-do-cons (sic) in the long war I have carried against that ignorance which has so terribly taken captive the flower of our youth . . .' About twenty-three, of a mild disposition and accomplished mind. He would need to give three months notice and ought not to go to Ireland for less than £200 pa. On the 26th of that month the Kildare Place Society wrote back that the salary was too high.

By December Joseph Lancaster, with a multitude of other worries on his mind, was sick and tired of the business. John Veevers was worth double the sum asked for him. The good that such a young man could do did not lie only in a local school, but in all Ireland. Anyway it might be very difficult indeed to get him away from Birmingham. He added a postscript. As the correspondence, which he had understood was to be solely with him, had now been opened with others perhaps he would be better to withdraw.

John Veevers, however, was keen to take the Dublin post and wrote to his old Master to say he would be quite willing to accept a smaller salary rather than lose this chance. Seven days later, January 26th 1813, he announced that he had agreed; could Joseph help him with advice about giving notice to Birmingham?

The Birmingham Committee, when John Veevers went to see them on February 2nd, were gravely displeased at having their brilliant young master removed after three years and wrote an angry letter to William Allen about being kept in the dark. John promised to train another man during the three months of his notice, but Birmingham remained unmollified.

John Veevers was supposed to arrive in Ireland in May, but it was late June before he left England, having been delayed to look after the Tooting school during one of the recurring crises of Joseph Lancaster's life. When, at last, he did step on the boat for Dublin he carried with him a glowing recommendation from Joseph Lancaster, who described him as the first and best of all his young men. John would train splendid school masters and 'I shall imagine I have become a great Grandfather to all the Youth of the Empire'. The Birmingham Committee had also recovered sufficiently to pay tribute.

'The Committee feel themselves called upon to acknowledge the benefit which has been derived from the energy, abilities and fidelity of Mr John Veevers, the master of the school. He has seconded their efforts with unremitting zeal, and under his intelligent care the school has been carried to a degree of excellence, at once verifiying the efficiency of the Lancastrian system, and fulfilling the expectations of the benevolent founders'.

John Veevers was to stay with the Kildare Place Society until 1833.

Parallel with all this activity and while, in public, Joseph Lancaster and the Committee were each maintaining that their respective establishments were going on very well, a rending climax was being prepared behind the scenes. Neither party any longer had faith in the idea that, with rational discussion and rigorously drawn Deeds, a modus vivendi might be arrived at. Joseph saw everything that he valued, work, reputation, his young people themselves, slipping away from him, the Committee feared that in his rage and distress he might bring down the whole edifice of the Lancastrian System about their heads. In the wings the National Society was quietly growing, ready to pick up the pieces.

One of those who remained a Lancastrian supporter was David Holt. Towards the end of 1812 he launched a subscription to raise a capital sum of two thousand pounds for Joseph Lancaster's personal use, and a further sum to be invested, in the names of a committee, to give an income for the support of his relatives. The sponsors did not wish to set up a rival to the Society's subscriptions, but hoped that donors would feel able to give to both.

With great generosity a number of early and old friends did so. The Dukes of Kent, Sussex and Bedford headed the list with one hundred pounds each: lower down the names of William Allen, Joseph Fox and William Corston appeared – the first two for £100, the last for £50. In February 1813 David Holt had already sent out fifty circulars which he intended to follow up with personal visits, and had his whole family engaged on the business. When he had finished with Manchester he meant to attack Derby, Nottingham, Sheffield and Birmingham.

David Holt was not blind to Lancaster's increasing wildness and extravagance, but he felt his merits outweighed any such aberrations. In a letter to Joseph announcing these plans he enclosed a draft for £200 with the admonition, 'Do apply it with care, for self and Family and indulge in no speculations'. He might as well have spoken to the wind. On March 3rd he wrote sorrowfully that one of Joseph Lancaster's bills had been dis-honoured, and he heard many objections to Joseph using his paper 'Friend of Man' to hurl abuse at the clergy. Nevertheless he, David Holt, would do all in his power to help. He was also concerned about the situation in the school at Tooting, on which a friend had recently reported. The domestic arrangements were comfortless and discouraging, the grounds in disorder, and no female in the house; poor Hannah Enoch having presumably found herself, as she had feared, inadequate. David Holt felt that the conditions were not good enough to warrant fees being asked.

In April 1813 something happened which, while ostensibly joyous, may only have added to the unhappiness and confusion surrounding Joseph Lancaster. Elizabeth his wife, whose bills had been disowned by the Committee a month before, was said to be cured of her madness. At the recommendation of the Duke of Kent she had been transferred from Thatcham to Isleworth, to an establishment run by Messrs Delahyde and Lucett who purported to offer a New Curative Process for Insanity. Joseph was informed that Mrs Lancaster had greatly benefitted by this change and that it was thought essential that he and Betsy should come to Sion Vale to be with her, and that Betsy should stay a while. It was four years since the little girl had seen her mother.

Joseph put other work aside and went at once. John Veevers, en route to Dublin was waylaid and asked to hold the fort at Tooting. For her own peace of mind Elizabeth Lancaster could hardly have chosen a worse moment to be cured. With threatening clouds all around him, her husband pressed her into the service of the cause. He insisted that she volunteer to take part in his public lectures relating to female education. The pressures on her gentle, pliable nature could hardly have permitted her to resist. Through the Duke of Kent Joseph arranged an introduction to the Princess of Wales, who agreed to attend two lectures by Mrs Lancaster herself. Her husband thought she acquitted herself well, but he had failed to take into account the other husband in question. Rumour reached Mr Lancaster that the Prince Regent, who considered his own wife deranged, was greatly displeased. Once more there was talk of the withdrawal of a Royal subscription. Hardly surprisingly Elizabeth Lancaster's recovery was to be no more than temporary. In June necessity drove her again to Sion Vale.

Meanwhile the Committee prepared for a showdown. The annual meeting took place as usual on May 8th 1813 at the Freemason's Tavern. The Dukes of Kent and Sussex 'behaved nobly'. The Marquis of Lansdowne, whose appointment to the Committee Lancaster had opposed, contending that he was only a 'milk and water friend', made an excellent speech, as did Sam Whitbread.

On June 17th William Allen met the Duke of Kent at Kensington Palace and unburdened himself as to the full extent of his alarm respecting Joseph Lancaster's conduct. He and Joseph Fox were trying to produce a new Constitution for the school, and no doubt that too was discussed. Matters had reached such a pass that the Committee no longer felt able to function properly so long as Joseph Lancaster retained the power to harass them with complaints, ignore their decisions and confuse the public image of the work of the Society. They wished to restrain him, but had no idea how. Probably now they wished to be rid of him if such a step could be taken without irretrievable damage to their own position and that of the Borough Road school.

An offer was made to Lancaster to appoint two outside persons to meditate. He agreed. They were to be Francis Place and John Bone.

Francis Place, whose son was at Tooting, was a man of quite extraordinary gifts and a singular sense of his own virtue. He had worked as a leather breeches maker and struggled through an early life of great hardship to achieve the goal of freedom to pursue his own interests by the time he was forty. He was, par excellence, an observer of the social scene, disciplined, hard working, with a passion for facts. Disliking any appearance in the public eye, he worked through other men as a radical reformer. The tiny library in his house off the Strand became the meeting place for Whig members of Parliament and those men with commitment to social change. For Francis Place the real talent in political life was persistence. He was a man of absolute integrity who feared the emotions, did not suffer fools gladly, and was totally wanting in humour. He was also an atheist. He admired Lancaster's System, having himself nine children living and finding it difficult to get the kind of education for them that he could afford. At this stage he was on friendly, if not intimate, terms with Joseph Lancaster who had written to him at some length about the iniquities of the Committee.

The second mediator, John Bone, was a nonentity. He was also poor, and Francis Place wrote later that this meant that he was never quite accepted by the Trustees. Quite erroneously Francis Place himself had the reputation of being rich, probably because his frugality and application had made it possible to give up working for a living.

After a meeting between William Allen, Joseph Fox and William Corston and the two new mediators a proposition was put to Joseph Lancaster. It was that he should take the office of 'Inspector of Schools in the Borough Road', with only two days attendance required for a salary of £4.4s a week. It was a generous offer. To Joseph Lancaster it was enslavement in a situation where he should rightfully be master. He maintained still that the Trustees themselves held their own position by his gift, and he could retain or dismiss them as he pleased. Thomas Sturge, who had known him since he set up the first school in his father's house, urged him to accept. So too did David Holt. But it was impossible for Joseph Lancaster to do so. His temperament, his character and his past achievements all militated against such a course of action.

He was being dunned on every side; bills for carriage hire, food, clothing, children's toys, stationery, poured in. Elizabeth had had a relapse and her future care was uncertain. Mr Delahyde was threatening to take out a warrant for an unpaid account. The Tooting school had begun to disintegrate. Joseph was rarely there. John Veevers reported that a Mr and Mrs Muchett had arrived late one evening and asked for their sons, one of whom had written complaining of a box on the ear for idleness. In fact, John Veevers said candidly, all the senior boys were impudent and out of hand. The Muchetts were not the only parents to remove their offspring. Yet David Holt was writing about the opening of the Manchester School beseeching Lancaster to 'put thyself into the Mail and come down': it would have a good effect. In Bath and Bristol private subscription lists had been opened on Lancaster's behalf. He was said to have taken two houses in the Blackfriars Road, one to convert into a printing office, the other for his boys, and was also attempting to write the 'Life and Travels of Joseph Lancaster – including travels in Ireland and Scotland, to be sold for 5/– to subscribers, 7/6 to non-subscribers – to go to press when two thousand copies had been spoken for'.

Francis Place and John Bone tried to pin down this mercurial man with a series of questions.

'What do you consider your proper and peculiar duties?'

'What is the extent of the power you wish to possess?'

'What remuneration from the public's money, through the hands of the Committee, do you expect?'

The rational Place could have answered such queries as precisely as they were stated. Even had he not been consumed with wrath and pain, Joseph Lancaster's emotional temperament would have utterly rejected the limitations so placed on a vision.

He answered:

'My proper and peculiar duties have been to train masters, to organise schools, to deliver lectures, and to preside with undivided authority in the Borough Road as to education. This involved as much of finances as may be indispensibly consequent of those duties being properly performed'.

'In order to effect this I have had the complete power of a master over an apprentice and a teacher over his scholars. I cannot in justice to the System suffer any other person than myself to certify any person as qualified to teach without my knowledge and consent, as unqualified masters have been sent out to the great injury of the System, when I was ready to examine them first. The power I have had I must have, or my name is a cypher to add to the consequence of the units among my Trustees.'

'As to remuneration I want none nor ever did. But as remuneration as gain by services is different from repayment of actual expenses I do expect that all expenses should be generally covered . . . My past expenses are a loss to my family: the advances of the Trustees are no loss to them.'

He was less than fair to the Trustees, who had borne the principal burden of his enormous debts. Though well off, they were not immensely rich men. They gave out of the depth of their commitment rather than from an overabundance of wealth.

Francis Place spurned these answers as not 'precise', as he now totally rejected all Lancaster's grievances against the Committee in which he had once believed there might be some substance. Among those accusations; which included the alienation of the hearts of young people, usurption of his rights, and refusal to recognise a mythical sum of money as being the debt to Joseph Lancaster which had been accumulated by the nation was one that the Committee had passed a resolution that any boy who went from the Borough Road to Tooting 'and slept a single day' should be expelled. In the middle of July 1813 John Pickton, master at the Borough Road, began to enforce this order.

For Joseph Lancaster this was a major betrayal. John Pickton had come to the Borough Road in 1804 to be trained as a schoolmaster. He was one of the Family. That he should carry out the orders of the Committee, now revealed as the enemy, cut his old Master to the heart. He threatened the direst retribution.

John Pickton, who was to spend the rest of his life in the service of the Society, was in a very difficult position. His affection for Joseph Lancaster remained unshaken, but he was only too well aware of the chaos and disruption that the wild

Lancastrian behaviour was bringing to the school. He must have seen clearly that in the struggle to progress it was the Committee who would eventually triumph. It was perhaps a tribute to Lancaster's training that he put the welfare of his school first. Many years later John Pickton's oldest son would write to Joseph Lancaster and tell him that the Master's likeness had always hung in his father's room and that the Pickton offspring were constantly told that this was a wonderful man, through whom millions of children had learned to read. But that was in the future, when time had gradually begun to close the gulf that opened between them in 1813.

At the same moment John Lovell, another member of the Family at the Borough Road, was also writing to Joseph Lancaster to tell him that a Society of Teachers had just been formed, with himself as Acting Secretary. It was not merely a Benefit Society, but an association of experienced persons to carry on the System, subscription one guinea per annum. So, very slowly, the profession of teacher, on which Joseph Lancaster set such store, was becoming organised and respectable.

On July 17th William Allen went again to Kensington Palace, this time accompanied by Joseph Fox and William Corston. There they met the Dukes of Kent and Sussex and the Duke of Bedford, and discussed the Lancaster business. Always just, William Allen suggested that the Dukes should hear Joseph's side before further steps were taken. This was agreed, the Duke of Kent however remarking that as Mr Lancaster was a man of violent temper it would be better to 'have some indifferent person present'. The choice fell on Samuel Whitbread who, when approached, agreed to meet all the Trustees at Joseph Fox's house in Argyll Street. It was as if Lancaster were possessed by the Devil, Joseph Fox wrote. But he was persuaded that 'nothing is required at the present moment but to restrain Lancaster so that the Committee may act without interruption'.

Francis Place, in the meantime, had grown weary of the whole affair. No two men could have been less compatible in nature and temperament than Joseph Lancaster and Francis Place. The more they saw of one another, the less they liked what they had discovered. Place, cold, logical, disliking publicity, clear thinking and decisive: Lancaster, hot, emotional, given to gestures of wild extravagance, loving with a full heart and hating with a will. Francis Place thought Lancaster dishonest, childish and perverse.

He had no patience with men who did not pay their debts.

Joseph Lancaster asked to see John Bone alone but the meeting was abortive. On July 26th Bone informed Fox that negotiations with the mediators had failed.

In this impasse the Duke of Kent agreed to play a more active part. Joseph spoke of him as a personal friend, and did indeed feel that he had a special relationship with every member of the Royal Family. The Trustees were willing to accept His Royal Highness as arbitrator. The Duke requested that all correspondence relating to the dispute between Lancaster and the Committee be reported on by Joseph Hume, late Tory Member of Parliament for Weymouth.

Fox had recently introduced Joseph Hume to Francis Place who took a poor view of him as being 'officious in respect, and active in such matters of business as were likely to please the two royal personages'; later he amended this to 'active, diligent and careful'. In fact Francis Place was to have a major influence on Joseph Hume's whole future career. Hume was to become Place's political pupil, realign himself as radical Member for Aberdeen and move the repeal of the corn laws in 1834. He became the mouthpiece in Parliament for the man who sat in the back room off the Strand meticulously researching, collating and annotating facts and figures.

William Allen gave Joseph Hume the Trustees' statements and accounts; Francis Place, on the instructions of the Duke of Kent, handed over Lancaster's correspondence which was prodigious. Those letters, many of them intemperate, vilifying the Committee, had been a major factor in changing Francis Place's attitude towards Joseph Lancaster. Lancaster must have known that they would do him harm. He now accused Place of violating his privacy by turning them over to Joseph Hume, only to be told that it was his friend the Duke of Kent who had authorised the transaction.

The meeting between Joseph Lancaster, the Trustees and the Duke of Kent was held in Kensington Palace on August 13th. The two outsiders present were Samuel Whitbread and Joseph Hume, both of whom had been made privy to all the documents in question. Joseph Hume, whose detailed, factual report simply reproduced an account of the arguments on both sides to date, was already of the opinion that settlement was nearly impossible. He warned Sam Whitbread:

'By the correspondence between Mr Lancaster and Messrs Place and Bone, you will discover that Power and Money are the two points on which everything rests, and so uncertain are the opinions of Mr Lancaster as to the extent of either, which he would require or might be requisite, that I have great doubts whether any final arrangement can be made unless both parties agree to the arbitration and are determined to abide by the decision which you may give on the subject.'

Francis Place, who had now joined the Committee was also at this fateful meeting.

The Duke of Kent presided and Joseph Hume's report was read. It occasioned little discussion. The Duke of Kent, his 'personal friend', then presented Joseph Lancaster with a fait accompli; either he stayed with them and agreed to resolutions taken by the Committee, or they were 'determined to maintain the cause without him . . .'

The bald statement that the Committee were prepared to jettison him, though he cannot but have feared that they might, must have struck Joseph Lancaster with terrible force. He had told himself that he was indispensible to the Society and the System, now he saw his reputation stripped from him; and by the Royal hands that he had trusted. He knew very well that the alternative offered gave no compensation for the pre-eminence that would be lost. The men facing him were bent on a just and sensible arrangement; but for Joseph Lancaster it was his whole life that they were tearing away. Already overwrought, he launched into rhetoric, boasted of his triumphs, dissolved into tears, challenged the Trustees to prove the outrageous things they were saying about him, gesticulated frenziedly. Francis Place, to whom such scenes were abhorrent, decided to end it. He announced coolly that Lancaster was in no state to conform to any proposition and that he, Place, was satisfied that Joseph Lancaster was insolvent and ought to be made bankrupt.

The storm of hysteria that this statement induced in Joseph Lancaster brought other members of the meeting, especially the Duke of Kent, to his defence. Francis Place then set out to prove the accuracy of his accusation. True to his own nature he had made scrupulous enquiries and knew to the last pound what bills had been dishonoured, which were due in the next few days, the amount of advances obtained from parents at Tooting – of whom he was one, what purposes they were not used for when they should have been, how much was owed to tradesmen. With a mercurial change of position Joseph Lancaster confessed that it was all true and threw himself on the mercy of his friends. Once more, with great generosity, they agreed to take his affairs into their hands and attempt to sort them out.

This time everything would have to go. Joseph Lancaster owed two or three thousand pounds more than he woud be able to pay when every asset had been taken into account. Subscriptions raised by various friends had simply vanished away. Francis Place and Joseph Hume recommended that he call a meeting of creditors and offer them everything he possessed to release him from all further claims. Two days after the encounter on August 13th the Duke of Kent wrote to William Allen.

'With respect to the unfortunate Joseph Lancaster I cannot help fearing that vanity and distress united, have bereaved him of the power of judgement; but I trust, in a little time, we shall be able to convince him of the folly of the former, and relieve his mind of the latter; and that we shall yet be able to avail ourselves of his services, by remunerating them liberally, and marking out his line so that he cannot possibly stray from it.'

At Tooting, where Maurice Cross was helping and John Lovell visiting to do what he could, all was confusion. Joseph Lancaster was not there. John Lovell wrote to him that the Family at Salvador House might appear small but it was too large for such a time of trouble. Twenty boys, who did not regard Joseph Lancaster with affection and duty or they would not be as indiscreet as they were. Soon there would be no food. There was nothing left that could be turned to money.

On August 18th the Trustees met and noted Joseph Lancaster had thirty-five lads at Tooting who had been removed from the Borough Road. In the existing circumstances they might be expected to return. If so it must only be if Lancaster expressly stated that they would in future be under the control of the Committee. Thirteen of these boys were apprentice printers, seven schoolmasters in training, and fifteen without any formal indentures. The Committees agreed that the establishment should be cut down and only those young men who might be expected to become masters retained in it. Joseph Fox was to write to the Society of the Benevolent Sons of St Patrick and ask them to accommodate the Irish boys elsewhere.

Joseph Hume wrote to Lancaster that his situation required

resignation and patience; that his only enemy was himself. It may have been good advice, but neither virtue had even been at Joseph Lancaster's command.

Joseph Lancaster did his best to avoid the calling of a creditor's meeting. Persecuted, haunted, he disappeared from sight, so adding to the clamour of those who were owed money for it had now become public knowledge that Joseph's credit was failing. At last, reluctantly, having tried and failed to raise temporary loans, he agreed. A meeting was called for September 2nd at the Three Tuns in the Borough and conducted by Joseph Hume. It was attended by numerous outraged tradesmen; a butcher claiming £377, a baker £324, a chaise driver £80, a coachmaker £270, a postmaster at Mitcham £104, a cheesemonger £105, a stationer £400, a coffee house keeper £60, etc. etc. The total amounted to the staggering sum of £7222.1s.7d. The impossibility of getting even half this amount back was apparent to all those present and the creditors generally voted for bankruptcy.

Joseph Hume, however, tried to delay this outcome; not so much for Lancaster's sake as for the sake of the cause. He succeeded in getting a motion passed for fourteen days adjournment, during which time he would try to see whether things could not be arranged by a Deed of Trust.

The next morning a group of men, headed by Joseph Hume and Francis Place, set out to visit each creditor in the attempt to get a memorandum signed consenting to such a Deed. Many creditors refused. Joseph Hume suspected that they thought that, at the eleventh hour, the Committee would step in and pay. Many indeed felt that, as a large number of bills referred to the Borough Road, the Committee was bound to honour the debts. The Committee, however, was in no mood to do so, even had it been possible. A docket was struck and the bankruptcy commission went forward.

On September 11th the Tooting school was closed and the remaining boys sent home. On the same day Joseph Hume wrote to Sam Whitbread that he had drawn up a 'Code of Regulations for the Publick Institution in the Borough Road which we propose in future to designate The Royal British System of Education'. Nothing of Joseph Lancaster was to remain to contaminate his creation.

Joseph Lancaster, his world in ruins, had gone to Manchester to David Holt. The latter wrote to the Duke of Kent on Lancaster's behalf, pointing out the disasters which public exposure in the Gazette as a bankrupt would bring upon him. The Duke, while admitting Lancaster's merits as a benefactor in the cause of universal education, felt that 'candour requires me to say, that I much fear his conduct has recently been of such a nature as to deserve no more from Private friendship or support' Many of the creditors were going so far as to allege that there was a degree of criminal misappropriation in Joseph Lancaster's behaviour. The Duke of Bedford too felt that it was more important to back the System than the man. Joseph Fox thought it might be a good idea if Lancaster went to South America, where there was a great wish on the part of Bolivar's government for persons capable of introducing the System. Joseph himself talked wildly of America. David Holt, however, while in no way blind to the catastrophe which Joseph had largely brought in himself, had no thought of deserting his friend. He continued to correspond with the solicitor in charge of the proceedings, suggesting this expedient and that to avoid the final issue.

It was to no avail. Even in this extremity Joseph himself seems to have considered, as was his wont, that something might yet turn up. With exasperation the solicitor informed him that he must obey the summons to appear at Guildhall and admonished him that it was proper to rely on Providence; but no mortal had a right to expect a miracle in his favour.

Joseph Pen Selling, the Danish prisoner of war, left for Copenhagen on October 18th. On the 30th an enlarged Finance Committee met at Kensington Palace. A new Constitution and a set of Rules and Regulations was accepted, and a sub-committee directed to write to Joseph Lancaster and offer him the post of Superintendent in the Borough Road school at a yearly salary of not more than £400. An evasive reply was to be regarded as a negative. Francis Place had no doubt he would not accept.

On November 10th a General Meeting of subscribers was to be held at the Freemason's Tavern, for the specific purpose of ratifying the new constitution and a new title. The latter was extremely cumbersome; 'The Institution for promoting the British System for the Education of the Labouring and Manufacturing Classes of Society of every Religious Persuasion'. Within a year it was to be changed again to the British and Foreign School Society.

There must have been considerable apprehension among the Committee as to whether Joseph Lancaster would come to the meeting. They were men of goodwill, and many felt compassion for a man who had so disastrously ruined a life which had done so much good. But at least they thought they saw their way out of the morass into which his arrogance and financial illiteracy had plunged them. Good administration of the Borough Road Institution was now only a matter of time. That subscribers should not be further frightened off was of supreme importance. If possible nobody meant to mention Joseph Lancaster or his affairs.

Joseph Lancaster, however, had no intention of slipping quietly out of sight. He saw an opportunity to appeal to the public and compel those 'who had usurped his authority and possessed themselves of his property to abandon the one and restore the other'. He had a handbill printed, 'An Appeal for Justice', and this he sent round to subscribers and had distributed at the door of the Freemason's Tavern. In it a sentence declared, 'I have nothing I know of wrong in me, that I wish to excuse or palliate'. Clearly he hoped to raise a Lancastrian party.

In the event Sam Whitbread saved the day for the Committee, though some on that body did not altogether approve of his method of doing so. No doubt experience in Parliament had taught him ways of isolating an undesirable speaker. He carried the meeting through 'by preventing Lancaster, from making an impression, however false, upon persons at a distance, that he had been neglected by the Committee'. After a most solemn exhortation Joseph Lancaster agreed to render himself to the Society 'of which he could no longer be the conductor' in the post of Superintendent, at a salary of £365 per annum.

For him the day was lost; though he did not yet despair of gaining the battle.

'Elevation of new building for B&FSS — after contemporary engraving 1817'

Chapter 10
THE WILDERNESS

'I possess the spirit of a soldier's son'. (Joseph Lancaster to Richard Lancaster)

'. . . poor Joseph Lancaster is to commence his superintendence next week and his salary begins from the 1st inst . . . it affords the poor infatuated man one chance more and at all events will leave him without excuse – there are already some feeble signs of regeneration which afford a glimmer of hope – the cause, however, is saved . . .' William Allen wrote on December 4th 1813.

William Allen, out of the goodness of his nature, may have persuaded himself that he saw signs of a change of heart, but it was never within the bounds of probability that Joseph Lancaster would accept the new situation. His rage against the Committee, who had cheated him out of all that he had worked to build up, had become a destructive madness where the Borough Road was concerned, blinding him to his own interest as well as to his errors. Humiliation, a word often on the lips of his friends, was not something with which his pride could come to terms. For some men submission might have subtly reinforced a spiritual arrogance, but Joseph Lancaster's vanity was born of achievement and conquest in the market place. Everything he valued was bound up in the work that had borne his name. He was thirty-five, accustomed to adulation and independence, with the great vision of national education still far from fulfilment. It was true that he had been grossly extravagant; it was also true that privately he owned no more than he ever had. His wife and child, father and siblings, lived in the same humble circumstances that had always been their lot. The clothes, the carriages, the outward show, were in Joseph's eyes necessary to advance the cause in an age when appearance counted for much; though there is no denying that he enjoyed them. Those who were owed money should be happy to bear such a burden for the sake of the grand objective. That others might, in friendship, hold a different view was beyond his understanding. Even David Holt despaired when he saw how Lancaster alienated his friends and patrons and wrote that he could only recommend him to God, though he loved him still.

It soon became plain that everything was not well at the Borough Road. Joseph Lancaster was a subversive influence among the lads. John Pickton, who had earlier been said to be such a good master that what Lancaster did in the school was of little moment, must now have found himself in an impossible position, his loyalties unbearably stretched. Insubordination grew. Joseph boasted that he would worst the Committee at the next meeting. 'If we mean to support the Institution we must disencumber it of this man, he has done the cause more injury than all its professed enemies put together,' William Allen wrote to Sam Whitbread.

In March 1814 the Committee were informed of scandal. Thirteen years later Francis Place recorded among his papers what had happened. If any written note was made at the time by those concerned, none survives.

A young man called William Brown, one of Lancaster's former apprentices about whom nothing else is known, told William Corston that Joseph Lancaster flogged his lads for his own amusement. William Brown put this complaint in writing and it was brought to the Committee, who felt it their duty to institute an enquiry.

The Committee asked Joseph to appear before them, showed him the letter and told him that they had set an enquiry on foot. Joseph Lancaster appears neither to have admitted or denied the accusation, being more concerned with the enmity which he was sure the Committee felt for him and the impossibility of their being unbiased judges. In the end it was agreed that two dissenting ministers, a 'half-quaker' called Henry Newman, and Francis Place should form a sub-committee.

Though flogging was commonplace in many schools, and used in horrifying form as a disciplinary measure in army and navy, in the Lancastrian context it was a serious charge. Joseph Lancaster was a Quaker and the System had been built round reward and emulation, with shame rather than physical violence as the means of punishment. But there was worse to come.

The sub-committee, aware that it was treading in a minefield, set to work very cautiously. They examined William Brown, and a number of other lads whom he indicated 'had been often flogged by Lancaster for his amusement', as well as when he was displeased. They reported that 'His (Joseph Lancaster's) practice was to hug and caress and kiss them to induce them to consent to be flogged . . . sometimes he laid them down upon the sopha and sometimes several of them stood before the fire with their trousers down and their shirts tucked up round their waist while Lancaster flogged them . . .' In this connection it should be noticed that Francis Place himself used the words caress and kiss when describing normal greetings among members of the Committee. The sub-committee had no doubt that the case set out by William Brown had been proved.

Francis Place gives no indication of the actual time involved in these incidents, or how long they were thought to have gone on. It seems unlikely that such activities could have been concealed during all the years when the Borough Road school was at the height of its fame and under constant outside scrutiny. In years to come, though many other criticisms were made of Joseph Lancaster's life and conduct, the hint of sadism or homosexuality was not one of them. Nor, in the considerable correspondence that has survived, did any of the Family whose loyalty and affection he retained, make even a glancing reference to such a possibility.

Joseph Lancaster was an emotional man, given to public expression of his affections and of his hatreds. He loved his lads and found much of the fulfilment of his own life through them. No doubt, as with other men in similar professions, there was an unrecognised sexual element among the motives that drove him to choose his lifework. That it led to open practice is hard to believe. It is true that Elizabeth was jealous of her husband's concentration on and delight in the company of his boys. How much this was one factor in her mental collapse or, on the contrary, how far the fatal disruption of his domestic life reinforced Joseph Lancaster's dependence on his lads it is impossible to ascertain. What seems certain is that, at a period when his whole world was disintegrating around him, when the manifestations of his wife's inability to offer support were only too clear, when some of his boys appeared to have betrayed him, Joseph Lancaster's own hysteric unbalance led him into actions of which in happier days he would almost certainly never have been guilty.

The sub-committee put forward their report without comment or recommendation. The Committee was at a loss what to do. They hoped that if Lancaster were told of the report he would quietly withdraw from the school. They were even willing to consider making up his salary in some other way. He was called before the Committee and the report read to him. The reaction was not what they expected. Indeed he gave no indication of caring what the report said and, disconcerted by this brazen indifference, the Committee failed to make any decision at all.

By doing so they handed the initiative to Joseph Lancaster. At the next School Committee meeting on April 16th he sent in his resignation as Superintendent. Along with a document listing his reasons for taking this step, he presented a letter to Joseph Fox, for the perusal of the Committee, which was to have the effect of a time bomb on that sober, devout body. In it no mention was made of the report on flogging, nor indeed of the fact that Joseph Lancaster intended to open a rival school. Its explosive charge concerned Francis Place who was not himself present at the meeting.

'To the Chairman of the Borough Road Committee.

'Joseph Lancaster, Superintendent of the Borough Road School addresses with all due respect the note and papers which accompanies this, and requires that they may be communicated to the Committee who have taken upon themselves the Government of an Institution, which has never prospered since it improperly ceased to be his. Being unexpectedly summoned to attend an Assignee and an Accountant on the ground of ascertaining the precise amount of money to be paid forthwith is the only reason why he is not present this day as he intended. Under these circumstances and for the reasons stated in the enclosed papers he being a weekly servant at a salary of one pound per day, gives them by this instrument notice from the date thereof, that he shall finally quit, give and resign the situation of Superintendent of Borough Road School and the duties and pay attached to that office, on the day called Saturday the 23rd instant of the present 4th month April 1814. For that the public faith to him being broken by them, his usefulness destroyed and having no alternative, but to see his system liable to be perverted to infidel purposes, to dishonour his pious Patron the Sovereign and to honour those who deny his Saviour unless he resigns – he with heartfelt satisfaction, performs his Christian duty, and will not associate or be committed one day longer than the law requires with any single individual on a committee where there is in that committee a man who has shown himself anxious to extirpate the Scriptures from what are called Lancastrian Schools . . .'

Francis Place was an agnostic. It is hardly conceivable that some members of the Committee had not known this at the time when he joined them. Though he did not flaunt his 'infidelity', neither did he conceal it. Perhaps it had been simpler to leave sleeping dogs alone. Now however, in his desire for revenge, Joseph Lancaster made this convenient course of action impossible.

Joseph Fox, whom Francis Place was beginning to dislike almost as much as he did Joseph Lancaster and to think equally insane, was flung into extreme agitation by this revelation and William Allen scarcely less so. The whole of the Lancastrian System was based on a broad Christian education. It was on this it took its stand against the narrower, Established Church, National Society. Suspicion of condoning atheism would have presented their rivals with a useful weapon.

There were few men in this age of almost universal religious profession with the courage to stand against everything their society and nation believed in and say that they were without faith. For a public man in particular it would have been to put his reputation at risk. Perhaps only someone of Francis Place's stern self-sufficiency and icy integrity would have refused to compromise when the accusation was made.

Since about 1811, when Francis Place first met James Mill the utilitarian philosopher, both men had been interested in the possibility of setting up a West London Lancastrian Association to extend the non-sectarian Lancastrian System to all poor children living west of Temple Bar. In July 1813 a meeting at a coffee house in Cockspur Street had brought the WLLA into being, and appointed Joseph Fox as Secretary though there was no formal connection with the Borough Road School. Francis Place was determined that the Association should be established under tight control, both of finances and management. A system of inspection and enquiry was set up to ascertain the numbers of poor children in each of the districts into which the area was divided who could take advantage of schooling. Francis Place made arrangements for a detailed survey-which was never carried out.

It was at this time that cordial relations between Place and Fox began to disintegrate. Joseph Fox, accustomed to the laxity of the Borough Road Committee, where as major creditor his views were deferred to, took badly to being overseen by Francis Place. He also became convinced that 'Deism', the very charge that Mrs Trimmer had brought against Lancaster, was to be taught in WLLA schools. For his part Place now came to see Joseph Fox as a 'shallow gloomy bigot' and exceedingly artful.

When in April 1814 Fox received Lancaster's letter inditing Francis Place he was already antagonistic to much that the latter stood for. Immediately, and without informing the absent Place, he persuaded the Committee that another investigation must be held, at Kensington Palace, in the presence of the Royal Dukes.

Having no information about what had happened at the Committee meeting, Francis Place wrote to Joseph Fox asking for minutes and papers concerning Lancaster's resignation. He was told that everything had been sent to the Duke of Kent.

Joseph Fox was visited by Francis Place who told him coldly that as his 'infidelity' had been well known to the Committee it was mere affectation in them now to pretend ignorance and worse than foolish to hold a meeting at the Palace. Unless he instantly got copies of all the papers he would himself write to the Duke. The value of his efficiency to the Committee was well-known, and Joseph Hume, who was a prodigy of the Duke, would stand by him.

Place got the papers, but arrangements for the meeting at Kensington Palace on April 30th went forward. Joseph Fox circulated information. There were many members of the larger Committee who knew very well that, if challenged, Francis Place would admit the charge of infidelity; others were horrified. Quite a number, including Sam Whitbread, Joseph Hume, Fox and the Duke of Kent himself, thought he would not attend. Once the centre of anxious consultation before a meeting of importance, Francis Place now found only James Mill and one of the dissenting ministers prepared to talk to him.

There was an irony in the fact that less than a year after Place had confronted Joseph Lancaster before a Committee in Kensington Palace, he found himself facing the same situation.

By design he arrived late, accompanied by James Mill. The two men had agreed that Francis Place should remain silent until everyone else who wished had spoken. Place recognised that discussion of the issue would lead the group into very sensitive areas. When in Committee he had never spoken against Christianity or the use of the Bible in schools. What was under scrutiny then was his private opinion; and whether a man should be publicly condemned for opinions he held in private was a matter on which Committee members themselves held widely differing views.

When he entered the room, a man of fine presence and piercing eye, there was a larger company assembled than the Committee had ever before brought together during Place's membership. Caustically Francis Place remarked that it was extraordinary how the Quakers turned up when the meeting was at the Palace.

At his appearance a hush fell over them, with the faint sound of indrawn breath, 'such an expression of feeling as is usually evinced on the unexpected entrance of a disagreeable intruder, whose presence was neither desired nor expected'.

Taking no notice, he sat down and began to speak to those he knew. With uneasy shrugs a number 'shuffled away' from him. There was whispering and delay. Sam Whitbread came in and went out again. So did Joseph Hume. Francis Place watched with contempt the ludicrous and cowardly evasions of his fellow men.

At last, in an atmosphere of trepidation and suspicion, the two Royal brothers of Kent and Sussex made an entrance, preceded by more senior members of the Committee. With ceremonial bustle chairs were set and the Duke of Kent took his place as president. 'Whitbread looked knowing.' Joseph Hume engaged in obsequious conversation with the Duke. 'Enough to make a dog sick,' Francis Place noted.

There had been a conspiracy to seat Francis Place at the end of the long table, isolated from the body of the meeting. Seeing this, he immediately made his way into a position high up on one side. A profound silence fell over the group. Sardonically Francis Place noticed how Whitbread whispered to the Royal patron and Joseph Hume bowed constantly 'like an unwieldy elephant'.

The Duke of Kent roused himself from his embarrassment and opened the meeting. Having described the manner of Joseph Lancaster's resignation, though with no mention of William Brown's allegations and the enquiry into them, His Royal Highness, delicately spoke of the charge against an individual of the Committee brought by Joseph Lancaster.

He waited for observations. No one stirred. One or two of the bolder looked over to Francis Place. Francis Place said nothing.

The Duke said;

"Mr Place I suppose you have seen Mr Lancaster's letter?"

"I have."

Another lengthy silence ensued, none of the Committee wishing to expose his views in front of his fellows.

Desperately the Duke appealed to Mr Place.

"And?"

Then Sam Whitbread intervened, saying hurriedly;

"Let him alone."

The Duke of Kent, a good-hearted man who was seldom disconcerted, said cheerfully;

"I suppose every gentleman present has seen Mr Lancaster's letter . . . which contained so much inadvisable and indecorous matter and improper accusations that, as he has separated himself from the Institution, it might be advisable to take no notice of it, but to go on to other business."

Very loudly Sam Whitbread said;

"Certainly."

Whereupon the Duke of Sussex shouted across the table:
"Prosecute him Place!! Prosecute him Place!!"

'Thus terminated the mighty affair,' Francis Place wrote. He
walked back across Kensington Gardens with Thomas Sturge,
whose simple honesty he found refreshing.

If Joseph Lancaster had hoped, which undoubtedly he did, to
divide the Committee against itself, he had not succeeded.
Nevertheless tensions remained. Francis Place was to continue to
put forward meticulous plans for economic retrenchment and the
development of the Institution in the Borough Road along
strictly utilitarian and selective lines. But he was increasingly
disenchanted with his fellow members. As they had found it
impossible to accommodate Joseph Lancaster's charismatic and
individualistic presence within their orthodoxy, so now Francis
Place found it impossible to come to terms with a Committee
which, in its turn, he considered inefficient and without any
notion of the management of money. The fact was that the
School Society continued to run into debt. Francis Place drew up
plans, plotted out districts, made detailed projections for expansion based on charging parents 1d per week and confining the
Borough Road entirely to teacher training. Nothing ever came of
any of them. Nobody had the least idea how a well ordered
Society should be conducted. He thought William Allen, whom
he admired, too credulous, affectionate and compassionate to be
any good as a man of business, and at the beck and call of Joseph
Fox. They had saved the System, but were not equal to the trust
reposed in them.

In 1815 an explosive row within the Committee on whether the
boarding establishment should discontinue resulted in Francis
Place withdrawing his plan. In June that year, at a public
meeting which he did not attend, his name was not put forward
as a Committee member and he severed his connection with the
Society thereafter.

In the West London Lancastrian Association too all was not
well. Francis Place never hesitated to tell unpleasant truths and
the rift between him and Joseph Fox was irreconcilable. 'Fox is
as base a wretch as Lancaster', Place wrote to a friend. In July
1814 a scandal, the accuracy of which remains obscure, broke
about Francis Place. He was accused of being a Government spy,
and resigned from the Association. At that point the Association

had started no new schools.

May 21st 1814 saw the fourth Annual General Meeting of the Society at the Freemason's Hall with the Duke of Sussex in the chair. On this occasion the Society's title was again changed. It became, and was to remain, the British and Foreign School Society. The report, which Francis Place called a 'most finished piece of trickery', spoke in glowing terms of the 'unbounded prospects' of spreading the System to Europe, Asia, Africa and America. Joseph Pen Selling had left for Copenhagen: Robert Ould was working for an extension of the System in America: there were enquiries from Canada: Sierre Leone was expecting two trainees. The Princess of Wales was present, the hall was full, everything went off admirably and William Allen brought home upwards of three hundred pounds. Joseph Lancaster's resignation was announced.

'On this subject the Committee do not want to say anything further, than that having toiled to support the man as well as the System, it must produce great regret in the mind of everyone who values the cause of Universal Education, that the only enemy to Joseph Lancaster had been Joseph Lancaster himself', the report stated. There had been no quarrel. '. . . the whole must be attributed to one of those mental delusions that sometimes lead men astray and cause them to commit the most fatal errors'.

But everything was going smoothly and, while his loss was deplored, the cause of general education was saved. Joseph Lancaster had been told that he was no longer necessary to his System. That was what they must not see suffer.

The Committee also reported with regret that overtures made to the National Society, in an effort to come to some agreement in country places which could not afford two schools, had failed. In fact the rivalry remained as bitter as ever. In December 1813 Sam Whitbread had approached the Prince Regent, through Colonel McMahon, seeking His Royal Highness's patronage and protection for the reconstructed School Society, now purged from the errors of Joseph Lancaster. The Prince Regent had directed that the new 'Rules and Regulations' of the Society should be sent to the arch-enemy, the Archbishop of Canterbury, for his opinion. Dr Manners-Sutton wrote a careful, damning reply. Of course people should be free to educate their children according to their own religious opinions; provided those opinions were consistent with Christianity, good morals and good order. But there was a distinction between individual and national education. Church and State would be upheld by wise religious toleration, but it would be unreasonable to expect that the Church of England would maintain its footing when people were educated indifferent to its doctrines; which meant hostile to them. This scheme of education had a strong tendency to national infidelity. If this System was introduced, it was the Archbishop's opinion that the ecclesiastical establishment of the country would be placed in the greatest possible danger and Christianity itself would hardly be safe.

Colonel McMahon replied to Joseph Fox that HRH was under the necessity of declining the proposal that had been made to him; though that would make no difference to the continuance of his subscription.

On April 25th, two days after his resignation had taken effect, Joseph Lancaster acknowledged receipt of 'One hundred pounds for His Royal Highness' Annual Subscription to the Lancastrian Free School in St George's Fields and for training schoolmasters, and promoting schools in this country'.

There was consternation on the Committee when it was realised that Lancaster, who had always contended that the Royal subscriptions were given for his personal work, intended to keep the £100. Joseph Fox wrote to the Comptroller explaining that the connection with Lancaster had been dissolved and asking whether the subscription was understood by HRH to be for the personal use of Joseph Lancaster or for the Society. The Comptroller replied that no news had reached him of Joseph Lancaster's departure from the Free School, and it was for the support of that institution that the subscription had been paid. By June, however, the Committee were no nearer laying their hands on the £100.

Even before he officially resigned Joseph Lancaster had been planning to open another school. Though travelling and speaking had come to occupy much of his time, it was in the school that his talents had first flowered, the school was the base that gave him security and identity, and took the place of home. Tooting had become a shambles through neglect; in the Borough Road he had set out to destroy the basis of discipline and confidence that had once been his pride. Nevertheless he needed a school to prove to himself and others that the name of

Lancaster remained synonymous with education.

Still of sufficient address and presence to carry conviction, he had persuaded an official Spanish visitor, who had come to the Borough Road to learn about the System, to bypass the Committee and advance £2000 to fit up a new schoolroom adjoining Bushnell's wheel factory off the Westminster Road. At the moment when Joseph Lancaster was handing the Committee his resignation, broadsheets were appearing on the streets of Southwark and being sent to subscribers.

'Royal Lancastrian System of Education
Joseph Lancaster
Founder of the above system under
Royal Patronage
Has now removed the Institution under his superintendence, to
The School Rooms
near the Asylum, in the Westminster Road
St George's Fields
Application for Admission may be made every day from Ten
o'clock till four
in the afternoon . . .'

By May 1814 Joseph Lancaster's certificate of bankruptcy had been signed. As a result the Society of Friends disowned him at their Yearly Meeting.

Joseph Lancaster's relations with the Quakers had always been ambivalent. He shared with Francis Place the opinion that they could be ill-informed and of narrow understanding, easily offended and unforgiving. His nature was the opposite of the Quaker virtues of prudence and sobriety; his strong individuality had never found it easy to accept the corporate counsels of Meeting. He was a soldier's son and not ashamed of his father's militant profession. Yet, in the depths of his being, he felt himself to be a Quaker and the principles of Quaker belief and worship were dear to him. It was Friends who had supported him from the earliest days; it was Friends who now disowned him and who had, in the shape of William Allen, been instrumental in his downfall. The closeness of the connection made the emotions involved more violent. A common creed exacerbated sensitivity. Public disownment changed nothing in the heart of Joseph Lancaster, where he knew himself to be a Quaker, but it rubbed the edges of his spirit raw.

From the beginning the new school was a disaster. Joseph

Lancaster, in fact, did not want to be in London, where his financial position laid him open to constant embarrassment and harassment; but nor did he mean to leave the capital in the hands of the enemy. He appointed a young man called Bennett Cross, who under pressure of circumstances proved both sly and dishonest, to look after the new Institution, which had attracted about one hundrd and seventy pupils. But the principal burden of responsibility fell on Richard Lancaster, his father.

The family of blood and kinship had now become all-important. There had never been any separation. Joseph's fame had not broken his close links with parents and sisters. Now that he was in trouble their attitude to him remained unchanged. Richard Lancaster had feared for his soul in the days of his glory; he feared for it still, but that did not prevent his doing everything in his power to help his son.

Elizabeth Lancaster had come home, probably because paying for her board elsewhere was no longer possible, and Betsy was with her mother in the house in Elliott Row, the Borough, where a number of lads, Bennett Cross among them, boarded. When upset Elizabeth's derangement led her to lose all interest in her appearance, to refuse to keep herself clean, and to question, continually and audibly, whether her husband loved her. The circumstances in which she now had to live made such regressions hardly surprising. John Lovell, who knew her, testified that she had a warm heart adding, perhaps with some insight into his own gentle nature, that they were always the weakest.

Betsy was nine years old in the September of 1814. She was a well-grown, personable little girl, adored by her grandfather. Everyone who knew her spoke highly of Betsy. Against all odds she was growing up stable, sensible and loving.

Joseph Lancaster had always been fond of his only offspring. Now he began to find in this sturdy child a human being whom he could love unreservedly, a pupil ready to learn and a daughter whose dearest wish was to stand by his side. He also saw that she might immediately play a useful part in the never-ending pursuit of financial solvency.

The letters that Joseph Lancaster wrote to his family, at this moment of dire distress and for the rest of his life, contrast strikingly with his public communications. The latter were often strident, hysterical, full of recrimination and self-pity. Little of this appeared in the former. They were sensible, practical letters, replete with kindness, affection and optimism. Complaints were few, and mention of his traumatic disasters and the men whom he considered responsible for them rare. To Betsy in particular he wrote with the enthusiasm of a teacher who enjoys imparting knowledge and at the same time with the open assurance of one friend to another. He had always believed in the potential for growth and responsiblity in young people. He did not deny this confidence to his daughter.

By September Lancaster was in Manchester, staying with David Holt, having spent some time on the way with brother William in Liverpool. The new school was in deep trouble. So also was the home at Elliott Row. On August 27th Elizabeth Lancaster had written despairingly that household goods, on a species of hire purchase agreement, had been seized and she had nothing left but a counterpane and two sheets. It did not seem to have occurred to Joseph, indeed it never seems to have occurred to him, to take any special thought for those he left behind to face dire situations not of their own making. His Micawber-like temperament looked only to the future with a conviction that something would turn up.

Nor indeed do his families, who suffered most in this way at his hands, seem ever to have lost the expectation that he might indeed be right. Elizabeth entreated him to let her come to him in the north. 'The house is unpleasant, to be left with such a parcel of lads as they are'. She was having trouble with the rent, and did not know what to do with his desk, the boxes of papers in the closet, the lessons and pictures. Her father-in-law was worried about the printing machine, the bedstead at the office and the future of the school. 'I think he said, he was afraid thou wouldst not bring things to an even settlement,' she wrote to Joseph. 'I expect it is not much wonder if he is a little anxious to know about things in the present circumstances, poor dear Man I think he seems tolerable considering his age. Betsy sends love'. She added that if she got a pair of shoes or slippers and paid for clothes washed she would badly need money but he was not to hurt himself, and ended 'with dear love to thee . . .'

For someone of fragile mental health, uncertain what might happen to herself, her child or the roof over her head, it was an extraordinarily mild letter. Bennett Cross, whom she detested, had written a violent and impudent communication to Lancaster the week before. He complained of bills and debts and Joseph's inability to run a printing office, indeed to run anything while so engrossed in public work. But his principal invective was reserved for Elizabeth, her unkempt appearance, her dislike of the boys against whom she would defend herself with a knife or a poker if they 'checked her', and above all her jealousy, her pathetic longing to be reasurred that her husband loved her. She should be put in an institution, Bennett suggested, if anyone who had heard about the Place investigation heard her he knew what they would think.

Bennett Cross was obviously aware of William Brown's accusation. If a number of boys were involved it could hardly have been kept secret, which makes lack of information from any source other than Francis Place the more extraordinary. These were not squeamish times. Those who fell from grace, especially if they did not belong to the ranks of wealth and privilege, could be cruelly treated. Joseph Lancaster's reaction to this letter is also interesting. Writing to his father on September 6th, nearly a month later, he apologised for Bennett's lack of proper attention to Richard Lancaster but went on to defend him. 'I believe Bennett is faithful, but he is in his manners, one of the oddest boys in existence'. It was not until three weeks later, when Bennett had begun to make away with goods that did not belong to him, that old Mr Lancaster, who had always thought him a rogue, was given permission to dismiss him if he thought fit.

On August 29th Joseph had written from Manchester to his father, enclosing £12.10s for a quarter's rent and thirty shillings for family expenses. He added that he was now in sight of port and had met with kind and generous friends. He spoke hopefully of a young and zealous committee. Three days later, when he had received his wife's letter, he wrote again at greater length. Once more £12 was enclosed. His main concern was for his many letters, papers and minutes left in the house at Elliott Row. He wished to make Richard Lancaster responsible for removing them and also legal protector of all the remaining property in the school and printing office for he hardly knew who else to trust. Elizabeth could come to stay with William. 'There is a new cheap coach which comes to Liverpool without coming through Manchester – she may come in that – I believe the fare is not above two pounds inside . . . I think the sooner she is off from London the better for I fear she will only be a grief to thee there'. Betsy should remain for a time with her grandfather. A week later he had another thought. Betsy and Elizabeth were to come to Manchester where he was sure their presence would move the hearts of his friends to liberality.

Richard Lancaster, an old man of seventy-two with every right to be anxious, had considerable difficulty in carrying out these commissions. Elizabeth seemed lost to her own preservation and had been taken to live with Quaker friends. He could not get into the house. 'I fear thou wilt be wise for thyself'; he wrote. 'thou left the Boys to themselves without any person fit to take care of them or thy Property – and thy long absence has made them absolute Masters'. He had eventually to climb in through a window. The house was a wreck. 'I fear much for thee, for thou, always, keeps thyself in troubled waters.'

On September 14th, however, Elizabeth and Betsy were put on the coach for Manchester, Betsy in a new great coat which Joseph had instructed his father to buy for her. Two weeks later, after they had met the Manchester committee, they were on the way to Liverpool, where Betsy was to spend the next three years in the house of her Uncle William.

David Holt had his own problems. A daughter, who had been seeing a young man of whom her parents strongly disapproved, suddenly married him without their knowledge while her father was in Liverpool. Nevertheless, he prepared to involve himself in a great deal more work and worry on Joseph Lancaster's behalf. Under no illusions about the difficulties of the task, a small committee was set up whose main effort was to try to give Lancaster some financial stability. Joseph saw it as a promise to 'secure my usefulness; to enable me to write my life and publish my defence against my London enemies as well as to provide for my wants and I hope ultimately for thy (Richard Lancaster's) old age which I will never neglect while I can do anything to promote its comfort'. A circular was to be issued, and he had already written thirty-nine sheets of a book 'The History of the Rise and Progress of the Royal Lancastrian System of Education'.

A public meeting was held in Manchester, to try to get enough money for an annuity. Only ten people came, but Lancaster persisted in taking a rosy view of proceedings. 'I am drawing no more pictures – I am telling thee a truth, that as my friends prosper in their plans – I shall yet be able to see thy old age happy . . .' He prided himself on the 'intrepid manner' in which he had acted over the last twelve months; the daring spirit with which he had confronted 'in penury and privation' a host of 'bedizzened titled and untitled cowards'. 'I possess the spirit of a soldier's son, he boasted to his poor bewildered father who, as yet, saw little sign of the promised £500 annuity.

By an ironic chance the Committee of the British and Foreign School Society had also decided in September 1814 to try to raise a basic fund. Their aim was £10,000 in gifts of £100 each. By January 1815 only twelve hundreds had come in. 'Eighty eight hundreds more wanted,' William Allen noted.

Cheered by the backing of his Manchester friends, convinced of the rightness of his cause, disregarding appeals from Richard Lancaster and the new young man who had taken over from Bennett at the school, Joseph was once more making public appearances in the Manchester and Liverpool areas and visiting schools. He left it to his friends to worry about the realities of his situation, choosing to believe that worldly embarrassments were of little importance beside the furthering of the great cause. Yet he must have known that the Westminster school, which was in utter disarray, was not only an appalling advertisement but a fruitful source of fresh debts. It is hard to see why he did not close it down. Even his illogical optimism cannot have blinded him to the impossibility of his returning to the metropolis for some time to come. But the school, any school, even a bad school, with the Lancastrian name, functioning however feebly within a short distance of the Borough Road, must have represented a gesture of defiance which he was reluctant to relinquish.

For David Holt and his friends, however, the situation appeared very different. As fast as money was collected, Joseph Lancaster spent it; and never on the repayment of old obligations. On October 21st David Holt was asking asylum for him from John Jackson, because there was a writ out for Lancaster in the county. Hardly surprising then that, although they continued to stand his champions, they packed him off to Ireland in November to further the cause of education in that country.

He was to be in Ireland and Scotland for the next year. During that time, on July 6th 1815, Sam Whitbread, who had been suffering from an unidentified disease, committed suicide. Within a year, on April 10th 1816, Joseph Fox was dead of a rupture of the gall bladder at the age of forty. Joseph Lancaster considered that Providence had dealt justly with them both.

Joseph Lancaster's Irish journey followed the pattern of earlier visits, seemingly unaffected by events in England. Maurice Cross was in Belfast, where he was to remain in charge of the Lancastrian school until 1830. Their meeting was full of affection and delight. John Veevers, who during the period of Lancaster's superintendency at the Borough Road had written of himself that he was but a poor consoler, was in Dublin. There were successful lectures everywhere and the aristocracy continued to attend. The Catholic college at Maynooth received him with honour. Nuns and priests were kind.

Money was still a problem, but something of the old panache came back in the various appeals that he addressed to friends and strangers alike. He had not paid the bill at the Belfast hotel, on the pretext of a speedy return; and had left a trunk with books and documents there, probably because they demanded some surety. In a letter to a supporter, laying out the necessity for Maurice to bring back the box to Dublin, Lancaster managed to make payment of this bill appear a trifling favour by which no one would ultimately be the loser. Every now and then a small amount was forwarded to Richard Lancaster, sometimes £15, sometimes £6, sometimes £4. Instructions were to keep the school going.

In July 1815 Joseph Lancaster left Ireland for Scotland, arriving via Portpatrick. He announced his coming by broadsheet. Lancaster had many faithful friends in this country, notably Alexander Henderson in Edinburgh, but Joseph Fox had recently visited the north and there were some towns no longer willing to receive Joseph Lancaster. Nevertheless he continued to write optimistically of lectures in Edinburgh and Glasgow, 'one unclouded blaze' in Aberdeen, presents sent to Betsy from Elgin, adulation in the papers at Perth, blessed usefulness in St Andrews, birthplace of Andrew Bell. In Edinburgh he had published a small pamphlet, 'A Narrative, etc' which abused William Allen and Joseph Fox in the grossest terms and caused the former much pain.

Joseph Lancaster came back to England early in November 1815 and again divided his time between Liverpool and Manchester. In the latter place he had a severe bout of rheumatic fever which left him ill and penniless. But the real shock was to discover that Elizabeth had gone back to London and been taken into the care of the Quakers. The Friends intended to send her to their retreat in York, for persons in a state of lunacy.

Once again the sense of betrayal was strong. One moment Joseph was swearing that he could never live with her again, the next that he would remove her from them sooner than they expected. The only excuse that he could find for her was that she must indeed be mad.

On the other hand, having seen Betsy again he had a longing not to be parted from her. In spite of the companionship of a cousin, Mary Ann, of whom Joseph Lancaster was very fond, Betsy disliked living with her Uncle William. Considerably older than Joseph, William was a difficult man, a manufacturer in whalebone whose trade rarely enabled him to live in any comfort. Joseph now felt that the ten-year-old Betsy could be of help to him and even earn herself a living as a teacher. Betsy too very much wanted to join her father. It was, however, to be another year before she did so. In June 1816 he sent her a box of mugs, jugs and rugs from the Potteries. At this time Elizabeth had returned to stay with Richard Lancaster and the family rift had been patched up. Joseph wrote to Betsy that her mother was a great deal better and joined in sending 'our dear love to thee'.

Joseph Lancaster had been importuning Sir Robert Peel, now Chief Secretary for Ireland, on behalf of education in that country. In June 1815 in a debate on the Irish budget the principle of religious toleration in education was sanctioned. There had been a proposal, how well founded it is impossible to say, that Lancaster should settle in Ireland. It hung before him like fairy gold, the solution to many problems. He put out a broadsheet, 'Education for All the Youth of Ireland', to try to stir up interest and appeal for money. It stressed that the friends of the System in Ireland did not think it needful to establish a public body, committee or trustees; 'the work to be done being an exertion of individual energy and talent, which public associations may shackle, but can neither create nor command'.

In the summer of 1816 Lancaster was travelling to Bristol, Bath and the West Country, proving once again to himself, and attempting to prove to others 'that my heart is alienable from the work . . .' There were good friends in Bristol, the Cumberlands, and he hoped that they would get up a subscription for him. He could still retain the affection of intelligent and influential men. Sir Richard Phillips, author and bookseller-publisher, patron of radicals, who produced The Juvenile Library in 1800 and made a handsome gift of books to the Borough Road school, was a strong partisan. He sent Francis Place a copy of 'Oppression and Persecution', printed that year in Bristol and written in Lancaster's extravagent public style, full of vituperation against Allen and Fox. Sir Richard Phillips, to Francis Place's extreme annoyance, remarked that it merited serious attention.

'Oppression and Persecution', the very title is significant, gave Joseph Lancaster's version of the events leading up to the final break with the Committee, and was his justification. The preface was addressed 'Impartial Reader'. His self-image was clearly very different from that perceived by the larger outside world and much closer to the private person whom Betsy and his father knew. He insisted that he was the last man to say a word in his own defence, and it is probable that he believed this statement in spite of the torrent of printed matter in which he vilified his enemies, as he also had difficulty in relating his own view that financial prodigality was of no importance with Place's opinion that it came close to criminal dishonesty. The imaginative leap of seeing himself as others did was denied him by the strength of his own inner commitment to an overriding idea. Inward contemplation of his own intentions enabled Joseph Lancaster to forgive himself much that others, working in the chaos where intentions and worldly considerations met, could not.

The heart of Joseph Lancaster's anguish was plain and beside it nothing else mattered. It was the way in which his 'late Trustees' had 'broken their compact, and literally choused me out of a local institution, which I had reared from its foundation, until it proved a blessing to thousands'. Then they sought to alter the name, 'as if Britons and Foreigners had combined in its invention'.

Such an appeal evoked a sympathetic response in others beside Sir Richard Phillips. What was less easy to agree with was the view of the Trustees as having usurped Joseph Lancaster's funds and filched the money which was intended to support his aged father, afflicted wife and interesting child. In the violence of his feelings the thread of his argument was often lost and the abuse of former friends unrestrained. Every action of the Committee he saw as a betrayal, culminating in the Act of Bankruptcy and the suggestion that he might leave for Caracas. However, though now deprived of an effective field of labour and persecuted in the press, Joseph Lancaster remained undaunted. With a last dart at the decreasing numbers of pupils at the Borough Road and its general state of deterioration, he asserted that Ireland still beckoned; and characteristically ended with a call for £600. In fact remittances which he daily expected from Ireland never arrived, nor did the projected journey ever take place.

In March 1817 Joseph Lancaster was in Portsmouth staying with Sir George Grey, Resident Commissioner of Portsmouth Dockyard, younger brother of Lord Grey a future Whig Prime Minister. From there he wrote to Colonel McMahon, Keeper of the Privy purse, asking what had happened to the Prince Regent's annual subscription. He feared it had fallen into the wrong hands. It is unlikely that he ever got the interview which he requested.

He was still travelling and lecturing, but in spite of all his cheerfulness it was becoming only too apparent that the time had gone when Joseph Lancaster created a sensation on a platform. His patrons had changed their allegiance; power was no longer on his side, and the people followed patronage and power. Richard Lancaster even began to suggest that, if the Committee made him a fresh offer he should accept it.

There was never any such intention. Things had begun to go better for the British and Foreign School Society. The first Auxiliary Society had been formed in Bristol in July 1815. Others followed. The Russian Emperor was interested in training for Russian teachers; a Lancastrian school flourished in Calcutta, India, and New York had opened its third school house; there were six potential teachers for Ceylon at the Institution, Borough Road. William Allen was working on 'A Manual of the British System of Education'. In May 1816 Henry Brougham had moved for a Committee of the House on the education of the poor and obtained the appointment of a select committee to enquire into the state of popular education in London, Westminster and Southwark. He urged State intervention to supplement voluntary effort, and William Allen was examined at the House of Commons on the nature and progress of the British and Foreign School Society. By the end of that year it seemed certain that the £10,000 invested fund would soon be reached. In January 1816 the decision had been taken to build a new school, and in June 1817 fine new buildings were opened in the Borough Road.

In fact, in a euphoria not unlike that which had once possessed Joseph Lancaster, the Society had extended itself far beyond what was possible or practicable. They were to remain in debt until 1829. Hayti, Senegal, Malta, Poland, Russia, France, Spain, often hotly pursued by the National Society, the B&FSS sent teachers off to every corner of the globe, sometimes ill-prepared, certainly without proper support, at considerable expense and with few lasting results. Meanwhile at home, in the Borough Road Institution, the old inspiration had vanished and the narrow rigidity that was taking its place led inexorably to the inflexibility that was eventually to discredit the System.

Whatever his faults and extravagances, Joseph Lancaster was a charismatic teacher. None of his successors on the Committee had ever conducted a school, and indeed it was charged that too often masters never saw a Committee member from one month's end to the next. With the discipline of the System, Joseph Lancaster had encouraged a vigorous, joyful energy. He understood young people and their need for change and challenge. Ceremonies and parades, generous rewards, punishments geared to a youthful sense of fitness, the accessibility of books, toys, any new or interesting invention that caught Lancaster's fancy, all made for a stimulating and exciting environment. By 1816, under pressure from the National Society, the Bible was the only text book used in the Borough Road, and the children were required to report on Monday morning where they had worshipped the previous Sunday. No less than Joseph Lancaster, William Allen felt strongly about non-sectarian education, but he also felt impelled to prove that he did so. The days when the Borough Road school had been the most exciting educational establishment in Europe were gone.

In November 1816 Isaac Walters, who had acted as steward at the school for eight years, was told that, as the result of a paralytic stroke, he could no longer be retained in his job. 'The Committee therefore direct that notice be given to him that it will be expected he shall leave the Institution at the end of the year and they hope his friends will then provide for him.' Maybe William Allen helped him privately, but it is tempting to speculate that Joseph Lancaster, who was generous with what little money he himself possessed as well as with other people's and always ready to provide warm recommendations for needy young men or hard-pressed widows, would not have parted with a faithful servant so coldly.

On June 3rd 1817, when the new buildings were being opened

in the Borough Road by the Duke of Kent, Joseph Lancaster was in Gosport, writing to his wife, 'Thou knowest that I love thee and yet thou give way continually to that disease which makes thee unhappy by doubting it – and this injuring my peace without a cause'. For all his optimism, assurances to Betsy that things were better and promised to be better still, there was simply more than Elizabeth's health to disturb Joseph Lancaster's peace. His father was old and ill. Lucy Edmunds, a kindly neighbour and great gossip, looked after him and sister Sarah and acted as Joseph's agent in buying pens, quills, ink, etc., taking messages and getting in subscriptions, some of which she spent on provisions for Richard Lancaster. Lucy Edmunds was worried about Betsy who she thought needed some female attention and not to have too much expected of her. Though the contrast in his financial situation was never mentioned in Joseph's letters home, it was clear that very little came into his coffers at this time; and that usually begged from a friend or former acquaintance. Any income from lectures had practically disappeared, due as much to severe winter weather as to failing audiences. Joseph Lancaster was close to destitution. It may have been when famine and contagious fever in Ireland finally made a return to that country impossible that America was seriously mentioned. There were, after all, Lancaster relations there.

In December 1817 he was back in Manchester with David Holt and Betsy had joined him. It must have been about this time that Samuel Sharwood commissioned a portrait of Joseph Lancaster from John Hazlitt. No one looking at this picture would guess that the plump kindly man portrayed had suffered traumatically and been publicly humiliated. Some years later Lancaster was to tell his friend John Robinson, miniature painter and pupil of Benjamin West, that he had an objection to having his picture placed in a museum for public exhibition. He thought it an abominable vanity – and in any case did not care to hang in the same gallery as Tom Paine. Yet, convinced of his own importance, on the national and indeed world scene, he carefully kept every scrap of writing relating to himself and had no hesitation in counselling Betsy that these would one day be of considerable monetary value. Irrepressible, Lancaster had provided himself with a punning coat of arms; inside a circular border hung a bell with 'J. Lancaster Me Fecit' engraved on it.

Lucy Edmunds reported that Richard Lancaster's reaction had been to exclaim, 'The Proud Fellow'.

Once again David Holt, in conjunction with Samuel Sharwood, decided to raise another subscription. The printed circular was headed 'Distress of Joseph Lancaster'. 'Since the much regretted division between Joseph Lancaster and his former Trustees, it has fallen to the lot of a number of friends of his cause, in Manchester, to witness his unabated zeal and exertions for the spread of general knowledge. In England and Scotland they may have been useful, – and in Ireland they have yielded a harvest of blessings.' It went on to describe Lancaster's illness, Elizabeth's affliction, the effect of a bad winter on his lecture takings. In short Lancaster was destitute and without his Manchester friends he and Betsy might sometimes have starved. Once, even in this emergency, of which his own letters gave no indication, Lancaster had been forced to pawn his Bible to buy food. The time had now come when the prospect of America beckoned enticingly. To David Holt's subscription William Allen sent £25.

In the end the American venture seems to have matured quite suddenly. In April 1818 Lancaster was lecturing in Huntingdon-shire and concerned with the distribution of a long, anonymous, religious essay. Betsy was with her grandfather and Elizabeth at the Friends' Retreat in York. From St Ives Joseph wrote to Betsy, 'Dear love to Grandfather and aunt and tell him that this country is fen land full of oziers and skean rods. The price on the spot without carriage is ten shillings a bolt – I think I shall get one bolt and send it up as a present to him . . .' He had also bespoke a sucking pig for grandfather, about 9d a pound. John Lovell and Richard Madox Jones, two old apprentices, were in the house at Elliott Row. One of Richard Jones' jobs was to teach Betsy writing, geography and arithmetic. Her father sent her puzzle questions to tease her young tutor. 'If one terrier dog can worry six rats, how many rats can worry one terrier dog.' She was to ask it seriously, thus inducing him to give a serious answer then she could laugh at him.

In May Joseph's niece Mary Ann wrote that she supposed the American voyage had been given up. On June 8th John Lovell hoped that it was not abandoned. David Holt had enough money to pay for a comfortable passage. On June 23rd 1818 Joseph Lancaster, Elizabeth, Betsy and Richard Jones sailed from Gravesend on the 'Washington', Captain Foreman, for the New

World. It was nearly two years since Elizabeth Lancaster had last seen her daughter.

Richard Jones and Betsy with José, Carlos and Ricardo *(after a picture painted about 1833 probably by José Mariá Venerte.)*

Part
2

UNITED STATES

Joseph Lancaster — after engraving (1813), probably from earlier silhouette'

Chapter 11
A NEW WORLD

'The kindness I have experienced here from all classes and those of the society of Friends in an especial manner is truly American and endearing' (Joseph Lancaster to Governor Clinton)

Joseph Lancaster arrived in America with a double edged reputation. In many parts of the east coast the Lancastrian System was already known and admired, and there was a fund of goodwill for the inventor. On the other hand the close links between the Quaker fraternity on both sides of the Atlantic meant that his disownment and the reasons for it were common knowledge. The latter fact did not prevent his being graciously welcomed, but it lurked in the background ready to surface at the first incautious step.

The 'Washington' arrived in New York on August 24th 1818. It had not been a particularly good voyage. She was a square rigged three master of about three hundred tons, registered in

New York and already eleven years old. Both Betsy and her mother suffered considerably from sea sickness. The passage was in fact rather more salubrious than it might have been as David Holt's benevolence had ensured the Lancasters a cabin; Ed Baker, a Lancaster apprentice who had gone to America in 1815 went steerage from Liverpool for ten guineas, finding his own provisions. From London the fare was five guineas dearer.

Ed Baker had had a much worse crossing. '. . . 74 days with a drunken Captain an inefficient and mutinous crew and three storms are enough to sicken one . . .' he wrote to Francis Place, who had asked for minute details as to the process of emigration. His provision chest, 'much against my will', had been flung overboard in mid Atlantic to trim the ship and he landed in New York destitute. Nevertheless he provided Francis Place with a great deal of interesting information.

On leaving Liverpool, in order to get through the Custom House, he had had to get a passport from the Lord Mayor, or a Certificate from a Justice of the Peace, or the Minister of his Parish and churchwardens, stating that he was not an artisan or a manufacturer, neither of whom were permitted to leave the country. Edward Baker, not having access to any of those people, turned up a person who had known him since he was seventeen to swear for him and then he had to discover an old established inhabitant of Liverpool to give a reference for this sponsor.

Once on board, and recovered from his sea sickness, he enjoyed the diversions; drafts, chess, cards, Fox and Goose, dancing and skipping. The food was less pleasurable. Finding it impossible to cook for himself, 'the act of cooking destroys the appetite', he nearly starved for the first two weeks.

The sailors survived on a daily diet of oatmeal, water and molasses boiled for breakfast, salt beef, hard coarse biscuit and soup for dinner and supper. Had he been given a second chance Ed Baker would have come to an agreement with two or three other passengers to mess together, and then asked the Captain for someone to cook for them. As far as clothes went he advised one or two flannel shirts, to be washed in the sea; linen shirts were destroyed by this process. A hammock, a small mattress, pillow, blanket and sheet, a tin saucepan and steamer, caster oil, rhubarb or salts, he now saw as being essential items of baggage.

The Lancasters' voyage was swifter and less burdened, their

food being provided. It is probable that Joseph, with his naturally resilient temperament, enjoyed it. Had they been travelling steerage he would no doubt have participated with zest in those amusements which his Quaker profession permitted; among the staider cabin passengers he himself may well have been the chief source of liveliness. Elizabeth Lancaster's mental health profited from the company of her husband in a situation where he could not escape her. At any rate she landed in New York equable and happy. But the person for whom this sea voyage effected a transformation was Betsy. Until now she had been her father's 'darling', his 'jewel', the daughter to whom he sent loving messages and small presents. From the moment the family landed in America 'Betsy' became 'Elizabeth', Joseph Lancaster's lifeline and his chief support. The old name was laid aside and with it the twelve-year-old girl moved away from childish things.

Betsy, for whom it is easier to retain the diminutive, loved both her parents. When her mother was with the Friends in York, in the immediate harsh months before the decision to leave was taken, Betsy had written asking if she could have a silhouette of her. She added that her father 'encourages me to love thee, which I do very dearly,' and hoped that Elizabeth would soon be well '. . . for then I shall have thyself and however much I may be pleased with thy profile that will be much better'. Now they were together and Elizabeth may have perceived with pain that her jealousy of her husband might well have yet another focus. But Betsy was a young woman of character, courage, tact and sterling common sense. She saw those whom she loved clearly as fallible human beings, but that made no difference to the strength and loyalty of her affections. Richard Jones, their fellow passenger, had begun to watch her developing with growing interest.

Both Lancasters had relatives in America. In the early years of the eighteenth century an uncle of Richard Lancaster had gone from Warwick to Philadelphia and left descendents in that area. Elizabeth Lancaster had a kinsman in New York, by name William Shotwell. Quaker communities in Pennsylvania and New York were strong and cohesive and Joseph probably remembered his youth when he had been impressed by the religious visits to England of Thomas Scattergood, David Sands and William Savory. Then too there were his lads, the Ould brothers who had been in America since 1811, and Ed Baker. Joseph Lancaster never anticipated rejection. He expected always to be welcomed, and if rebuffs were in evidence to administer them himself.

In the event the arrival was propitious. Lancaster was an honoured name in New York education and Joseph was met by the Mayor and Recorder of the city, and by the State Governor, the Honourable de Witt Clinton.

De Witt Clinton, whose own wife had just died, was a powerful supporter and was to remain a faithful friend to Joseph Lancaster. He was a large, handsome man from a public spirited family, energetic and intelligent, pragmatic and able. For ten years, before becoming State Governor in 1817, he had been Mayor of New York City and had been responsible for much urban improvement and philanthropic innovation. One of his important interests was the promotion of the Lake Erie-Hudson canal which became known as 'Clinton's ditch' and was to help establish New York as the nation's major commercial centre. He had removed the political disabilities of Catholics in the city, and was patron of the Orphan Asylum and the City Hospital. In 1806 de Witt Clinton had opened the first New York Free School and prophesised that the Lancastrian System would launch a new era in education.

The new Constitution for the Union, which came into being after the War of Independence, did not mention education. In the Tenth Amendment of 1791 it was, by default, left to the individual States, in which attitudes to schooling varied widely. Two years after Joseph Lancaster landed in the New World, of the twenty-three States then composing the Union, ten made no mention of education in their State constitutions. Until Independence, and in some States for many years after, education for the poor was largely dominated by the pattern of English charity schools; but the effect of the War of Independence had been to close many educational establishments, particularly in New York, and this led to a break in traditions inherited from the United Kingdom.

The Union Constitution had established the free exercise of religious faith and forbidden the setting up of any state religion or the requirement of any religious test or oath for government office, thus beginning the emancipation of education from church domination. The Lancastrian System, with its non-denomina-

tional emphasis and its efficient, effective and disciplined procedures, enabling large numbers of children to be taught economically, offered an answer to American needs, which seemed
scientific and peculiarly suited to American ideals. Americans
liked to say that monarchies rested on an education of status,
fixing each class in its proper place; republics required an
education of virtue, to motivate men to choose public over
private interest.

New York had been almost entirely rebuilt since the peace. A
city with a growing population, it was beginning to suffer from
urban pressures and their associated problems. In 1795 New
York State Legislature had passed a bill to provide aid to
common schools, appropriating twenty thousand dollars a year,
for five years, to be apportioned to counties on a population
basis. The counties were expected to match one half of their
share with school taxes, the money to be used to maintain schools
teaching English, arithmetic, and other subjects necessary to a
good education. In New York City, where there were nearly one
hundred teachers offering a common education, the distribution
of this subsidy was a problem. The Common Council, which
acted in place of school commissioners, applied in 1796 for legal
provision to establish 'public' schools and to shift the emphasis
from financing teachers to providing buildings. The legislature
agreed. The new public schools were to be styled free schools,
but through lack of community interest the school law expired in
1800 and was not replaced. The accumulated monies were
divided among the city's eleven charity schools, which were then
called free schools.

In 1804 a Quaker, Thomas Eddy, active in social reform and
prominent in the efforts to provide more schooling for the city,
became aware of Joseph Lancaster's work in London through his
friendship with the metropolitan magistrate Patrick Colquhoun.
On June 20th 1804 Eddy wrote to Joseph Lancaster telling him
that he had been so impressed by the pamphlet 'Improvements
in Education', which Patrick Colquhoun had sent him, that he
had had a thousand copies printed in New York and Philadelphia.
In 1805 Thomas Eddy founded the New York Free School
Society, to provide schooling for the churchless poor, and on
May 6th 1806 de Witt Clinton, their President, opened the
Society's, and America's, first school on Lancastrian lines. In the
next three years the Free School Society gained both State and

municipal assistance, built a large school specially for monitorial instruction on Lancaster's plan, and decided to establish more 'for all children who are the proper objects of a gratuitous education'. Benjamin Perkins, the Free School Society's Secretary, went to England and paid a visit to the Borough Road.

By 1818 the Free School Society was responsible for over a thousand scholars in three schools. In 1815 Ed Baker, now in Philadelphia, had been offered the job of master of the New York Lancastrian school. And even while Joseph Lancaster was on the high seas Thomas Eddy had concluded a deal with William Allen and the British and Foreign School Society for a teacher to perfect monitorial procedures in the city's school system. Charles Pickton, an early Lancaster apprentice, and his wife sailed in July on the 'Emily' to take up this work. The B&FSS had stipulated that he must not teach in any school where Joseph Lancaster was working.

The Free School Society was already well established when Joseph Lancaster arrived in New York. As the founder of the System his was an honoured name; but as one who might wish to play an active part in school organisation there was no place for him.

A week after landing Joseph Lancaster gave his first lecture on American soil in the New York Free School room, by courtesy of Governor Clinton. Approximately three hundred people came to hear him and the receipts were a satisfactory hundred dollars. The next morning he and Betsy left with the Governor, by the steam boat 'Paragon', to visit the State capital at Albany. Richard Jones and Mrs Lancaster remained in New York in a small house at 37 Dey Street. Elizabeth was agitated and upset by the prospective hazards of river travel for her husband and daughter. Perhaps too she resented being once again excluded.

But for Joseph and Betsy all must have seemed well. De Witt Clinton was a powerful man and Joseph Lancaster had not yet grasped that this was a society without patronage as he had understood it on the other side of the Atlantic. In this country to possess influential friends did not automatically open doors.

It was a pleasant leisurely journey and much in the landscape on either side of the Hudson river seemed familiar. Betsy was 'highly delighted with seeing America so much like England'. The Governor and his friends were attentive and Joseph was introduced to local senators coming up to the State capital for a meeting.

They arrived in Albany on September 2nd. The Governor's son acted as a guide to the town. For some of the time Governor Clinton lent them his carriage. Joseph wrote at once to Elizabeth asking for 'Sutcliffe's Travels' to be sent him, so that he could take a more informed interest in all these new places. September 8th was Betsy's thirteenth birthday. The Governor invited them to breakfast and her father gave her four dollars as a present. Betsy was delighted. She and Joseph spent the day together exploring the town. They witnessed an incident, which Joseph used as a lesson for Elizabeth. Walking up a hill they met a stage with four fine horses. One of the four fell dead. The driver kept his head, controlled the other three and the passengers got out safely. So it was not only steam boats that accidents could occur. In this case, however, the 'dead' horse got up again, twitched his ears, looked very sagacious and went on as usual. If only Elizabeth would not give way to anxieties, often unnecessary, and an interruption to her husband's public duty.

Things seemed to be going better between Joseph and Elizabeth. She had been called on by Mrs Thomas Eddy and another Quaker lady, and taken breakfast with William Shotwell, to whom she appeared happy and agreeable. Joseph, particularly wary of the protestations of Friends, warned her to be cautious. He had no doubt that the long arm of calumny would stretch across the Atlantic and do him damage where it could, and the rumour of the ban on Charles Pickton working with Lancaster was already known to William Shotwell. But he cannot have felt friendless. Letters had now caught up with him, sent on by Richard Jones. There was a warm welcome from the Ould brothers from Washington, with Robert offering his own house as a home for the Lancasters and Henry adding his 'inexpressible pleasure' at the news of their arrival. John Lovell had written from England, thanking Joseph for his liberality before he left and admitting that he found the separation painful. 'Pray don't delay sending for me', he pleaded. He would leave his aged parents and a few friends with sorrow, but believed utterly in Joseph Lancaster.

From Philadelphia Ed Baker too had communicated. He wrote in affectionate terms and, with great generosity, enclosed twenty-five dollars as a mark of his gratitude to his old master, because he himself knew what it was to land in a strange country with little money. Like Robert Ould, Ed Baker offered shelter under his own roof till something better came up; and his son, if a little boy, would help Joseph Lancaster to develop the System. This open-hearted letter was not to receive the answer it merited.

Among a packet of letters from local wellwishers was one from the Corresponding Secretary of the Teachers Society of New York (City and County) announcing that Joseph Lancaster had unanimously been elected a member; and a number of applications from young men wishing Lancaster to take them on as teachers. Richard Jones forwarded all this correspondence with some notes of his own about the present situation as he saw it. There was gossip about the choice of Betsy, rather than her mother, as a travelling companion. Thomas Eddy thought Lancaster should publish a manual to subsidise himself, others suggested that he open a pay school. Ominously Richard ended with a statement that he and Mrs Lancaster were without money. David Holt and his group of friends in Manchester had made an arrangement through a lawyer in Liverpool, J. D. Moxon, to pay Joseph Lancaster £25 per month for the first twelve months, but this assistance was slow in arriving and, as Joseph was to discover, Americans did not care to pay advance subscriptions for any publication not yet through the press; or sometimes even written. They preferred to hand over the cash when the volume was actually bought.

So lectures remained the major source of revenue. But the lectures were going well, though William Shotwell cautioned that American audiences did not appreciate 'sallies of pleasantry'. No jokes, please, Mr Lancaster. There were two lectures in Albany, where he had been given a fulsome address of welcome by the Trustees of Albany Lancastrian School, which had been incoporated by the legislature in May 1812. During the rest of September Joseph and Betsy visited the other three big towns in the State, Troy, Schnectady and Hudson, lecturing in each, as well as in Waterford, Lansingburgh, Poughkeepsie and New-burgh on the way back down river to New York. The result was nearly two hundred dollars, sufficient to justify optimism about adequate provision in the future.

Joseph Lancaster had very quickly settled down and begun to make plans. These he confided in Governor Clinton along with his guidelines for behaviour. 'My rule of action is first to be publicly grateful to those who have from principle, and not knowing me, or expecting even to see me – promoted for a series of years that system which is as dear to my heart as ever. Second to keep my movements as much in the line of public harmonious feelings – free from the discordance of political spirit – as possible. To shun rather than mix, with violent men. To neither make, nor meddle in politics. Legislation is out of my province unless where humanity, benevolence or education bring it within my line of march. Third to strike fire on as few religious feelings and sectarian interests as possible.'

The practical side of this blueprint included establishing a school, which he would like to be in New York if a suitable room could be hired. Though he did not say so, it was plain that he hoped de Witt Clinton and his friends would provide the capital for such a venture. From this base a seminary for schoolmasters could be formed. Publishing school books and a new manual, corresponding with the friends of education, travelling and lecturing throughout the States were the other component parts of this master plan.

It was the teacher training on which he set most store. On September 7th he expounded his own ideas on this subject to Governor Clinton.

'A teacher otherwise a good Scholar may acquire a knowledge of the System in a month or six weeks – one month to three is a desirable portion of time. The latter will render a man practically expert, as well as theoretically in the principles of the system.

'The qualifications of a Teacher should not merely consist of his attainments, which as to knowledge are obviously indispens-able – but a mildness of character combined with firmness – a love of the duty of tuition with capacity and affability, sufficient to make appeal to the good sense and reason of his pupils without professing such an object when doing it but acting naturally as a Teacher at home in his work and in the Society of his pupils. The greatest difficulty of finding a proper Teacher lays much more in finding a person of proper capacity and attachment to his pursuit than in the attainments common to teachers.'

By early October Joseph Lancaster was back in New York. He had written to Elizabeth that when he returned he would take her on a journey to Long Island 'where I suspect we shall find a number of Lancasters of the "ancient flock"'. It was not to be. He found her once more in a state of mental and physical disorder. Nor was there the compensation of a successful fulfilment of his plans. He tried to get the use of the Court House for a public lecture, as had happened in Hudson, but was refused, the court being in session. And the Committee of the Free School Society were less than enthusiastic about his setting up a school and teacher training institution. It is unlikely that they could have stopped him, but he saw plainly that they did not wish it. He decided to take his family and spend the winter in the great Quaker city of Philadelphia.

It was natural that the Free School Society should have been wary of welcoming Joseph Lancaster in an active capacity. At this time the New York schools were the best in America. They received State funds in proportion to enrolments and were controlled by their boards. Procedures, which were what the System was all about, could be perfected by young men like Charles Pickton; Joseph Lancaster with a name and a reputation, and a personality not easily absorbed into the communal group, was quite a different matter. His employment could bring embarrassment; independent action on his part might be productive of schism and jealousy and in conflict with the development of schools in the city.

The fact was that America did not need Joseph Lancaster. They had the System and it was working well. Though he promised many embellishments, Joseph brought nothing new in educational thought or practice. The honour that was done him celebrated past achievements: it had nothing to do with present employment. Nor is it by any means certain that Joseph would have made a success of a school. He was forty, and for the last few years had spent more time lecturing and publicising than teaching. Francis Place wrote in 1827 that the credit of making the System known in England belonged solely to Lancaster. He did it well. He enjoyed travelling and speaking and meeting people. He had not lost his affection for young people or his natural aptitude as a teacher, but the constriction of the schoolroom was irksome to him now.

Philadelphia too prepared to receive Joseph Lancaster with honour; but they had been warned. Samuel Emlin, a Quaker, wrote from Burlington, New Jersey, where Lancaster was delivering a lecture on route, to his kinsman in Philadelphia, Roberts Vaux, on October 15th.

'. . . I understand that Joseph Lancaster, who has this evening given one of his lectures to a pretty numerous auditory for this place, intends going to your City tomorrow and I suppose will soon make himself known to some of you who are interested in the system of general School Education . . .

'I suppose it is no secret to thee that he is unconnected with our religious Society, or the British and Foreign School Society and therefore now stands independent of both . . . Whilst we carefully avoid throwing anything in the way to prevent his regaining the ground which he has lost and making a provision for himself and family, it may also be best to exercise a care not to bestow too much attention, lest by inflating a mind which has been represented as but too susceptible of vanity, the benefit which he may have derived from the experience of the events of the last few years, be lost to himself and produce inconvenience to others as I suppose it has heretofore . . .'

Robert Vaux was three years younger than Joseph Lancaster. He had retired from business before he was thirty to devote himself to philanthropic works, and was interested, as was his counterpart Thomas Eddy in New York, in penal problems, hospitals, work with the insane and education. It was his first year as President of the Board of Control of Public Schools in Philadelphia.

After the opening of the Lancastrian school in New York in 1806, Philadelphia had followed suit with enthusiasm. In March 1818 a special law permitted the city to organise a system of schools for the education of its poor children, and the Board of Control was established. A Committee was chosen to find a building and a teacher for a Model School, and in May an agreement, endorsed by the British and Foreign School Society, was made with Ed Baker, who had been conducting a private Lancastrian school in the town. He was asked to run the Model Boys School at a salary of one hundred dollars a month.

Joseph Lancaster had treated Ed Baker very badly. Not only did he never reply to his first generous and welcoming letter, but news reached Ed Baker that Joseph Lancaster had refused delivery of that letter, saying he knew no one of that name. Hurt and upset, Ed Baker wrote again on October 9th, reminding Joseph that he himself had taught him the Lancastrian System. He had always defended and admired Lancaster, who knew that the B&FSS had taken over his school in Westminster, as indeed it had Lancaster's own, by compulsion. Surely Joseph could not blame him for that, or the fact that he had accepted some help with his travel to America from the Society. He hoped they could remain friends, and thought that Joseph would find him a useful ally in Philadelphia.

Tragically this appeal fell on deaf ears. Even the smallest and most innocent association with the British and Foreign School Society smacked of gross betrayal to Joseph Lancaster. So, and not for the last time, he deprived himself of a friend and prejudiced his own future for the sake of a vendetta that he could never win. The situation was the sadder because Ed Baker was one of his lads; a fact which in Joseph's eyes may have made his supposed defection the more heinous.

Joseph Lancaster arrived in Philadelphia on October 19th. He was welcomed by a deputation which included the Mayor and the City Recorder. The new school law was explained to him. The city was divided into sections and the Directors of the first section, the inner city, chose a small committee to go round with Mr Lancaster visiting the schools. The three men designated for this duty were Joseph Reed, the Reverend George Boyd and Ebenezer Ferguson JP Inspector of Lumber. Thomas Steward-son and Ebenezer Ferguson were also delegated by the Controllers to confer with Mr Lancaster about his superintending the Model School until its operation conformed strictly with his original System. The new school building was approaching completion.

On October 23rd the two men reported to the Board that Mr Lancaster was willing to organise the Model School and instruct the sectional teachers at a hundred and twenty dollars a month. The old school was to be closed and Ed Baker to remain on the payroll for three months. Joseph wrote to Governor Clinton that he had 'offered personally to organise their model school – and make it not only what it ought to be, a perfect model – but a seminary for training teachers – and they fell completely into my terms and plans – and I have now taken a little house furnished it and am preparing to winter here I have only bound myself as to time for the term of six months.'

Potential causes of friction were already clear. Joseph, whether with justness it is impossible to tell, condemned the work that Ed Baker had been doing since May in the old schoolroom as bringing the System into discredit. Ed Baker, who had offered hospitality and financial help to his former master, now found himself superseded and unappreciated. The Controllers seemed to imply that they expected Joseph to remain in charge of the school for a reasonable period when Ed Baker had worked out his three months notice; but Joseph was writing to de Witt Clinton that he hoped in the spring to get back to New York. He had also stipulated for two or three weeks off in the New Year to visit Congress and to lecture. Into the bargain he immediately attempted to gain an advance on his salary, a request that was not viewed favourably by the Board. Joseph was deeply offended by their dilatoriness in replying, especially when he considered, wrongly, that he could get much better money almost anywhere else.

At last, on November 26th, the Board agreed to advance two months salary. Ebenezer Ferguson voted against this decision.

The Board were in a very difficult position. The opening of the new Model School was delayed owing to the slowness of the carpenters. It was only a few months since they had set out to build up a system of publicly controlled schools for the poor, and the idea that money for such a venture should come out of the public treasury was a new, and not very acceptable, one to taxpayers. They were anxious to raise teaching to a profession. Now the old school was closed, the new one not yet opened; pupils had drifted away and were failing to reregister, and the Board were having to pay 100 dollars a month to Ed Baker, who was no longer working, and 120 a month to Joseph Lancaster, who had so far done nothing.

By December the upper room of the new Model School was ready and it was decided to open the boys school there; though this top storey had originally been intended for girls. On December 21st the boys school began to take in pupils and, in a few weeks, had registered four hundred and thirteen. Again a small committee, Thomas Stewardson, Ebenezer Ferguson, William Fry and James Ronaldson, were chosen by the Board to discuss with Joseph Lancaster the subject of a girls school, with Betsy to teach needlework.

On the 1st of January 1819 the matter of a salary for organising the girls school was agreed. On January 2nd Joseph Lancaster, having slept over it, decided the salary was insufficient and withdrew from the contract. He wrote to Roberts Vaux to justify this decision, stating that it was indifferent to him whether the terms he had now laid down were acceptable or not. What he asked was the same salary as he had been granted to oversee the boys school. He would be involved in double trouble and should be paid accordingly. 'I am grieved that there should be any controversy or discussion on subjects of finance', he added. 'It is not my wish to make the system expensive. I think I had estimated my services at twice the salary received by any teacher in the United States I should not have overrated them'. Alas, he had miscalculated his market. Though, from where he stood, Joseph Lancaster appeared an undoubted and valuable asset to the United States; America, already conversant with the mechanics of his System and aware of his tarnished reputation, did not see it that way.

To Thomas Stewardson he wrote more forcefully. There would be two school rooms to oversee and, as he could not be in both places at one and the same time, he needed a full time assistant. If he used Richard Jones it could not be for little or no remuneration. 'The sum voted for a teacher in so responsible a situation as that of a model school is utterly unworthy of any respectable teachers acceptance. The situation is more highly responsible than any other school. The office of training teachers is more arduous, if there should be several. It will require labour, thought and experience to succeed even with a few and can 4 dollars a month more than common teachers be equal to such responsibility?' He added, 'In any proposition I have made I have always studied economy – In my last application – I have overstudied it – I find I shall be a very considerable sum out of pocket if I persist . . .'

On January 3rd the Board discharged the original committee and appointed three fresh members, Joseph Reed, George Boyd and James Rowlandson to reopen discussions with Lancaster. On January 12th this group brought back Joseph's proposals to the Board. They were that he 'open and organise the female school and establish the teachers thereof, including the instruction of female teachers for the Sectional Schools in the same way as the Masters: visit and superintend the Sectional Schools after the teachers had been instructed in the Model School: and receive compensation of five hundred dollars, in addition to the $120 per month'. It was a very considerable sum of money.

In the meanwhile Joseph Lancaster had left for a lecture tour, which was to included a triumphant visit to Washington. He put Richard Jones in charge of the 'partly organised' boys school. In a letter to Governor Clinton Joseph described it as an 'Elysium'.

It is doubtful whether the Board felt so euphoric about their own dealings with its teacher at this particular moment, and perhaps they would have been even more harried if they had known that he was trying to make arrangements to have himself appointed to organise a new Lancastrian school in New York.

In Washington, the Union's capital, a broadsheet was published.

Lectures on National Education
Joseph Lancaster
Presents his respects to the Members of the
National Legislature . . .
Two lectures on 25th & 26th

1) On the power of knowledge in developing the intellectual talents of man, and improving the moral and intellectual conditions of nations.

2) On the nature and advantages of the Lancastrian System of education.

The visit was to be the highlight of Joseph Lancaster's American life. He was received by the President, permitted by the Speaker to lecture in the Congress Hall, and met a number of distinguished persons, including the French and British ambassadors. Once again he was lionised. The early days of his success in the circles of the great had returned and he was what he felt himself to be, Joseph Lancaster, the man to whom thousands of children owed their ability to read and write; whose name was in every man's mouth.

After the first lecture the Member for Virginia, Burwell Bassett, moved that the House of Representatives pass a motion 'That Joseph Lancaster, the friend of learning and of man, be admitted to a seat within the hall'. Congressman Henry Clay of Kentucky advocate for the Spanish-American republics, said he had never seen the chair on which Lancaster sat better filled. Joseph made a punning reply to this compliment, asserting that man at his best could never be better than a piece of clay. Both these remarks might have been interpreted differently, for the 'Weekly National Register' reported that Mr Lancaster was 'of middle stature and fat withal. His appearance very Quaker-like'. Little dignity, less polish, no grace, strong discriminating mind and pleasant temper. They saw him as an energetic speaker who would make a contagious preacher, but did not altogether approve of his method of lecturing. 'He is familiar and ludicrous in some of his illustrations, sometimes descends to a pun'. No one doubted his sincerity but the Register considered that it was ill-judged of him to flatter Americans. Henry Ould took great exception to this notice, and then went on to admonish Joseph that Americans were no better than other people, indeed it was surprising that they were as good considering the riff-raff that immigration brought in.

But the warmth of his welcome must have stirred Joseph Lancaster's heart. Congressmen crowded round and pressed him to visit them in their home States and to undertake lectures all over the Union. He wrote to Roberts Vaux back in Philadelphia that he only wished the whole Board of Control could have been present to see his triumph, and sent them an ironic message, 'My respects to the Gentlemen of the Board – and tell them they may have confidence, that the polar Star of Education in Pennsylvania will not be eclipsed by any other Star in the Union'.

Robert Ould warned him not to put his faith in Congressmen. Burwell Bassett advised that Congress would not patronise the System for fear of creating a precedent. In America Joseph should not rely on patronage. He should publish by subscription, but not expect any money at the time of subscribing. Costly books would not sell. William Shotwell added that there would be difficulties if the book had already appeared in England. It was Robert Ould's opinion that three dollars was the maximum charge for lectures. There was plenty of good advice, but for the moment it was the fact of recognition that occupied Joseph Lancaster's mind.

The Board expected him back on February 1st and arranged to open the Girls School on that day. Roberts Vaux wrote, however, that they could spare him a while longer. 'Richard Jones manages his little army admirably and had no doubt that the Girls School can be conducted for a week without thy presence'. Roberts Vaux would keep an eye on it, even if it was only to see that the girls sat still and said nothing.

Joseph got back on February 8th, having lectured in Baltimore and Harrisburg on the way. The heady atmosphere of success was immediately exchanged for the harsh realism of practical schoolmastering. The Board, though still patient, was increasingly disenchanted. Ebenezer Ferguson was downright sceptical. Joseph did not help matters by complaining that the Girls School had been opened too hastily with a novice in charge; it is unlikely he was referring to Roberts Vaux's supervisory eye, 'and a set of lessons – the worst adapted to the Lancastrian system of any in the world by the most stupid ignoramus breathing . . .' Perhaps this was poor Ed Baker, who had received his final salary cheque on February 4th and was now attempting to make some money by selling a new gunlock mechanism invented by Francis Place.

There were three hundred and fifty girls in the female school, with Betsy as 'President'. But by March 3rd Joseph was threatening to resign. The Board were dissatisfied with the lack of action in the matter of instructing the masters and mistresses of the sectional schools. They drew up a series of Rules and Registrations, the very title of which must have revived ominous memories in Joseph Lancaster. The 9th stated that 'Every sectional teacher is to be instructed in the principles and operations of the Lancastrian System of education by attendance at the model school; to be admitted by an order from the Board of Control.' Roberts Vaux was asked to find out what day Joseph Lancaster would be ready to receive them.

Joseph was beginning, once again, to feel like a 'hired servant', and resenting it. He asked that the Board consult him before adopting any measures. The Board replied on March 18th by resolving that 'from and after the 24th May next ensuing the further services of Joseph Lancaser will not be necessary'.

Joseph himself was still writing to Governor Clinton with glowing accounts of the state of the Philadelphia schools; though in the same letter of March 5th he was also asking if there was any chance of his services in New York State being supported financially by the legislature. He suggested the grant of a sum sufficient to train and pay the expenses of a number of teachers and maintain one or two model village schools. Preferably the remuneration might take the form of a grant of land which would provide a legacy for Betsy.

By April 5th, having had no satisfactory answer, he was considering starting a pay school in Baltimore, where he felt the situation to be more open than that in either New York or Philadelphia. Once again he put to Governor Clinton the possibility of his having 'an opportunity of organising the model schools now building in New York – I do not wish to make this proposition myself or that it should be understood by the committee as originating with me before it may have succeeded – as thou must be fully sensible a refusal and a preference to the mere boy you have now engaged will tend very little to the credit of any other persons – to say nothing of myself . . .' For about $2500 or $3000 dollars he would come for a year, with Betsy in the girls school and Richard Jones in the boys, and an arrangement to be absent occasionally lecturing.

On his last day in the Philadelphia Model Schools, May 25th 1819, Joseph wrote to Roberts Vaux. 'This afternoon Joseph Lancaster takes his last leave of those who have provisionally been "plants of his hand and children of his care".' He considered the young man who had been engaged to take over from him, John Ely, intolerable. Two days later the newly appointed teacher for the girls school fell ill, leaving a vacuum. Joseph Lancaster offered his services free to the Board 'for ten or twelve days, in conjunction with such female teacher as the Board of Control may approved of'. The Board accepted, though Ebenezer Ferguson protested strongly against this decision.

In June de Witt Clinton and Roberts Vaux, two of the most important men on the educational scene in New York and Philadelphia, wrote to Joseph Lancaster. De Witt Clinton apologised for Joseph's April letter having been mislaid during the Governor's absence and told him that nothing could happen in the State until the next meeting of the legislature. Roberts Vaux said:

'As an individual I shall always entertain an ardent and affectionate solicitude for thy welfare and best interests. Human praise cannot add to the precious reward which indulgent Heaven has no doubt in store for that Mind, the energies of which are devoted to the promotion of the happiness of mankind. This durable inheritance in view could but have constituted thy 'morning joy'; may its blessed assurance be thy 'evening song'.

Both men were to remain the friends of Joseph Lancaster until their deaths.

'Betsy Lancaster — after photograph of miniature in possession of R. Lancaster-Jones'

Chapter 12
FAITH, HOPE AND CHARITY

'My dear son! take my advice I pray thee, and regulate thy finances with discretion'. (Richard Lancaster to Joseph Lancaster, 1.12.18 AAS)

The patterns which shape the lives of men have their origins in character and temperament as much as in fate or circumstances. Joseph Lancaster might have stayed in Philadelphia and in time made himself an honoured place. The developing school system with its emphasis on training teachers could have afforded ample scope for his pedagogic talents and a secure base from which he might have sallied forth to conquer America. For all their wariness, and Ebenezer Ferguson's hostility, the Board would have been flattered to have him if he had shown himself as a man whom their prudent carefulness could trust. But his genius, both for good and evil, drove him to seach for wider recognition, to make certain that people in places which he did not know yet knew him; and his lack of financial acumen, or even common sense, was proof against every inducement to be warned and take care.

Early in June 1819 Joseph Lancaster left Philadelphia armed with introductions, to look for backers. His brother William, after the death of his own wife, had also emigrated to America, arriving in February of that year. He spent the first months in New York, finding life extremely hard. 'Poor Uncle William Lancaster has been here now 4 months – and earned only 26 dollars', Joseph wrote to Betsy on June 11th from New York. 'Living on his own little all till his few dollars are nearly exhausted.' Joseph hardly knew how to help and found William's case very distressing because he was genuinely industrious and 'has been very much our friend when friends were scarce'. This reminder was to soften up Betsy, for William presently arrived in Philadelphia, where there were Lancaster cousins, and Betsy, who did not like him, was not very pleased.

Betsy was at the centre of the little household left behind in 83 Wood Street, Philadelphia. Inevitably the Lancaster finances were in a parlous state. Less than a month after he had ceased to work for the Board of Control little remained of the not ungenerous salary which that Board had paid. Betsy now became both housekeeper and treasurer, guarding carefully the money that her father remitted to her whenever lectures went well; fiercely cherishing her independence. Joseph was anxious that everything of importance should be under her care. He had confidence in her, and wished her to be used to accepting responsibility. It was part of her education. He wrote to her often, occasionally twice a day, and trusted her entirely. His letters were always cheerful, never complaining and full of information about the new places he was seeing and the flora and fauna of the America countryside.

The letter from New York on June 11th enclosed five dollars and promised five more. The lectures in that city had not been a success. Joseph recognised that he had ceased to have novelty value; and it may be that those connected with New York schools were alarmed to see this unpredictable celebrity return to their neighbourhood.

In Philadelphia the family were close to starvation and Betsy lived from day to day as the posts came in. Richard Jones must have lost his job when Joseph Lancaster left the model school and in any case he never seems to have had any separate contract with the Board which would ensure him a salary. He hated being idle and wrote heatedly to Joseph Lancaster reminding him of their distress. On June 17th Betsy reported having received seven dollars, but the extra she expected through a friend had not arrived, 'which has placed me in an awkward situation to be sure I have managed for our dinner today and I counted four cents remaining and as I have not any money of my own and I do not expect a letter today as it is past the time that the postman calls but I fully expect one tomorrow but if I am disappointed I really can not imagine what must be done but I will live in hopes a custom which thou art apt to follow', she wrote breathlessly to her father. Could he please send an answer quickly, for she was in very great anxiety. If they were alone they could live on bread and butter, but 'as our friends are here we are necessitated to buy meat which at this time of year is very expensive'. The friends were Henry Holt and his wife, presumably staying because Joseph's abundant good nature never refused aid where needed. Mrs Holt was in bed with a suspected miscarriage, so any money her husband had was naturally needed for her comfort. Betsy averred that the family ate from five to six pounds of meat a day, nearly one dollar's worth, a statistic that Richard Jones, writing by the same post denied. 'I assure thee', Betsy went on, 'that our diet has been equally moderate as when thou wast with us . . .' But she urged him to pay special attention because she was really becoming quite uneasy. There was no one who would give them credit except the grocer and the baker; alas an all too familiar situation. She ended with an apology for worrying him, as she knew that he was depressed by his lack of success since leaving Philadelphia. Mother sent love. She had a rash on her neck and the doctor thought leeches would do some good. Mrs Lancaster had asked how many. The reply had been fifty; but American leeches were not so ravenous as English ones.

Joseph Lancaster had left for Connecticut, Massachusetts and New Hampshire. On June 21st Betsy received eleven dollars, with which she was very pleased having had to borrow for several days from Uncle William, 'which I have found a very arduous task as I have naturally an independent spirit'. She was very alarmed. Uncle William now in Philadelphia, had suggested that he might take a house and have them all to live with him at his expense. He had begun to sell a few of his whalebone articles.

Betsy could not bear the possibility. They would then all remain as much indebted to him as ever, and he would expect her to keep house and 'plat his whalebone and help him with the chairs and blinds'. She remembered the years in Liverpool and how disagreeable he would sometimes be, and she was sure that whenever he was affronted he would remind them that they were dependent on him. 'PS please excuse all defects for I am in a very great hurry'. 'PS but above all and everything else pray don't let us live with my uncle.' When Joseph did mention Uncle William again it was to ask Betsy to be kind and tell him to cheer up. He did not allude to the housesharing. In the event it was Uncle William who came to live at 83 Wood Street. When this happened Joseph took the trouble to remind his daughter that her uncle had no authority over her.

On June 24th Joseph wrote from New London, Connecticut. He had arrived at 5am from New Haven by steamboat and immediately booked a meeting house for a lecture. Before leaving New Haven he had posted a letter with three ten dollar notes payable in New York, and would send more if that night's lecture was any good. He would not rest until Betsy had a good reserve, 'not doubting but my little Lord Treasurer in petticoats will take great care of it.' Instead of charging for lectures he had now decided that a collection produced as much.

By June 28th he was in Providence Rhode Island, in good health and with a lecture in prospect. Though not getting on as fast as he would wish, there seemed no doubt that he would make one hundred dollars a week for two or three weeks to come. As usual his optimism betrayed him.

Betsy was having drawing lessons from John Robinson, the miniature painter, who had emigrated to the New World in 1816. For ten years he had known and admired Joseph Lancaster in England and now, living in the same city in a strange land, a friendship developed between the two men. John Robinson had a wife called Mary and two sons and a daughter. The family was to become intertwined in Joseph Lancaster's life in a way that Betsy could not, at this time, have imagined.

John Robinson took an interest in Betsy and in her struggles to keep the difficult Lancaster household afloat. Not unnaturally he saw her as a child burdened by responsibilities beyond her years. It was not a view that Betsy herself accepted and some friction developed between them. She wrote indignantly to Joseph that

she had been astonished to find that he had agreed to Mr
Robinson reading her father's letters. She resisted this intrusion,
but had eventually had to agree concerning the letter actually in
her hand when she was in his house. Later she concealed any
letter she thought important.

Joseph Lancaster wrote back placatingly. It had been a
mistake. John Robinson must have misunderstood something he
said. Let him enjoy the pleasure of his mistake. In future private
letters would be addressed to Betsy care of Cousin Moses
Lancaster and she need only show the ones that came to 83 Wood
Street. But John Robinson must have admired Betsy Lancaster
and felt confidence in Joseph's method of bringing her up for,
when he died seven years later, he left his only daughter Mary to
his friend, as a legacy.

Being treated as a child was something Betsy greatly resented.
She was feuding with the mistress of a school, which she must at
one time have attended possibly acting as senior monitor. Two
of the junior pupils reported hearing her spoken of as 'nothing
but a Child'. Describing the incident and what followed Betsy
wrote to Joseph, '. . . you must know that you have not got a
Child to deal with now'. She would go back and deliver the two
books that her father had promised, spend a short time in the
school and see how it was conducted; though she almost wondered if the mistress would let such a 'Child' into her establishment. Altogether Betsy was very much mortified, 'because I was
never looked up to as a Child while in that school I am certain I
never tried to lower her in the Children's estimation but I
consider it all of no consequence whatsoever', she ended loftily.
'What poor Eliza Eastburn says is not worth minding'. Betsy was
thirteen and a half years old. Joseph Lancaster wrote back
consolingly.

On July 2nd Joseph Lancaster was in Boston. He hoped to
find himself a niche in that city, 'a comfortable settlement,
usefulness in education and a prospect of bringing forward his
beloved child as a teacher'; so he wrote to Betsy, in a letter
enclosing five dollars and giving an account of the money that he
had forwarded from other places. He was to spend the better part
of three months in and around Boston and had great hopes of the
lectures there. With more leisure he set out to give Betsy a long
description of all that he had seen, advising her to look up
'Worcester's Travels' as she read and learn American geography

at the same time. The country was very fine. The New England
States had people of a steadier habit than either New York or
Philadelphia, they were also better instructed and hospitable. He
had met a gentleman who told him of Jamaican Lancastrian
schools; and been in New London nearly on the anniversary of
the day they left Old London, 'and the boys there look very
much like some of our finest London boys'. Not many beautiful
birds, but he had seen robin red poles and canary birds and a
mocking bird, also water snakes.

Betsy had a tame squirrel called Bunn, whose antics and well-
being interested them both. She wondered if the New England
'ground and ferret squirrels' he mentioned were handsomer than
Bunn who was fat and liked having his back and head rubbed.
Joseph often asked how Bunn was getting along.

Betsy's education was continually in his mind. He told his
cousin Moses that he spent all his spare time writing to her,
hoping in this way to make up for some of the instruction she
missed by his absence. He sent her a sketch of the nine-year-old
Merrimack chain bridge at Deer Island near Newbury in Massachusetts, and told her he had bought a hammer to investigate the
structure of the country. She was to look at 'Phillips Geology'
and, as he rode along, he would collect stones and seeds to bring
her. He gave the name of a friend in Philadelphia who would
teach her French if she wished. Her mathematical education was
still entrusted to Richard Jones. In another letter he agreed that
she should not labour copying Goldsmith to send him. It was
enough that she read the articles to which he referred. The flow
of words would come as she became accustomed to speaking in
company; 'my jewell', he admonished her, 'obey what I am going
to say do not make thyself a slave in the house so as to neglect thy
reading etc.'.

He sent her anecdotes as he heard them, and recounted
incidents. He met a preacher who had been asked by the males in
his congregation to resign, because they had been outvoted by
the women – 'the women thou see are of some consequence in the
world'. He tried to impress on her the advantages of learning to
draw, which the practical Betsy with little talent in this direction
was inclined to dispute. It was useful for the botanist, besides the
day might come when her attainments would be a blessing to
multitudes of dear young people as well as a comfort to her
father. The study of drawing ranked among the fine arts.

He did not neglect her religious teaching, writing long separate letters on this subject to the 'Darling of thy Father's love'. He approved of her regular attendance at Friends Meeting.

On financial matters, which were her cross and his downfall, he wrote that the wish of his heart was that his darling should learn a sense of the value of money without contracting a love for it. A purse proud wretch appeared to him worse than the beasts of prey, destitute of fellow feelings for their own species. Alas, he often found it impossible to distinguish between those whom he thus castigated and the true friends, sometimes themselves very poor, who tried to save him from his own weakness. In October 1819 Robert Ould, who had done so much to make Joseph Lancaster feel welcome in America, fell under his displeasure for refusing him a loan.

Each letter from Joseph to Betsy, and back again from Betsy to her father, contained its quota of concern over money. Postage was a worry, as it had always been. When Joseph had been away over three months, Cousin Moses one day refused to accept a letter for Betsy. He did not reveal the reason, but by now she knew it intuitively. He suspected that he would not get repaid. Betsy, who had understood that her father had a special agreement with Moses Lancaster about postage was indignant. '. . . I will go to them this afternoon and will pay him to the last cent'. She would not even ask why the letter had been refused. In fact she would make as little use of his help in future as she could.

The landlord was constantly coming round for his rent and Betsy, out of what her father regularily sent her, seems to have managed for a time to appease him. But Richard Jones, who had hoped long before this to have been settled with Joseph Lancaster in a school or training centre, was distraught and discouraged by the uncertainty of the whole situation. Unfairly, Joseph accused him of being too fond of money. It would have been nearer the truth to say that Richard was fond of Betsy and had a clearer idea than she had of the precarious nature of their circumstances. Joseph Lancaster wrote to him that he should be devoting his time to improving his mind, rather than worrying about money matters and trying to find himself a job. 'Hast thou known me so long to doubt my word – what ground can I have given thee to lose confidence . . .' 'Dear Boy arouse and cheer up.' It was easier for Joseph, riding round the beautiful New England countryside, meeting fresh people and finding plenty to occupy and interest his mind, to give this advice than for Richard Jones stranded in Philadelphia and living in constant fear of debt or scandal, to accept it.

It is likely too that Richard Jones, eight years older than Betsy, found himself in the unenviable situation of not knowing exactly how much money was coming into the household. Betsy and her father were at one in the desire to keep to themselves the exact amounts that passed between them. The postal arrangement with Moses Lancaster, which he was enjoined to keep secret from both Mrs Lancaster and Richard Jones, meant that Betsy had no need to let anyone know the size of the notes that came to her purse. She was asked not to double up her letters with Richard's for the sake of saving postage, for then he might see what she had written. Betsy kept two account books, one for housekeeping and another which dealt with expenses that concerned only herself and Joseph Lancaster. Though often angry over money matters, there is no sign that she ever felt the need of a confidante, or that she blamed her father for the situation in which they found themselves.

Indeed Joseph, according to his lights, was doing his best. The returns from his lectures varied greatly, but he sent home a regular portion after keeping enough for his own expenses. Nor does it seem to have occurred to him that those same expenses must sometimes have seemed unduly extravagant when Betsy read of them at 83 Wood Street. At the end of July he detailed to her the outfit which he acquired in Boston. Several pairs of new stockings and three pairs of new drawers; two silk waistcoats, two dark jean (sic); a pair of silk breeches, a pair of silk trousers, a new coat, six new shirts, etc. all paid in ready money; braces of red and yellow leather; which unfortunately dyed his shirts in a very disagreeable manner when he perspired. He added that Betsy herself could spend ten dollars on anything she liked for a summer dress, keeping in mind the sweet simplicity of Quaker garb.

Poor Elizabeth Lancaster, for whom the deceptive freshness of the New World had soon faded, longed for letters from her husband and was constantly put off with promises. She felt slighted, treated with contempt and indifference, '. . . poor me may be shuffled off just as it suits'. In every decision of any importance to their life and her own she was passed by. Her daughter kept the details of the housekeeping from her and spoke to her with kindly superiority. She no longer went to Meeting, nor was Joseph anxious that she should, and no Friends now visited her. She wandered like a ghost about the house, once carrying a bundle which Uncle William took from her and opened. It contained five or six dollars, which Betsy thought showed how careful she was with her money. Mrs Lancaster did not greatly like Uncle William and objected to his living with them, but he was said to be the person who dealt best with her when her disorderly fits came on her.

She loved her husband and still suffered from jealousy. In July Joseph lectured at Marblehead, a small seaport on the coast north of Boston. Most of the men were at sea, so the audience was largely female. 'Now it will not do to tell poor mother this or she will think Lecturing to the women in the absence of their husbands a mortal sin and be jealous of the whole congregation', Joseph wrote to Betsy. Pathetically Elizabeth said she would send him her love if she thought it would be valuable. But Joseph was beginning to resent her very existence, and he did not hesitate to make his feelings plain to her daughter. He was determined that 'poor mother' would not continue to be an annoyance and interrupt their comfort and business. If she did she must go. 'Will not ruin thy temper and my own, destroy our peace and impede her interests as well as our business.' He was uneasy too in case the Friends might once again try to help her. 'I will allow no interference of our beloved friends we have had too much of it. My regard for her is undiminished but I am decided that she will never live with me again if she plays any of her games among them. I have been too long harassed by parleying with them. I will do so no longer.'

In an undated letter, probably written some months later in 1820, Elizabeth Lancaster approached her husband with her own testament. She wished to compensate for things in her conduct which might have disturbed him. She was sure that she had never publicly disparaged his character and implored him to forgive her for anything '. . . I may inattentively have said or done. I truly hope that love which thou hast at times shewn me, by many kindnesses conferred upon me will not easily be removed from thy mind'. Perhaps he could explain any misunderstandings between them. She was really distressed by the way he was behaving to her '. . . be assured I will for the future endeavour to be very cautious of vexing thee – pray don't sleep from me tonight, as I promise faithfully I will not disturb thee. Accept my love and do attend to my requests'.

If Joseph Lancaster had hoped to be received with open arms in Boston and heartily supported in his efforts to start a new Lancastrian Institution, he was much mistaken. In a sense he came too late. Though the real thrust of educational interest in New England was in academies and higher education, the three States of New Hampshire, Massachusetts and Connecticut all had some form of State school law, town tax or school fund. Schools and academies were on the whole non-denominational and there was none of the sectarian rivalry which in England had undoubtedly stimulated educational debate, even while it also inhibited government support. Small rural communities in New England were tight knit, responsible for their own affairs. A Lancaster lecture might arouse interest in the method; but they did not need a stranger to organise their own children for them, and there was little financial backing for an individual on his own. Boston already had well organised school committees in different wards, and in 1818 the city had appropriated five thousand dollars for infant schools to prepare children for the grammar schools.

There were indeed places for teachers who would work under a school board or committee. But Joseph Lancaster had never been accountable to this kind of control, and he did not intend to be so now. The citizens of New England and its large Quaker community were prepared to accord him recognition for his original discoveries; they were not ready to accept such an uneasy bedfellow into their midst.

Everywhere he went, and almost regardless of the kind of welcome he received, Joseph Lancaster wrote to Betsy with optimistic hopes for their future. Everywhere he went he left a trail of debt. On August 24th, from Salem north of Boston, he told her that they had 'heightened prospects' and were in many respects much more comfortable than in England. He would look for a house in Massachusetts and they would all live together. This may have been to divert Betsy's anxious enquiries as to whether they would not be better to move into a smaller dwelling in Philadelphia. By September 18th he was telling her that he fully expected to be setting himself up in Boston and to be sending for his family. There was to be a meeting to open a subscription to pay for scholars, six hundred at ten dollars per annum, and 'The Institution will be altogether my own. In this city no trial on a large scale (say 50) has yet been made'. On the 27th he was still full of this plan. A meeting of gentlemen calling themselves the 'Friends of Joseph Lancaster' had been held. Twenty-nine scholars were now engaged and more promised. It was true he had enemies among the local school masters, but there were also those who were well disposed. He hoped to be settled before the winter.

Nothing came of it. By the end of October he was in Richmond, Virginia, castigating the Bostonions as mean and comparing the Virginians favourably with them. He hoped to have the organisation of a girls school in Richmond. But by November 7th he was in Baltimore, where he had many loving friends and was quite sure that they would settle there. Meanwhile he continued to tackle an enormous correspondence and to attempt to raise interest in possible publications. There was a 'Proposal for a publication to diffuse correct knowledge of the Lancastrian System throughout the USA'; a plan for a 'pacific march to the Ocean of that name'; ideas about the education of Red Indian children; suggestions about raising a grand collection of minerals and fossils for the nation; 'Letters on National Subjects . . .' to senators and other distinguished citizens. There were many begging letters too.

In September 1819 John Lovell had arrived in the United States. He sailed from Gravesend on August 5th, being seasick the moment he stepped on board, and arrived at 83 Wood Street when Joseph was absent in Boston. In a letter to Betsy, Joseph sent him a welcome and a message that when he knew how many stripes the American flag had he had only learned half the lesson, now he must find out how many stars and shine brilliantly among them.

It was not to be easy for John Lovell to fulfil this cheerful prediction, though he was honourably to do his best. He was a tall, shy, tender-hearted young man who hero-worshipped Joseph Lancaster, and he was delighted to be once more under his roof, along with his great friend Jones. But at the very beginning there were the usual financial difficulties. A subsidy that Joseph had promised never arrived so John had had to borrow twelve pounds sterling from Captain Turley on whose ship he had travelled. This debt must be paid as soon as possible for the sake of both Lancaster and Lovell's good name, so he wrote to Joseph

Lancaster care of Boston Post Office.

Whatever reply he got to this appeal it did not contain money for, on October 28th, John Lovell, who found himself in the middle of a situation which cannot have been wholly unexpected but was nevertheless alarming, was writing desperately to Joseph Lancaster in Virginia that he had given Captain Turley a note of hand on his own responsibility and was now haunted by fears of prison. A rumour had reached John that Joseph Lancaster believed him to have more money than he was admitting and this upset him very much. He might have faults, but his veracity had never been questioned. By November 20th he had received no answer; and even on January 6th 1820 he was still trying to get satisfaction from Captain Turley, who had a needy family of his own.

John Lovell joined the little group who tried to keep the Lancaster ship afloat. It was already so waterlogged as to be not far short of disaster. The landlord was owed forty dollars, soon to run to seventy, then to two hundred and seventeen; by which time the family had been evicted and taken in by John Robinson. The grocer was refusing more goods, bills were beginning to appear from printers and other merchants who now saw that the Lancaster credit was shaky. There was no longer a servant to help with the work. John Lovell was of a nervous, modest nature. It must have caused him intense anguish to find himself being looked upon as a disreputable, perhaps even dishonest, character, while all the time the man responsible, if he wrote at all, did so in terms of patronising encouragement. Yet his devotion to Joseph Lancaster never wavered. He had admired him when he was one of his lads. He admired him still.

He was also impressed by Betsy, though his position in regard to this fourteen-year-old must often have been a difficult one. The fact was that John Lovell had as poor a head for money as had his Master, but without the latter's jovial effrontery. Ten years older than Betsy, he had yet to ask her father to tell her to lend him money when he needed to buy a cloak in January; when Lancaster failed to do this and simply sent Betsy an additional twenty dollars John reproached him bitterly with neglect – when Joseph knew he was barefoot and in danger of arrest. It is good to record that Betsy, when she discovered his despair, freely offered him the ten dollars.

But it was John Lovell, perhaps because their natures had

much in common, who did his best for Elizabeth Lancaster. She had never liked Joseph's lads, and often resented sharing a house with them. Now it was John who stood between her and her husband with sympathetic understanding. Reading out a letter from Joseph one day, he passed on love to Betsy and regards to Elizabeth. She was very upset and John Lovell took it on himself to rebuke his Master. He should send affection to his spouse 'for she is a woman, your wife, and Elizabeth's (Betsy) mother'. She has a fond heart, he reminded Joseph, and, 'perhaps fond hearts are the weakest'. Maybe he was thinking of his own.

By December 1819 plans were well forward to set up a Lancastrian Institution in Baltimore, in the State of Maryland. It was to be a day school, with a small number of boarders. John Lovell approved of this plan, provided the house could be properly managed. Parents of respectable children expected them to be well looked after, and he considered Betsy too young to carry this responsibility. Such practical aspects of the plan do not seem to have occurred to Joseph Lancaster, at that time in Washington lecturing and lobbying for support. But on the negative side he had suggested that other arrangements be made for his wife. John was anxious and distressed. It seemed hard to blast her fond ideas of being happy with Joseph without at least giving it one more trial. He felt that she should move to Baltimore with the family, but that any house they settled in should have a sitting room where she and Uncle William could live separately. Though Uncle William was an excellent man, he was uncouth and it was not proper that he should eat with the boarders.

Richard Jones may already have been in Baltimore attempting to establish the school. Certainly Joseph Lancaster, though he was writing to Roberts Vaux for help, does not seem to have had his heart in it. John Lovell found it very difficult to get any clear indication from the Master as to when the family would be moving from Philadelphia, and this prevented him from making arrangements to take in pupils himself in order to add to the household finances. Once again, in a way that John Lovell must have found depressingly reminiscent of the last years in London debts were beginning to mount up, credit to be refused. Creditors in Boston, as well as in Philadelphia, were getting restive. Some scandalous articles had appeared. Richard Jones wrote urging Joseph to be open with those to whom he owed money. Did he not see the wretched consequences that would follow his silence. The Boston creditors would advertise him.

It was to be in the middle of February 1820 before Joseph Lancaster finally arrived to settle in Baltimore. Back in England the Duke of Kent, his old supporter, was dead. It is possible that Joseph felt that the Lord had at last avenged him. George III, 'the good old King', was also to die this year.

During the weeks in Washington Joseph had see-sawed between hopes and doubts. 'My spirit has naturally suffered much under a sense of our circumstances and resignation has been a difficult matter at times . . .' he wrote to Betsy on February 1st. Nevertheless he had some useful interviews, among others with the Secretary of the Treasury. Two days later he was once again optimistic about the latest subscription list, and enclosed twenty dollars; '. . . but it requires so much pressing'. The Russian Ambassador and various other high officials had joined the list but with all Joseph's diligence, calling, interviewing, importuning, he could not manage to collect more than twenty or thirty dollars a day. He did not forget, however, to send regards to 'dear four-footed friend Bunn – and tell him that though I have been too busy to give him an invitation to meet me at Baltimore as yet, yet I am in good hopes of seeing his beloved self and his more beloved mistress where I may say in person that I am her very affectionate and loving father'.

By February 11th he was still in the capital, with fifty members of Congress on the subscription list, preparing a pamphlet for the press. As soon as the river was free from ice he hoped to leave. At last, on February 23rd, he wrote from Baltimore to tell Betsy she could begin packing up. John Lovell had already arrived and was in high spirits at being reunited with Richard Jones. Betsy should sell everything that would be cumbersome to transport, including chairs and bedsteads. He hoped to make five hundred dollars out of the latest book, 'Letters on National Subjects . . .' He was looking for a house. They could all live much cheaper together and be content with little furniture and simple fare. Everything was going to be all right. They could look forward to being together again. On March 1st he sent her another fifty dollars and told her she could come 'as fast as wings can carry you'. The school promised well. Please ask mother to be careful of her behaviour. He hoped

Uncle William would be kind enough to wire up the old cage and make the gentleman's house fit to travel. He would not want her to leave Bunn behind.

Perhaps because she was excited at the prospect of a move and being once more with her husband, Elizabeth Lancaster was in better health. She had had several letters from Joseph, which she may have owed to John Lovell's gentle admonitions. Cheer up and trust was the burden of Joseph Lancaster's messages; an injunction which he carried out admirably himself, but which others involved in scandal and harassment on his behalf found more difficult to accept.

For many years now there had been little common ground on which these two could meet. Even Betsy, her father's daughter, had failed to bring them together. When he wrote to Elizabeth on February 17th 1820 Joseph still used the language of love, 'my beloved, thou joy of my heart, my darling precious jewell'; but he had taken it for granted that she would allow him to love all mankind first and be content to take her secondary place quietly at home. While for her love meant possession, that cruel jealousy which had been her torment and his bane, 'so much so that it has almost been better to be out than in a home where he had no comfort'.

On March 11th, when at last they were together in Baltimore, he wrote her a note.

'. . . cheer up then my dear heart lean on the bosom of one that so dearly loves thee, with confidence and without doubting . . . Thou wilt go to meeting with me always – and meet the Lord a present help there as well as at home – but quietness and soft speaking and obedience to thy husband's wishes are the only path to restore thee to Society – thy child and thyself – Cheer up then my treasure and be happy for a blessing surely will attend thee if thou cheerfully and willingly conform to the desires for thy welfare of thy affectionate friend and husband Joseph Lancaster'.

It was a moving appeal from a man whose own position in Society was being steadily eroded. It is to be hoped that it warmed Elizabeth's anguished heart and cast a glow over the next few months when they were to live once more in the same house. She died on December 6th 1820 at 43 Front Street, Baltimore, and for all her waywardness Joseph was sad without her. It had been a hard life for the pretty little Quaker who in

June 1804 had stepped out bravely on the road to Brentford, in a jaunty procession with her young husband and all his lads to visit Mrs Sarah Trimmer.

From the beginning the Baltimore Institution never really flourished. Though he gave little outward sign of it, Joseph Lancaster's own confidence may have been undermined by Tooting, Westminster Road and Philadelphia. It is possible that the sympathy which had existed in London between himself and his boys was less easy to establish in this new country. One of its own citizens wrote about the spirit of freedom, even licentiousness, breathed into all youth in the United States which made them more difficult to control than in Europe and of the morbid sensibility of parents. Lancaster himself, though individuals and Quakers as a group might arouse his talent for abuse, was rarely critical of American society and culture. Jones and Lovell also, devoted as ever, were nevertheless becoming restive as their own prospects of an independent working life seemed continually to recede into an uncertain future. The years 1820/23 were to be unhappy ones.

In England Joseph Lancaster had been at the centre of national controversy and, for all his religious pacifism, this son of a soldier had gloried in it. In the New World, where sectarian antagonism in education hardly existed and local differences took no account of his presence or absence, he knew himself to be on the periphery of the concerns of the nation. There were times when, for all the bitterness that the battle had engendered, he wished for an Andrew Bell in America to stir up an active committed debate and to bring Joseph Lancaster into the limelight.

There was surprising goodwill towards him among many of those eminent in the philanthropic world in the United States. Perhaps his own view that he had been abominably treated by his fellow countrymen in England inclined Americans to favour him. The War of Independence was still recent history and the late King George III a monster to many. Feelings towards their erstwhile rulers were ambivalent. But it must soon have become clear that the rumours of financial instability which had crossed the Atlantic were only too true, and Joseph did not bring with him the counterbalancing excitement of new ideas or profound educational thought. Most, probably all, of his influential acquaintances sooner or later found themselves being importuned for money to support the Lancaster family or further the Lancaster cause; often the same thing; some, having agreed to do the latter were frustrated by Joseph's lack of business sense which resulted in proofs not being returned to the printers, pamphlets never appearing, letters going unacknowledged. He was warned that his fall in the public esteem, 'from blood heat to freezing point', would go further if he did not keep his promises.

Yet many of these men, de Witt Clinton, Roberts Vaux, Robert Ralston the Philadelphia merchant, Burwell Basset the Virginian Senator, and others, not only continued to do all they could for him but did so in a spirit of admiration and affection.

Some kind of Institution did come into being in Baltimore, but it was dogged by debt and latterly by the illness of its founder. When Joseph Lancaster left to travel, as he still did from time to time, John Lovell or Richard Jones took charge. In August 1820 when Joseph Lancaster was in Harper's Ferry, Lovell was lamenting that it was always his fate 'to be left in these petit scrapes'. He meant settling debts, dealing with notes of hand that were falling due and attempting to get proofs of Joseph Lancaster's 'Ultimatum' through the press.

Harper's Ferry was a small place about sixty miles from Baltimore on the West Virginia-Maryland border. Most of its thirteen hundred inhabitants were connected with the Armoury based there, and its four schoolrooms all came under the Superintendent. There were plans for setting up another, Lancastrian, school, and one of the Committee, John H Hall, was in correspondence with Joseph Lancaster about it. It was to be June 1822 before the schoolroom was actually ready and then Richard Jones went to open it and train its future teacher. He was lonely and unhappy at this time, longing to be settled in life. Only letters from Betsy encouraged him.

It had become plain that Richard's feelings for Betsy were a good deal warmer than that of a disciple for his master's daughter. Two years before John Lovell had slyly remarked on this growing attachment. Sending his admiration to Betsy, for beautiful flowers were made to be admired and admiration was not love, he exclaimed, 'What an influential word love is', adding, 'ask Jones to define it in theory'.

In 1822 a Lancastrian school was opened at New Haven, Connecticut, where Joseph Lancaster had made a number of friends on his 1819 tour. Through one of them, Timothy

Dwight, who had himself run a famous school at Fairfield, Connecticut, John Lovell was offered the mastership. Very diffident and unsure of his own abilities, and at first homesick for his Lancaster family, John Lovell was nevertheless to make a success of this post and to remain in it until 1833.

For this young man, now twenty-seven, who had lived for the last decade in Joseph Lancaster's shadow, the move to New Haven was a momentous step. He continued to write often and anxiously, asking his Old Master's help and advice, but, as he remarked, Columbus when he left Spain could not have felt more importantly engaged than did John Lovell faced with the responsibility of the New Haven school. He organised it on the original Borough Road lines and was proud of how neat and well it looked. Feeling like a timorous and ambitious boy just going into society, he was surprised to find himself invited to the July 4th, Independence Day picnic in the woods and commended by Timothy Dwight. He supposed his 'Alpine' stature was part of the reason why people noticed him. Infinitely conscientious and extremely hard working, the only blight on his first years of independence was an unfortunate affair with a girl, Mary Shore, who insisted that he had offered her marriage and whose father and brothers actually appeared at New Haven to force him into wedlock. He summoned all the courage of which he was capable and withstood their assaults. It says much for his character and abilities that the school committee, who might easily have found the prospect of such a scandal too much for them, backed him up.

1822 was a bad year for Joseph Lancaster. He was constantly ill with rheumatism, fever, boils and the fear that his eyes were beginning to fail. Richard Lancaster, his father, had died in October 1821. Poor Bunn was dead. Parents of boys at his school began to withdraw them. A monthly magazine 'The Parents Friend', which had Roberts Vaux's support, seems to have come to nothing; maybe because he used his publications as vehicles of self-justification and abuse. He sent begging letters everywhere, some of which averred that he and Betsy were on the edge of starvation. In February they owed $220 arrears of rent. John Lovell wrote loving, fatherly letters full of sensible advice, regretting that his own salary was so small as to make it impossible for him to help, but urging Joseph to come to New Haven for a visit. Henry Ould sent fifty dollars as a six month loan, and recommended Joseph to show more Christian charity towards his brother Robert. Robert Ould himself wrote saying 'Let there be no strife between me and thee'. He had served Joseph in Swansea and taken his side in quarrels with the Trustees. He had refused a loan because he could not afford it, but one refusal must not sever the ties of a lifetime. Joseph was to remember that the Ould family was his. Robert had been married since 1814, and his oldest son, also Robert, was to become United States District Attorney for the District of Columbia.

1823 opened badly. John Lovell had a letter from Joseph 'full of melancholy expressions which wind about my soul like dark clouds'. In reply he quoted the old Lancastrian line, 'Pray Cheer up'. In truth Joseph Lancaster did not know what he was going to do. Though he still wrote to possible patrons of the satis-factory state of his school, it hardly existed any longer. He explored the possibility of taking United States citizenship; then toyed with the idea of returning to England where, he tried to convince de Witt Clinton, he was sure of a hero's welcome. With delicate generosity de Witt Clinton was sending him regular sums of money anonymously in the fall of 1823. But it must have been very clear to Joseph, ill and unhappy, that in American terms he was a failure. He may even have suspected that the time was coming when Betsy and Richard Jones would feel the need to strike out on a life of their own.

Perhaps this was why, when in the summer of 1823 he met a young Irish officer in the Venezuelan battalion of the Army of Colombia, Lieutenant Colonel Brooke Young, Joseph Lancaster set aside his earlier prejudice and wrote a letter to the place that had once represented exile, Caracas.

'Joseph Lancaster's coat of arms'

Chapter 13
CARACAS

'We are not new acquaintances. I expect our meeting after 16 years will be very interesting'. (Joseph Lancaster to Sam Sharwood, about Simon Bolivar)

Brooke Young was an Irishman of the Protestant Ascendency, originally a soldier of the 8th Regiment of Foot. In 1819 he came to Venezuela with the Irish Legion to fight in Simon Bolivar's war of liberation. In 1820 the new Republic of Colombia, which included Venezuela, Cundinamarca and Quito, was proclaimed and Bolivar, himself a Venezuelan, unanimously chosen as its President.

In June 1821 Bolivar marched into Caracas. Brooke Young had fought with a local unit at the battle of Carabobo which liberated Venezuela and had had his horse shot under him. He was promoted Lieutenant Colonel and appointed Field Officer of the Southern Battalion.

No doubt Brooke Young had heard of Joseph Lancaster in Ireland, where it is possible that the village school near his family home may have been supported by the Kildare Place Society. So, when the young man found himself in Baltimore in 1823 and heard that the famous Joseph Lancaster was living in the city, it was natural that he should seek to make his acquaintance.

Life for Joseph Lancaster was at a low ebb. For two years he had been in poor health. This, and the climate of Baltimore, was the excuse for seeking new pastures; the real reason for his physical breakdown was likely to have been severe mental depression arising from the failure of everything he touched. The deaths of his wife and his father no doubt added to unadmitted feelings of inadequacy, for in both cases he had in some sense abandoned those loving hearts and, however justified the actions a man has taken, regrets are close followers on the finality of death.

Lieutenant-Colonel Brooke Young, fresh from triumph in Venezuela and full of admiration for Simon Bolivar, recommended the mild climate of Caracas and offered to deliver a letter to the Liberator.

Joseph Lancaster and Simon Bolivar had already met in 1810 when the latter, on a diplomatic mission to London, had visited the Borough Road school. The request from Caracas for teachers, which came to the Committee in 1813, was probably also in Lancaster's mind. It showed that the System was looked on with honour in Venezuela; how much more likely then that there would be a welcome for its founder.

So, when Lieutenant-Colonel Brooke Young sailed for Venezuela on June 17th 1823 he carried with him a letter from Joseph Lancaster to Simon Bolivar offering his services to Colombian youth. 'I do not know the Spanish language,' Joseph added, 'but this is not an insuperable obstacle. It is very probable that a young and pleasant friend of mine will accompany me and he has already made some progress in the language and I will see that he avails himself of the time to achieve perfection in it.' The young and pleasant friend was Richard Jones, who would by now have found it impossible to let Betsy leave for another continent without him.

After Brooke Young departed in June, carrying this missive, a long silence ensued. Debts piled up and were ignored, or angrily repudiated. Loans were solicited with varying degrees of success.

De Witt Clinton's generosity during October and November kept the family afloat. Richard Jones was in despair and wondered if he should abandon all thought of schoolmastering. Joseph toyed with the idea of returning to England. He proposed to publish a book of his life and travels 'and perhaps a work more interesting to the public or more productive to its author could scarcely be imagined'. It was to be ten years before such a work appeared, and then its success was to be strictly limited.

De Witt Clinton did his best to warn and advise Lancaster against his continual and venomous criticism of the Quakers. The community of Friends in Baltimore had now joined those in Philadelphia and London as targets for his antagonism. The wound of his disownment had not healed; nor had his profound personal attachment to the religious principles of a Quaker profession diminished. The frayed nerves of the severed tie, of which the core strands still held, never cease to pain him, and whether the cause was phantom or real made no difference to the hurt against which he railed.

Simon Bolivar was in Peru when Brooke Young arrived back in Venezuela. Before sending on the Lancaster letter, which had been left unsealed for translation, he had shown it to the muncipal authorities in Caracas. On September 28th the Board of Patronage of Mutual Education of Caracas, which already had one Lancastrian school under its care, passed a resolution to accept Joseph Lancaster's offer to come to Venezuela. Brooke Young wrote back to Baltimore on October 2nd, justifiably pleased with himself at this successful outcome to his mission. General Soublette, Intendente of the Department of Venezuela, had forwarded the letter to the seat of Government in Bogota, and in the meantime the Corporation of Caracas had voted Joseph Lancaster two thousand dollars with a request urging him to come immediately. The money was in the hands of Mr Lowry, the US Consul.

Having in the interim had a letter from Joseph Lancaster enquiring whether anything was happening, Brooke Young wrote again on October 16th. He repeated the essential information and then went into more personal details. He himself would find a house if he knew when the Lancasters were coming. There was no need to be anxious about Betsy travelling on a schooner. Accommodation was reasonable and the passage only fifteen days. They should order fresh provisions from Mr R. Hall in New York; turkey in 41b cases at $1.25, chicken ditto, beef and gravy ditto $1, veal ditto $1.25, mock turtle one dollar, tripe one dollar, lobster meat 14 1bs $1.50, soup and boulle 81bs $2.50, oysters 41bs $75c, milk in half pints $2 a dozen. It was much cheaper than laying in livestock. Such a list, presumably with carriage added from New York to Baltimore via Norfolk, threatened to be of no help to Joseph Lancaster's finances.

This good news did not arrive till early December. In September Joseph had managed to get a draft from a ship owner in Baltimore, H. Daniels, on his agent in the Venezuelan port of La Guaira for three hundred dollars at a hundred and sixty days, cashable in Baltimore. It is likely that he achieved this result by speaking of employment in Caracas as an established fact, which at this date was not the case. By the end of December, however, there was real evidence not only that he had been offered a job but also that the offer was accompanied by hard cash.

Miscalculation, however, was still possible. On January 20th 1824 both Brooke Young and the US Consul wrote from Venezuela. The former was anxiously awaiting the Lancasters arrival; though he added, suddenly doubtful, 'Don't expect too much'; the latter simply said that he had received no money on the part of the municipality of Caracas, and greatly doubted if any such arrangements as had been suggested would ever be made. His somewhat cynical assessment of the situation was proved wrong. On February 11th he wrote again to say that Caracas had informed him that there was a sum of money in the hands of the Treasurer to be given to Joseph Lancaster on his arrival. Sensibly Mr Lowry replied that Mr Lancaster would need some money before that time, and he intended to send him five hundred dollars. Two weeks later he announced that thirteen hundred dollars had been deposited subject to Mr Lancaster's order on arrival at La Guaira; and as he had had no answer to his suggestion of an advance remittance the latter could not now be forwarded.

Money, however, was no longer needed at the Baltimore end. The certainty of official employment was sufficient to provide security. On April 9th, along with a draft for one hundred dollars on a Baltimore bank, Joseph Lancaster was being informed by one John Myers that passages were engaged on the brig 'Ann' which left on Sunday next, probably from Philadelphia.

Either the 'Ann' was delayed, or the Lancaster family did not take up those particular passages, but on April 20th 1824 Elizabeth Lancaster, daughter of the educator of youth Joseph Lancaster, married Richard Madox Jones at the house of Benjamin Kite junior in Philadelphia. Almost certainly the Robinson family and the Lancaster cousins were present; and possibly Uncle William, though the latter had been thinking of returning to England. Shortly after bride, groom and their father sailed for Caracas. One of Joseph Lancaster's last acts was to write a letter for John Lovell confirming his side of the story in the wretched case of Mary Shore, which had now to go to an attorney. John Lovell, uncertain whether he could bear to be left behind, had begun to learn Spanish.

In Caracas, briefly, the old vital flame was to blaze up again in Joseph Lancaster. It did not, alas, consume his besetting weaknesses.

They were off La Guaira by May 24th and were met by a welcoming note from Colonel Brooke Young. The Intendente, the supreme political and administrative authority, had been informed of their arrival. A Spanish marquis before the revolution he was a good man, punctilious and a stickler for etiquette. Joseph Lancaster was expected to write and announce his coming. He must do so, and then wait until he received a reply. The family was lodged in Marquetiá, a village about a mile from La Guaira, where HM Vice Consul, Henry Bold Hurry, had a house.

Venezuela, now a Department of the new Republic of Colombia, had only very recently, after bitter wars, achieved its independence from monarchist Spain. The republic itself had been proclaimed in 1820 by Simon Bolivar, whose vision of a Federation of the Andes was the driving force behind the movement for liberation. The First Congress of Gran Colombia, which comprised Colombia, Venezuela, Ecuador and Panama, was held in Bogota in May 1821. In 1824 the United Kingdom recognised the Republic.

The vision was splendid; the realities were very different. A vast land held many factions among the educated, whose loyalty to Bolivar was the only tenuous bond that kept them together; for the illiterate farmers and those of mixed blood it was often battle enough to preserve life. Between cities old rivalries still flourished. The struggling young Republic was economically bankrupt, and for many the dream that tried to build one nation out of a thousand disparate peoples had little or no validity. Simon Bolivar, who thought in terms that transcended all boundaries, saw his Federation extending from the Atlantic to the Pacific. In 1823, when invited to come with a contingent of his troops to help Peru step out from under the domination of metropolitan Spain, he did not hesitate; even though it meant leaving behind him two Departments, Colombia and Venezuela, riven by splits and ruled by those of often doubtful loyalty.

Bolivar's interest in education was very real. In his youth he had had a remarkable tutor, Simon Rodriguez, who saw schooling not as an institution for the production of aesthetes and aristocrats, but as a measure to create fellow citizens of the Republic. Strongly influenced by Rodriguez, Simon Bolivar was looking for ways to educate his people. It was natural that the Lancastrian System, with its emphasis on economy and the rapid, disciplined teaching of large numbers, should prove attractive.

It must have been with excitement and anticipation that Joseph Lancaster, his daughter and his son-in-law, came ashore in an open rowing boat at the port of La Guaira. This was a country such as they had not seen before. The climate at sea level was tropical. The small town, backed by high, forbidding mountains and still showing signs of the devastation left over from the catastrophe of the earthquake of 1812, had a population of five or six thousand. No doubt the US Consul Mr Lowry, who was to be dead in less than a year, met them and helped to see to the unloading and passing through customs of their goods.

When, ceremonial formalities completed, the little party rode over the spectacular paved mountain track to Caracas there must have been a feeling of release and exhilaration, the sense of a fresh purpose cancelling out the months of frustration, physical illness and spiritual unease. Officially at last Joseph Lancaster was wanted and among his papers was the draft, or its equivalent, from the municipality of Caracas which so signally ratified his contract, without making him any man's slave. For Betsy, newly married, riding behind the two men whom she loved, savouring the mountain air, it must have been a joy to feel that for both of them there was real, and satisfying, work in prospect.

It took four hours to cross the range to Caracas, three thousand feet up and set in a fertile valley. Though here too there remained many signs of the ravages of the earthquake, at first sight the wide streets and squares, ornamented with trees, flowers and fountains and lined by one-storey Spanish houses, made a gracious impression. Perhaps, as they rode along, there were troops of ragged little boys to be glimpsed in alleyways and courtyards, and among the ruined churches, reminding Joseph Lancaster of those original hordes of uneducated urchins in his native London and pointing to an urgent need for the gift that he could uniquely bring them.

The master of the Lancastrian school had resigned. He may, not unnaturally, have felt affronted at the prospect of demotion which Lancaster's arrival seemed to presage. Joseph, at any rate, inherited the school, with its forty or fifty pupils, and the master's house. To help teach and interpret there was a young Venezuelan, and eventually a multilingual Dane, Vigo Wadskiar.

At first all went well. From the beginning Lancaster determined to establish an Institution approximating as closely as possible to the Borough Road. He issued a series of 'Regulations for Boys training as monitors and intended to study language and science in the School of Joseph Lancaster patronized by General Bolivar.

'1) Each boy to live in the house on condition he teaches and does appointed duties at least one half of the time daily.

2) They shall form a class among themselves and study lessons appointed out of school hours.

3) On first days they will be exclusively under direction of their friends leaving school in the morning and returning punctually in the evening.

4) Their conversation in school and house with one another shall not be louder than a whisper.

5) As they all sleep in separate beds and apartments no boy allowed to return to his room after dressing in the morning – till evening without permission, and any two boys forbidden to be in the same bedroom by night or by day.

Expected to keep their own shoes clean, hair combed and clothes and hat brushed to sweep their own room and make their own bed.

6) Parents and friends expected to wash a boy's linen and provide him with clean every week.

7) There will be one month's trial, if they behave well they will be given a suit of clothes to be worn when the family walk out together or when the school is visited by special visitors – if after three months remittances come from

England, they will all get a second suit and the first will become daily wear.'

In July 1824 Colonel Brooke Young got command of a battalion of eight hundred men and, a month later, he left Caracas on the long journey to reinforce Bolivar in Peru. With him he took another letter to the Liberator from Joseph Lancaster, seeking patronage.

Dissension had begun to raise its head, and money worries refused to go away. The Lancaster family had not been long settled when a bill for $234.85 arrived in Caracas from Philadelphia. Issac Hopper, who presented it, was a distinguished Friend, about to become leader of the Hicksites when the 'Separation' of the Society of Friends in Philadelphia took place in 1827. By trade a tailor, he was the promoter of a negro underground escape route and outspoken in the cause of Emancipation. Probably he was encouraged to try his luck, as were others, by a report which had appeared in American papers saying that Joseph Lancaster was in the land of plenty and earning three thousand dollars a year.

In the school too there were troubles. The Board had published a notice which claimed that the catechism was taught. Joseph Lancaster refused to agree to this. His pupils might all be Catholic, but the Lancastrian System rested on the principle of non-sectarian education. After discussion the Board withdrew their notice. But then, as always, there were financial complications. The municipality, themselves in severe financial straits, fell into arrears with their half of the promised salary, the rest of which came from central government at Bogota. Joseph threatened to leave. Forty pupils were in any case not enough. The Board wished to inspect the school. Joseph replied no salary, no inspection. This impasse, which lasted for some time, with sundry efforts to mediate taking place, resulted eventually in the municipality ceasing to make any commitment to pay, the Board going into abeyance and Joseph Lancaster, undeterred, taking the school under his own supervision.

In February 1825 the Lancastrian Institute had moved into a Franciscan monastery in the centre of Caracas. By a decree of the Congress of Colombia in 1821 religious houses of less than eight friars or nuns were abolished, a measure aimed at acquiring fine buildings for educational purposes. The Franciscan monastery still housed a few monks, and was also used to quarter soldiers in times of civil disturbance. It was an immensely large building and Joseph's school was organised in the Chapel.

Always having perceived money as a commodity to be spent, rather than saved, Joseph determined to acquire a printing press, atlases, maps, engravings, books of all kinds, encyclopaedias, 'optical, philosophical, and drawing instruments', and to this end he wrote to everyone in England or America that he thought could possibly help; among them Josiah Wedgwood II and Rudolph Ackermann, art publisher and bookseller in the Strand. James Moxon, the Liverpool business man who sent news of the death of David Holt's wife, was also approached. Very quickly, and in the old pattern, Joseph had acquired a second Family of 'twelve superior native youths' who lived with him and 'who make me as happy as they can make a father'. Some were training as school masters, some as printers. To emphasise the importance of this whole venture Joseph had some fine note-paper printed, presumably on the school press. It carried the heading, 'Seminario de Jose Lancaster, Bajo el Patronato del Libertador Presidente, General Bolivar'. Underneath, the coat of arms with the Lancaster bell in its circle of leaves and the motto 'Lancaster me fecit' appeared on the left hand side.

After only eight months in Venezuela however, early in 1825, a change took place in Joseph Lancaster's life which, considering its nature and far-reaching consequences, seems at the time to have been taken very calmly by all concerned. It was suggested to Richard Jones by a Dr Forsyth, who was engaged in trade in La Guaira and interested in the dissemination of the Bible in South America, and the Mexican chargé d'affaires passing through on his way to Bogota, that he considered setting up a school in Mexico City, where there was already a Lancastrian Society.

Richard Jones certainly anticipated, or was led to believe, that there would be both official support and financial remuneration when he got to Mexico. Joseph wrote of a 'fine field of glory and usefulness'. It had probably become plain to Richard that he was never going to earn an independent salary as long as he remained in the position of his father-in-law's 'pleasant friend'. Betsy was newly pregnant and in any case there were no girls in the Caracas school for her to teach. Richard's Spanish had greatly improved. Bolivar thought of Mexico as ultimately being part of his Federation; as Lancaster saw his own aim to bring education to the children of all Colombia. In those heady days Mexico City may not have appeared so far distant from Caracas as it actually was. The young couple must have seen this as a splendid opportunity to strike out and make a name for themselves.

Joseph Lancaster seemed settled for a bright future. But perhaps, after all, he was not unaware of the patterns of his own life. At the same moment that Richard was considering this offer, Joseph was petitioning George IV for an annuity, payable when he reached Britain or any British colony, also the authority for free passages on any West Indian packet to Britain or elsewhere. Advancing in years, living in a new nation abounding in French spies and revolutionary plots, he felt that he and his family might at any time be driven to leave by 'invidious attacks'. At the moment such circumstances seemed remote, though there were rumblings beneath the surface of Caracas life.

By February 25th Betsy and Richard were en route to Mexico City by way of Philadelphia, and Joseph was writing to Roberts Vaux asking that a subscription be opened in that town to give the young couple a nest-egg of two or three hundred dollars. Both the Vaux family and Robert Ralston, another philanthropic Philadelphia merchant, provided generous hospitality to the Lancaster Joneses. Joseph Lancaster was never to see Betsy again.

Though it is likely that Joseph's own Spanish was never fluent enough to permit him to lecture in Caracas in his old style, in the early days he wrote frequently that he soon hoped to do so. To this end he had a set of transparencies made up by a pupil, perhaps as an aid while his language was still halting. What is more certain is that he learned to read Spanish and, living as he did in the constant company of his Family, came in time to converse reasonably well. And, as he was later to assure Mary Robinson, there was always the possibility of an interpreter.

By July 1825 Lancaster had received a generous and laudatory letter from Simon Bolivar, written in Lima on March 16th in answer to the missive which left Caracas with Colonel Brooke Young in 1824. In it Bolivar offered twenty thousand pesos, to be employed in advancing the education of the children of Caracas, to be paid in London by the agent of Peru, the government of which country had placed a million pesos at Bolivar's disposal for the service of the Colombians. He added that if Lancaster thought it could be usefully employed he would gladly send on an even larger sum. So two men for whom money had little concrete reality; Bolivar because wealth was his natural element, Joseph Lancaster because it was not; entered into a financial relationship which by the time they met was to destroy any possibility of fruitful co-operation between them.

Even before the promise was given, and certainly without any thought of using his present comparative affluence to wipe off past obligations, Joseph Lancaster was incurring fresh debts. During 1825 advice notices, or the goods themselves, were arriving at the new Institution in a constant stream. 'The whole of the Printing establishment' was forwarded in January from Le Guaira. In May Rudolph Ackerman sent off by the 'Dart' one hundred and thirty views, Oxford, Cambridge, etc., twelve drawing books, four portraits, one allegory, three songs, one subsidiary chemistry, two Mexico, one vol Persia, one Paley, etc. etc. Almost on the same date, on the brig 'Condor', a direct order was being shipped to Joseph Lancaster from London. The articles included: one large size compound microscope in mahogany box; one best 30m Pentograph; one diagonal mirror mounted in mahogany; one set of 6m best common drawing instruments; one large magnifier in ebony frame – two 5 inch prisms; one universal sundial in red case; one large improved ivory thermometer; one large phantasmagoria, etc. etc. In June James Moxon sent a box of books by the 'Bolivar'; Elizabeth Fry promised more volumes, adding that since she herself had known some fame she had often thought of Joseph Lancaster and the need for humility in those circumstances.

In September a parcel of books, which had been a year on the way, arrived from Professor Benjamin Silliman at Yale. Benjamin Silliman was Professor of Chemistry and Natural History, lecturer on mineralogy and geology, founder in 1818 of The 'American Journal of Science and Arts', the most influential scientific man in America. Joseph Lancaster, who took a keen interest in natural phenomena, corresponded with him on the geological structure of the mountains between Caracas and La Guaira, the prevalence of garnets, the power of attrition in forming pebbles on the beach, the incidence of thunderstorms and earthquakes in Venezuela and other such matters.

In November, however, Mr Ackermann wrote from London that Bolivar's first draft for ten thousand dollars was not being accepted by the Peruvian agent. A month later the news was still that only one of the gentlemen on whom the twenty thousand draft was drawn had arrived in London, and he said he could do nothing until his companion came. A more prudent man might have proceeded with circumspection after this warning. Such was not Joseph Lancaster's way. Indeed he published and disseminated in Caracas, in Spanish and English, a letter from de Witt Clinton which spoke of Bolivar and Lancaster in the same breath as benefactors of mankind; a view which did not necessarily coincide with that of most Venezuelans.

Late in 1825 two ships unloading at La Guaira landed men who were to become closely connected, not always pleasantly, with Joseph Lancaster. On November 27th Sir Robert Ker Porter, His Majesty's British Counsel came ashore; and on December 2nd the 'Planet' with thirty families of Scottish settlers dropped anchor in the roads.

Sir Robert Ker Porter, born in Durham, brought up in Edinburgh, student at the Royal Academy in London, artist and traveller, was a character. Appointed historical painter to the Czar of Russia, Alexander 1, in 1805 he fell in love with a Russian princess and eventually married her. He had journeyed widely, often in remote and exotic countries, and published accounts of those travels. Fastidious and eccentric, cultured and snobbish, reserved but with a wide circle of friends and acquaintances. Sir Robert, having left his wife and daughter in St Petersburg, was to spend the next sixteen years in Venezuela.

On November 29th, in company with Mr Hurry, he rode across the mountains. Sir Robert had Paris, St Petersburg, Constantinople and other cities of the old world for comparison and on this first short visit he did not think much of Caracas; nor indeed of one of the English visitors who called at the inn to see him, 'old Mr Lancaster of scholastic reputation'. Sir Robert was at forty-eight one year older than Joseph Lancaster. The two men were to be antipathetic from the beginning; not least perhaps because each in his own way had an instinct for the central role in the dramas of life. By a curious coincidence Sir Robert's father had been an army surgeon at the battle of Minden, where Richard Lancaster had served in the Foot Guards.

The Colombian Government was anxious to encourage foreign capital, technology and immigrants. In Britain a Colombian Agricultural Association had come into being and obtained grants of land from the Colombian Government. The London agents were L. A. Goldschmidt, T. Richardson and J. D. Powles. They aimed to select sites, provide free passages and dispose of the land in small lots for lease or for sale to settlers. The local agent, George Ward, was to provide transport, victuals, utensils and tools for eight months as well as advances of money, with titles and lien on stock and crops as security. One such concession was an estate at Topo, twelve miles north west of Caracas, in a valley two or three thousand feet high growing indigo, cotton and coffee.

The Association had an agent in Aberdeen, in north east Scotland. A recruiting campaign offered the possibility of fertile land under an equable climate, in a new country ripe with opportunities for wealth and advancement. The heads of families attracted by this opening, thirty of whom eventually entered into contracts, were not men driven to leave because of destitution and poverty. But life was hard in Scotland and work on the land brought very little reward. It was a poor country. The clan system had broken down and landlords were often absentee and uncaring. Small wonder that men saw for themselves and their sons the chance to do better in the New World. On October 1st 1825 just under two hundred souls sailed for Venezuela from Cromarty Bay. On December 2nd they landed at La Guaira and were transported up to the valley at Topo. Three quarters of them were MacDonalds, many were Gaelic speaking and some, though by no means all, were Protestant.

On December 28th Sir Robert Ker Porter, HM British Consul, rode over to see them. They seemed 'as yet pretty well contented', It was not to last.

Meanwhile, on September 22nd, in Mexico City, Betsy produced a 'fine large son', with big soft blue eyes, beautifully clear complexion and regular masculine features. They called him Joseph Lancaster in honour of his Grandfather, and Betsy hoped he would be worthy to perpetuate the name. There were times when Betsy could not understand how a country as illustrious as England could treat so shabbily a man as noble as her father. For the moment the baby was the only bright spot on Betsy's horizon.

Things had not turned out as the young Joneses expected. Betsy was very ill on the voyage from Philadelphia to the River Alvarado. When they landed she found the climate almost insufferable; and Richard the cost of travelling in Mexico far in excess of any provision he had made. At the very beginning he had to borrow sixty dollars. They arrived in Mexico City on the 5th of June, exhausted by the journey and with only twelve dollars in their pockets. The British Minister treated them with disdain. The next day Richard delivered his letter of introduction from Caracas to the Lancastrian Society. It proved to be much less influential than he had hoped. The Society took advantage of his arrival to arrange a debate on the subject of public education, but made it plain that there was no money to employ him; '. . . the body is poor, and without the assistance of the government it can do nothing'. Richard added that the Lancastrian Society itself had a bad reputation.

But for an introduction to a local merchant, given by Robert Ralston, they would have found themselves in desperate straits. This man, seeing the kind of accommodation to which they were reduced, took them into his own house for three months. Though Betsy thought Mexico City far preferable to Caracas in its situation and its fine buildings, she was very critical of local society. After six months she had no female acquaintances and was inclined to believe what she had been told, that the women were 'ignorant, hypocritical and unacquainted with the word friendship'.

But the worst of all was their poverty. Betsy was tired of being poor. To find herself once more in the situation which she already knew so well, with necessary expenses far outrunning their means, must have filled her with despair. For the next two years she and Richard were to beg, importune even, Joseph Lancaster for assistance, at first financial, later to try to obtain a vice-consulship for Richard. Betsy knew her father's open-handedness, but she must also have known that, even in the most favourable circumstances, he was always pressed for money. She knew him better than anyone, and his weaknesses must have been plain to her sensible, critical eye. Yet she retained a perception of him as a man who could be relied upon to help in a crisis; who, if he had the money, would give it away rather than keep it for his own use; and whose standing in the eyes of the world still accorded him influence and prestige.

Father and daughter kept up a regular correspondence, on Betsy's side anxious for his welfare, full of news of her 'little Mexican'; on his always optimistic about the way things were going. The school was doing well and prejudice dying down. He talked about his garden and the pet rabbit Betsy had left behind. Richard Jones wrote with political and commercial news; rumours of a Colombian invasion of Cuba. The election of a new energetic President for the Lancastrian Society in Mexico City brought a measure of hope, but there was friction between the Society and the municipal council, which had appointed a committee on public education. Richard Jones stood in the middle. He was now teaching English and copying and translating for the English Consul-General at a hundred dollars a month. In April 1826 he was beseeching his father-in-law to write to Canning, the British Foreign Secretary, to get him a position. In November that year he was thanking Joseph for two hundred dollars, commenting that they were 'truly, truly poor'.

It was the darkest hour. On January 5th 1827 the family left Mexico City for Guadalajara, twenty days journey to the northwest. Richard had accepted the post of 'Director Principal de las Escuelas Lancasterianas del Estado de Xalisco' at two thousand four hundred dollars a year, and was to set up a model school. Would Joseph Lancaster write a grand letter to H E the Governor on the subject of education, and congratulate the enlightened citizens of the province of Xalisco on the great step they had taken. In Spanish please. Both Betsy and Richard thanked Joseph warmly for his efforts on their behalf, and hoped he would not cease to exert them, for Richard Jones wanted further advancement. Among the sensible advice that his son-in-law passed on to Joseph Lancaster one sentence stood out. 'Don't let your inoffensive hat make you enemies.'

The hat had given particular offence to Sir Robert Ker Porter. It was probably inevitable that these two men should have disliked each other, but neither made any attempt to conceal the contempt he felt. Sir Robert set store by the forms and etiquette of polite society, as indeed did the wealthy upper class in Caracas for all their republicanism. The Quaker in Joseph Lancaster refused to debase the salute due only to Almighty God by removing his hat in the presence of any mortal, however illustrious. He had retained it in the presence of his monarch; how much more so before His Majesty's servant. Sir Robert may have despised Friends as a sect, or thought Joseph Lancaster's pretensions to be a true Quaker hypocritical, at any rate he refused to admit that there could be an admissable reason for a

British subject keeping on his hat in the presence of His Britannic Majesty's Consul. All Joseph's obstinacy was aroused by his no doubt cold reception when he appeared with it on. He felt himself more in tune with the true spirit of Colombian independence than the man he confronted, and the quarrel was the more bitter because they shared a common nationality. To de Witt Clinton Joseph made a joke of the encounter and, if as seems not unlikely, he even did so to Sir Robert's face this cannot have improved matters.

'I think', he wrote, 'if some ingenious mechanic can find a way that we outlandish folks of Caracas can unscrew our heads and take them off and on like the lid of a snuff box – then I may unscrew hat and all and keeping still the perpendicular I may gracefully wave the casket of knowledge like a true friend of education – as I would sometimes shake my glove in friendship not in defiance to a friend . . . He (Sir Robert) only wants my hat, now that I am determined he shall never have – to compromise the matter I wil give him my head if one of your American artists can only ensure my screwing it on and off – that may fit as close as it does now when on – and that my breathing may not affected nor I be likely to take cold when it is off'.

He may well have gravely miscalculated the reaction, in the great and powerful of the city, to his manner and appearance – though unlike Sir Robert their code would have prevented them showing open disapproval.

Throughout the first months of 1826 civil conditions in Venezuela were in a state of disturbance and unease. Long before this Bolivar had been expected back from the expedition to Peru. But week followed week, and still he did not come. General Paez, military commander in the Province, was a brave, patriotic leader, but at this period little more than a rough local chieftain, addicted to gambling and cockfighting, touchy where any infringement of his own independence could be suspected. Venezuela had lived under many years of disastrous and fragmenting wars. The Liberator was far away, small wonder that the civil population was jumpy; the loyalties of soldiers uncertain.

In January, and again in April, as though an echo to this situation, earthquakes shook Caracas.

The Scottish settlers too were disgruntled. There were delays in the allocation of land at Topo. The ground was not cleared of scrub and it was now plain that the area suffered from a severe lack of water. In the manner of men who hear what they wish to hear, the Scots had not realised, even if they had been told before leaving, that it would not be possible to cultivate their traditional produce, grain, vegetables and cattle. Coffee, indigo and cotton were unknown crops to them. It was sufficiently daunting to be in a strange country, with climatic conditions that they did not understand, land to be cleared and houses to be built by their own efforts, their accustomed implements of plough and harrow useless, without the burden of an unfamiliar end product to all their labours. They grumbled. They drank. Sir Robert quickly came to think of them as troublemakers.

Very early this year, or perhaps in the last weeks of 1825, John Robinson died in Philadelphia. Joseph Lancaster had greatly valued him as a friend, and during the family's first years in America he had been staunch and generous. When she heard the news Betsy forgot her irritation at his curtailing of her independence and wrote with warmth and sympathy. Mary Robinson, left alone with a family of young children, showed herself to be resourceful and unafraid. She proposed to open a small circulating library in Philadelphia to earn a living.

Joseph Lancaster, however, seems to have been cheerful and content. Even a letter from Nathanial Muggeridge in London demanding that, now Lancaster was successful and affluent, he remit £6000 to give his creditors in England twenty shillings in the pound did not disturb him. He was well able after all to ignore debts contracted on his very doorstep. He told de Witt Clinton that he found his pupils easy to govern, eager for knowledge, of the brightest capacities, fond and ardent. Carnival fell early in February. Sir Robert detested this uproarious feast, the throwing of raw eggs and squirting water at passers-by. Indeed for those from Northern Europe the rough uninhibited boisterous behaviour at Carnival could be as frightening as amusing. But for the Lancastrian school the great day was April 19th, Independence Day.

On this occasion the Intendente and the Cabildo or municipal council repaired in a body to a solemn Mass in the cathedral, walking afterwards to the City House to read the Act of Independence. 1826 was distinguished by Bolivar's gift to his native city, sent from Cusco in Peru, of the banner presented to Pissaro by Queen Isabella. This relic was to be paraded round the town.

Joseph had decided to make the most of the day. He had a letter of congratulation printed for distribution among the people, after he had presented a copy to the Intendente as he came out of church. As it happened the new Intendente, Dr Cristóbal Mendoza, had only been a few days in office. He was a strong Bolivarist, spoke a little English, and Joseph Lancaster had his eldest son acting as his interpreter for a while.

But there was more to the Lancastrian celebrations than the distribution of a complimentary letter. No doubt with memories of similar occasions in earlier days, Joseph Lancaster decided to mount a procession. Considerable preparation must have gone into the making of the twenty-one silk flags of the nations that had adopted the Lancastrian System. 'The star spangles of America marched with those of England.' The boys had new suits and stepped out proudly with Joseph Lancaster at their head. They were of all colours, black, white and every range in between, and each held a standard of the Colombian Republic. Even Sir Robert had to admit that the effect, though surrounded by crowds of richly dressed spectators and grandly uniformed men, was 'a truly gratifying addition to the cortege, and the young republicans fell in between the Cavalry and the Infantry and they all stepped off to the sounds of drums, trumpets, bugles . . .' Bells clanged. Volleys were fired. As darkness fell trees of liberty were illuminated and the Lancaster banners arranged round a Temple of Independence in the Grand Plaza. Joseph Lancaster who loved processions with his boys, enjoyed it hugely.

'I was much amused with the novelty of my situation and numerous mothers found their hearts leap for joy at the sight of their children – for most of the pupils and the family of my adoption are fatherless – The wiser part of the community expressed their satisfaction like men – but I have been often asked by the ignorant class when we should have another Rosaria having thought it a religious procession.'

Perhaps it was unwise, in a country where the Catholic church was dominant, and where, in a time of turbulence, men of God feared for their religious institutions, for this Quaker to bring so forcibly before the public his non-sectarian school. Traditionally the church had a monopoly of primary education. Joseph Lancaster's frequent mention of prejudice being overcome indicated that welcome for the System had not been universal. His refusal to teach the catechism would be remembered. Protestants were heretics, and there was nowhere in Caracas where they could bury their dead, being forbidden the use of the only cemeteries. But Joseph Lancaster had never shown himself sensitive to the atmosphere which surrounded him.

The Municipality of Caracas had ceased in 1825 to provide their portion of the money promised in Lancaster's contract, though Bolivar, in a letter written in 1826, reprimanded them for doing so. But news of Bolivar's twenty thousand peso draft had no doubt reached the Cabildo and must have seemed to exempt them from further financial aid. It is certain that the personality and the character of Joseph Lancaster was very different from that expected of the educator of youth and founder of the Lancastrian System. If they had visualised him at all, no doubt it was as a grave, cultured pedagogue whose ancestry, if not noble, was at least solidly respectable. But Joseph, for all his enjoyment of fame and desire to stand close to those of good birth, was himself a man of the people who never denied his own origins. Bluff and jovial, without a veneer of manners, easily upset and prepared to offend blatantly in return, he was an outsider in an aristocratic society where, ironically, he felt more at home than in classless America. Self made, he was prepared to struggle for his beliefs, to accept poverty for himself and his family as a normal condition of life. Small wonder that some in Caracas, even Bolivar himself, questioned whether he was an imposter.

On May 3rd 1826 news reached Caracas that a revolution had broken out at Valencia, a town to the west. General Paez proclaimed himself Chief of the Army and declared Venezuela a separate State. A deputation arrived in Caracas to find out what action the city fathers intended to take. The next day there was intelligence that General Santiago Mariño, one of the military heroes of the independence struggle, was marching on the city with a considerable body of troops. Sir Robert sent to Barbados for a ship of war to be dispatched to La Guaira in case British subjects had to be taken off. The merchants of that town were even more panic-stricken than those of the capital at the prospect of renewed civil war. On May 7th General Mariño entered Caracas, without his troops, to cries of 'viva Paez, Mariño and Venezuela! The Intendente acted cautiously and with diplomatic skill. General Paez himself arrived in Caracas on May 19th and was greeted with considerable enthusiasm. He undertook the supreme direction of civil and military affairs. Messages were sent to Bolivar beseeching him to come home to help the formulation of reforms, and by his prudence and wisdom direct the establishment of the Republic's new institutions. In the city itself daily activities returned to normal.

Joseph Lancaster, meanwhile, was engaged in a drama of his own.

In Philadelphia things had not worked out well for Mary Robinson since her husband's death. It was not easy for a woman alone to set up a business, however small. The circulating library was never more than an idea; a dry goods store failed. John Robinson had left her with a certain amount of property, paintings, prints and furniture, and a little money; but without a continuing income such assets soon disappear. There were also debts of about three hundred dollars. Then there was George, her oldest son, aged about nine and not easy to control. She had written to John Lovell to ask whether he would accept responsibility for George's education in the school at New Haven. Lovell, in poor health and low spirits, declined. Sensibly he replied that there was too great a distance between New Haven and Philadelphia, and he did not feel equal to being in sole charge of young Robinson. He suggested a school near his mother, where he would be out of reach of bad company, but still within the orbit of his home.

Mary Robinson wrote to Joseph Lancaster about her personal difficulties. He had known her husband for twenty years on both sides of the Atlantic, and she knew him to be a man of great kindness who would spare no pains to help those whom he loved. With characteristic, unthinking, generosity Joseph assured her that he could give financial assistance and offered one hundred dollars, which he sent in instalments through Robert Ralston. He also offered a job.

It was a Quixotic gesture probably arising in equal measure from warmth of heart, remembrance of the times when Mary and John Robinson had stood by him in difficult moments and shared their meals and their 'little mites' with the Lancaster family, and loneliness. Though he never said so to Betsy, Joseph Lancaster must have missed her company sorely. And with her had gone the last of his original apprentices. A Venezuelan and a young Dane, who knew nothing of the old days, cannot have been any compensation for the support, affection and common memories of Richard Jones and John Lovell. So, along with the offer of a job as schoolmistress, in charge of female education in Caracas, went an offer of marriage. It was the only condition that would make it possible for her to come at all.

She demurred. Her pride, as much as the newness of her widowhood, made her reluctant to admit that she could not manage on her own. He brushed her objections aside. Yes, language would be a difficulty, he wrote on July 1st:

'But so it is for all foreigners but time will conquer that when thou wilt live among people who continuously speak it. Thy difficulties would daily lessen and perhaps thou may be assisted as I have been with an interpreter.'

He saw no trouble about honourable fulfilment of her debts. If she came to Venezuela she would have occasion to sell:

'None of thy furniture and thy books. It is thy own and I hope can be so secured as to remain so perpetually. It may all be shipped when our arrangements are complete respecting thy stock.'

What she could not sell of the latter, he suggested, the creditors might be willing to take back at cost.

As for the actual journey. Joseph's friend Captain Ryan of the 'Colombian':

'Who has bought and paid for my types etc for the printing office – to the value of $700 will I am sure afford thee the very best accommodation his vessel a passenger can afford . . .'

He was a good kind man, and if she decided to come Joseph would agree with him for a conditional passage.

These details out of the way Joseph went on to discuss more serious matters.

'I am tied here by duty and expect no liberty to leave – lest I should unsettle at present the Institution I have so happily succeeded in rearing – in the very teeth of bigotry and opposition. In consequence of my daughter's leaving me I am unable to proceed in the cause of female education and this cause I feel bound in the fear of God and love of mankind to persevere in and on this ground I have given the invitation – I have always endeavoured to prefer virtue and good principle to every other claim – and it is on this ground – I offer thee marriage and should prefer thee with thy much loved family . . . I have a public family educated at Bolivar's expense who in regard to market and other expenses need a watchful eye and the feet of Christian prudence that what would clothe the poor, instruct the ignorant or feed the hungry may not be wasted – Here I look to thee as an economist. By such an arrangement all my children may be provided for in their own Education and as teachers of others – and whatever property there is or may be – may be secured to thee and them free and independent of me before marriage.'

For the time in which it was given, when no wife's property was deemed to be her own, it was a handsome contract, seriously offered. However future circumstances might distort the letter, Joseph Lancaster, with considerable anguish, was to hold to the spirit of it.

Regarding the wedding:

'A marriage might be made in Philadelphia by proxy (I think so) – before a magistrate and the same might be made before the American consul here which would be legal and most consonant with the principle of friends – of any mode I know out of their Society.'

Sir Robert Kerr Porter, HM British Consul, was not to be involved in any such ceremony.

Mary Robinson was not a Quaker. Joseph Lancaster wrote that all that concerned him was that she should love and serve the Lord and turn her back on the vanities of the world. In the first part of this declaration at any rate Joseph Lancaster fully lived up to the religious principles on which he had based his life's work.

This letter ended with an injunction to tell no one except Robert Ralston about the offer of marriage until she had agreed, the contract was completed and she had embarked for Caracas. Then he would have no objection to all the world knowing that he had honoured Mary Robinson above all other women.

On July 23rd Joseph wrote again. She had not yet received his first letter and was obviously still hoping to have some success in Philadelphia. But a sale of her husband's paintings had realised very little. Joseph immediately offered to pay cash for any drawings or drawing books that remained, undertaking to get the money to her by Captain Ryan. Once again he repeated the offer of a job as schoolmistress, urging her to consult Robert Ralston on this issue. He ended with an assurance of the depth of his feeling of indebtedness to John Robinson and herself. He could not find words to tell how much he felt for kindness received.

It took Mrs Robinson another five months to make up her

mind to accept his offer, during which time she must have tried many ways of keeping herself and her family afloat. She knew Joseph Lancaster and had watched Betsy struggling with the uncertain family finances in Philadelphia. She must have been well aware of the difficulties which would face any wife of this man. She had known Elizabeth Lancaster, and seen the suffering that marriage brought to both sides. But she knew Joseph Lancaster also as a man capable of great affection. She can have had no doubt that he would accept her children as his own. John Robinson had already bequeathed his daughter to his friend; George and John would find a father whom they could love and admire. Mary Robinson may have had qualms about the future, but by December 1826 she had decided to become the second Mrs Joseph Lancaster.

By August 1826 Bolivar had still not arrived in Caracas; and in London Bolivar's draft on the coffers of Peru remained unhonoured. In Venezuela Joseph Lancaster's bills with the merchants of Caracas and La Guaira accumulated steadily. Confusion reigned as to the state of the country and the intentions of the Liberator; trade was depressed, in Caracas troops were under arms. The Military Governor dared not call on the militia, whose loyalties were in doubt, and was anxious that the foreigners in the city should come forward to guard the monastery of San Francisco if the troops quartered there had to go out and deal with the mob.

For some time Joseph Lancaster and his school shared the monastery with soldiers; and not only with troops. In January General Paez had summoned all the citizens of Caracas to the monastery to enlist them in the army. Few had responded, so the General had ordered an indiscriminate arrest of all males. The Intendente protested and they were freed in the evening, but the city looked as though it had been looted by an enemy. At this moment the monastery was the barrack of the Regiment of the Apure. The battalion occupied the lower court, and the few remaining friars had been so intimidated by them, and by the civil power, that they were too broken in spirit to object to any use made of their once fine building. The troops came in:

'Like wild cats from the mountains cutting a multitude of idle capers for mischief so they gave great personal annoyance, however application after application to the acting authorities ultimately made them quite tame':

Joseph wrote to de Witt Clinton. If the friars were so;

'Beaten and bruised'; as he claimed, then the repeated applications were presumably Lancaster's.

'. . . though the monastery is no barrack and the troops who entered only by the permission of the superior of the house have no legal right to remain, but having no other place for a barrack they laugh at the law and say necessity has no law – How long we are to be pestered by these singing dancing fighting sots I know not, but I find myself at times a little like a fish out of water, amidst such a discordant set of neighbours though they dare not interfere with me or my pupils – who march out every day in companies with their members in regular order having the banner of education carried before them as the head national Lancastrian school in the nation.'

On August 28th the Regiment of Apure marched out of Caracas with colours flying. Though their loyalty had been suspect, the inhabitants were nevertheless filled with consternation at being left unprotected. On the 31st General Mariño with the Anzoátegui Regiment entered the town, the former in a rage at the defection of the Apure, the latter disorderly and undisciplined. A nervous uncertain atmosphere pervaded the city. But in spite of national crisis and local mistrust, the feud between Joseph Lancaster and Sir Robert Ker Porter continued to flourish.

The situation had become so bad that Joseph threatened to expose Sir Robert's conduct in print; for him always the final refuge when he felt himself to be losing a fight. He objected to being kept waiting or refused entry when he called at the consul's house;

'Either as a British subject or in his capacity as an important teacher.'

Sir Robert said he had only asked him not to come on the days that the mail arrived or left for England. The matter of the hat rankled. All the belligerence of the soldier's son rose up in Joseph at slights, real or imagined.

'Is it possible that my Government shall tolerate the idea of giving 2800 guineas to a Consul not to protect but to insult a true-hearted British subject like me in the face of the government that patronises me and of the natives that expect my countrymen to show me that urbanity, which I have received from Every British subject in Laguaira and Caracas – except the English

Consul.'

Sir Robert for his part was quite as outspoken. He considered Lancaster a rogue, whose inflated self-importance was based on false pretences. He wrote of;

'. . . that old serpent Mr Lancaster . . . who is the most black and dangerous being in the place. He has been (through his own want of principle) obliged to leave England in disgrace, in America for the same reason, and I have little doubt, but his extravagant folly and cruel love for defaming the characters of all will ultimately bring disgrace upon him in Caracas.' Sadly this prediction was to prove to have some truth in it.

So, when in October Joseph Lancaster decided to take a hand in the affairs of the Topo settlers, this move did nothing to help the state of war beween himself and the Consul.

That month news came from London that the Colombian Agricultural Association's bubble had burst. Their United Kingdom backers were bankrupt and, in consequence, rations and assistance to the colonists ceased. Already disillusioned, living in miserable conditions, the colonists now only wanted to return to Scotland or leave for America. Many were drinking hard. Some were tempted to try their luck in the city, others were sunk in depression, seeing no prospect for their wives and families but hardship and perhaps starvation. Sir Robert foresaw much trouble for himself, but he was not ready to take any official action on their behalf, maintaining that his powers did not extend that far. The colonists were the responsibility of the company and its agents, most of whom had now resigned their positions.

On October 22nd Joseph Lancaster, having learned that the colonists had been abandoned by the Association, rode up to Topo. He found one hundred and forty-three persons existing miserably in one block of buildings. He offered to do what he could, advised them to stick together, and came straight back to Caracas to write to Dr Mendoza, the Intendente. He reported that since March, when they had finally received their land, the settlers had cleared and cultivated about one hundred and twenty acres. The harvest had produced only two hundred bushels of maize and thirty of 'carroty (beans)', so they had no food in hand after six months and saw no prospect of improvement in the near future. Coffee, as a cash crop, took three years to mature.

Until recently the Colombian Agricultural Association had

provided rations, and at the end of eight months George Ward, the agent, had promised provisions for another four. Then, with only two weeks notice, allowances were discontinued and the settlers left to fend for themselves as best they could. They acknowledged that in many ways the Association had fulfilled its engagements with honour, and that the agents had behaved well. But the land had turned out to be some of the worst in Colombia. With this latter judgement Sir Robert Ker Porter agreed.

The colonists felt that they had been;

'Allured by great names and specious promises to a country whose language and customs are alien and now deserted in a wilderness.'

They felt themselves to be in a truly miserable condition and entreated the protection of the Intendente and the Government of Colombia. Agreement had been entered into with the Colombian Agricultural Association and in the name of the Colombian ambassador in Britain as President, and the papers signed by Goldsmith, Richardson and Powles with whom, or some of whom, the Government of Colombia had entered into public contract.

'They also hope, that in their general orderly conduct, they have not acted unworthy of the character of Scotsmen for Industry and that they shall continue to do credit to their own country.'

This document, written on his flamboyantly headed notepaper, was signed by Joseph Lancaster 'as a friend to the settlers of Topo' and witnessed by two of the colonists, Alex McDonall and Alex Rose.

In answer Dr Mendoza exonerated the Association, and offered to find work for individuals on neighbouring estates. No doubt mindful of Joseph's advice, and relying on him as their most likely benefactor, the colonists refused.

Sir Robert was very angry. He intended to stand aloof from these matters, but could not bear to see another man, and one whom he detested, taking on himself active responsibility.

'Mr Lancaster is meddling and speaking very illiberally respecting the Consul's not providing the means of support or exerting himself to send home these some 200 idle drunken Scotchmen . . .'

he wrote furiously in his diary on October 23rd. Joseph Lancaster saw only fellow countrymen who needed assistance;

and no doubt was not averse to showing his enemy in a bad light at the same time.

On November 1st Lancaster was in La Guaira. He wrote asking for an interview with George Ward, who had refused to act any longer as agent for the Topo project.

'I consider my interference in this case the same as any I should make for a family drowning or in a house on fire. I might rush into the water or into the flames to save persons with whom I had no regular connection before and whom I might never see again'; Joseph wrote.

He went on to reveal that he intended to raise a subscription among the British and foreign merchants to help tide the settlers over this difficult period, for he was convinced that if they did not quickly get some help they would come into Caracas and La Guaira 'in troops, begging for bread, and this would be bad for the cause of Colombian immigration and produce an unpleasant clamour in Britain. Whatever the merits or demerits of individuals, there were many unoffending persons among the settlers;

'I mean 80 children and persons under 14 years of age'.

This was Joseph Lancaster at his best, urgent to give help where he saw a need. He added in a postscript that he had heard that his efforts were attributed to hostile or improper feelings. But it was not causes with which he interfered, but effects. This was a situation of suffering humanity and nothing else.

Never slow where there was a benevolent object in view, Joseph Lancaster proceeded with his subscription and managed to raise close on eight hundred pesos. He wrote a letter to Robert Ralston, which appeared in Paulson's 'Daily Advertiser' in Philadelphia and eventually brought in three hundred dollars. He appealed to the St Andrew's Society in that same city. With what he received, and with his advice to the colonists to slaughter their livestock, on which it seemed the Association's creditors might place an embargo, for their own consumption, subsistence for the colonists was provided for a good many weeks.

Practical steps having been taken, Joseph then began to write back to England about them. He addressed a letter to the Earl of Harrowby and prepared to send a petition to 'Gentlemen of the House of Commons', signed by heads of families, two wives and some older sons, setting out their wish to travel to Canada and asking Parliamentary intervention to prevent companies speculating in the welfare of human beings.

Not unnaturally all this activity on their behalf endeared Joseph Lancaster to the Topo settlers. Sir Robert suspected that he was making promises with no possibility of fufilment, and it was true that Joseph's optimistic temperament led him to encourage those he had taken under his protection to believe that when Bolivar arrived they would be given fresh, good land, or that England would come to their aid with passages out of Colombia.

Meanwhile the political situation had become even more tangled. On November 25th martial law was declared in Caracas. The Intendente Dr Mendoza, was accused of intrigue and of opposition to the designs of General Paez. He resigned and was exiled to the island of St Thomas. On December 7th El Colombiano, a bilingual newspaper founded and edited by Colonel Stopford, closed. The Colonel, an Englishman, had seen military service in the Venezuelan war of independence and stayed on in the country. He owned lands and acted as a money lender. He was also at the centre of Protestant religious observance in the city. Between him and Joseph Lancaster there were bitter disputes about financial matters.

However misleading Joseph Lancaster's efforts on behalf of the Topo settlers may have been, in January 1827 Sir Robert Ker Porter received instructions from the British Foreign Minister, George Canning, that he was to enquire into the position of the colonists, to treat them as he would distressed seamen or British subjects, and be responsible for their repatriation. It is not unlikely that Joseph Lancaster's representations had something to do with this outcome.

January was a month of great excitement. There was news, at last, that Bolivar was in Venezuela and would be in Caracas shortly. Then rumours that he came not in peace but at war with General Paez. In the city the General's soldiers requisitioned every horse and mule that could be found. 'I never witnessed such Cossack like pillage of stables and horse furniture – that took place today by these plainsmen and their officers', Sir Robert wrote in his diary for January 1st. Two days later proclamations arrived from Bolivar, order was restored and the beasts returned; at least to the British subjects on whose behalf Sir Robert had made a protest.

By January 6th Joseph was in La Guaira to meet Mrs

Robinson and her children, and to see her goods through customs. She bought with her tea, furniture, bedding, books, prints and clothes as well as a piece of the best Irish linen for her future husband.

It was not an auspicious beginning to their new life together. The children were uneasy. Mary Robinson, although she gave little sign of being upset, was already perhaps wondering whether she had made a sensible decision. Owing to the raids of the military there was great difficulty in finding animals to carry the party over the mountain road to Caracas. When they did hire some mules the wretched beasts were so weak and miserable that even the soldiers had not thought them worth commandeering. Half way up the mountain they lay down and refused to move. No amount of urging, pushing, pulling or prodding could make them go on. In despair the travellers had to abandon their transport and, in gathering darkness, grope forward on foot down into the valley of Caracas.

The streets were full of troops. Joseph Lancaster had made arrangements for a separate house for the family, but when they arrived at it entry was refused by a sentry with a fixed bayonet. Not until they had made their way to the main guard house, where the name Lancaster at last evoked a response, was it possible to gain access to their accommodation. Joseph Lancaster, his sense of occasion uppermost, had hired the house formally belonging to the Grand Inquisitor, but it was quite unprepared for the arrival of a bride. For four nights, until Mrs Robinson's goods arrived from La Guaira, the family slept on bare cots without taking off their clothes.

On January 10th Simon Bolivar, General, Liberator and President of Gran Colombia, having issued an amnesty and become publicly reconciled to General Paez, entered Caracas with great ceremony. Windows and balconies were hung with flowers, streets were decorated with triumphal arches of laurel and pine. Slogans and draperies festooned every available space. There was an air of wild reaction after the tension and uncertainty of months. The foreigners resident in the city processed on their recovered horses, carrying their national flags, led by one bearing an allegorical flag of Europe.

'Then came the Municipal and Liberal officers of the city with their mace bearers. The Collegians and padres in their respective costumes, and an infinity of persons of all callings, colours, and political faith and feelings drunk and sober, to crowd, squeeze, and perspire on the glorious entrée about to take place.'

In the midst of all this excitement and rejoicing Joseph Lancaster, riding on a mule, led the procession of his boys, carrying the flags of the nations and the standards of Colombia.

Joseph Lancaster had waited a long time to meet Simon Bolivar, the patron of his dreams. He had had a number of friendly and encouraging letters from him and anticipated that with the arrival of the Liberator all difficulties would be resolved. His expectations were naive; his attitude one of hero worship.

Simon Bolivar and Joseph Lancaster were men of very different calibre, though they had in common a deep rooted desire to set their lifework in an international context. Each had a vision of personal glory, Bolivar's of the Napoleonic splendour accruing to the Liberator of nations; Lancaster's of the acknowledgment of millions of children to him as Father and Founder of their education. For both the moment of greatest triumph had passed.

Simon Bolivar, five years younger than Joseph Lancaster, was physically short, thin, of sallow complexion, with fine black eyes and, when he chose, great tact and charm. He was an aristocrat, a ruthless leader who for the last fifteen years had fought continuous bloody battles to create, by his ferocious will, a physical reality out of his vision of Gran Colombia extending, through the symbol of his person, from Guyana to Bolivia. Generous, brilliant, sophisticated, he was a man of war, hardened in the fires of experiences unimaginable to Joseph Lancaster and political events beyond the latter's understanding.

When in London, in 1810, in reality to attempt to enlist British help for the war in Spanish America, Bolivar, a rich and gay young man in search of interest and entertainment, had been taken to see the phenomenon of the school in the Borough Road. At that moment the Lancastrian System was expanding rapidly; aristocratic patronage was at its height and Joseph Lancaster, barely touched as yet by the creeping shadow of his debts, a man of wide influence, exuberant action and engaging presence. Impossible to tell what impression he made on Bolivar, if indeed apart from the acknowledged merits of his System he made any at all. But after sixteen years neither Bolivar nor Lancaster were the men they had once been.

Nor is it clear how far the Caracas school was successful educationally. The scholars appeared on the streets in good order, adding to the gaiety of carnival and celebration. But Sir Robert never seems to have visited the monastery to see the boys at work, or if he did he left no note of it, and, unlike the Borough Road, no record remains from either outsiders or Lancaster himself of what went on among the chemical instruments, atlases and books that made up the furnishings of the Institution. It cannot indeed have been an easy situation for anyone, with constant threat of disturbance without and the uncertain behaviour of troops within the shared accommodation. Nor was Joseph Lancaster any longer prepared, as in the days of his youth, to give his full time attention to the schooling of his boys.

At first all went well. There were eight days of rejoicing at the return of the Liberator and the bankrupt city indulged in banquets and balls. Joseph drafted a letter, to be signed by four of the settlers, congratulating Bolivar on his arrival and setting out the plight of the Topo colonists. Bolivar replied graciously, promising to do what he could. He contributed five hundred pesos to the Lancaster fund; but it was plain that he had no intention of providing fresh land for the project. He received the whole school and its Master in his salon, making and listening to the speeches that both he and Lancaster so well knew how to present on such occasions, and accepting a gift of books. He even agreed to attend the marriage of Lancaster to Mary Robinson.

The wedding took place on February 23rd 1827, just at the time of Carnival. Its form had exercised Joseph considerably as, being disowned by the Society of Friends, not a Catholic, and on bad terms with the British Consul, he found himself in a limbo, at liberty to devise his own ceremony. Bolivar's presence, as Chief Magistrate, gave legality to what was otherwise a simple exchange of words in front of witnesses.

The company assembled in the salon of the Grand Inquisitor's house. It was close to the monastery and Bolivar consented first to enter the chapel and look at Joseph's library and the instruments he had collected. Then he and his suite, the Intendente, Dr Mendoza recalled from exile, a number of respectable people, though Sir Robert was not among them, the Family and some of the Scottish settlers, collected in the large hall. Joseph Lancaster stood up in front of them and said;

'In the fear of the Lord and in the presence of this assembly, I take this my friend Mary Robinson to be my wife, promising to be unto her through Divine assistance a faithful and loving husband till it please the Lord by death to separate us.'

Mrs Robinson reciprocated. These were the same words that had been used in 1804 when Joseph Lancaster married Elizabeth Bonner.

The contract of marriage, which settled on his wife all the property she had inherited from John Robinson, along with books, manuscripts and furniture, and sundry other things belonging to Joseph Lancaster in the event of the latter's death, was then read out, and signed by a large number of those present, including the Liberator. Cakes and wine were handed round. Bolivar made a speech, addressing Mary Robinson Lancaster by her new name. In his gracefully turned sentences Joseph Lancaster heard approbation for everything that he had done since coming to Caracas. George must have found it all of great interest. For the Lancaster family it was to be the last happy occasion in Venezuela.

Simon Bolivar, anxious for the friendship and support of Britain, made himself easily available to Sir Robert Ker Porter who, however correctly he behaved, would have found it nearly impossible to disguise his contempt for Joseph Lancaster. In any case Simon Bolivar had more to occupy him than an English educationist whose standing with his own countrymen was equivocal. Family matters and political affairs were alike in confusion. In every town there were mutinous Venezuela soldiers. On either hand, personal or public, the Liberator's rule was threatened.

Mary Lancaster, probably from the moment that she had to grope her way over the mountains, disliked Venezuela. Carnival was the last straw. On February 26th Sir Robert wrote of it;

'As this is the disagreeable time when these people fill ambulators with eggs filled with fluid of various sorts and bedaub them sans respect all over, flour, starch, and other powdered annoyances, I shall keep the house until such folly ceases.'

It is not quite clear what happened. Joseph said that stones were thrown through the window when his wife and her daughter were standing watching what was going on in the street, and that a few days later Mrs Lancaster was struck by a youth when out walking. Whether this was deliberate, as he suspected, or over boisterous horse-play it is impossible to say. But, in the unstable mood of the country, there may have been grounds for Joseph's contention that Bolivar's favour had aroused the jealousy of the church.

That was not all. One day, while riding past a file of soldiers, Mary Lancaster was hit by a musket. In the confusion of her agitation the soldiers were gone before it could be ascertained what had actually occurred. But both she and her husband began to fear that they were being deliberately intimidated, and when, on leaving a social gathering, she was doused with water, almost certainly as part of the the carnival high jinks, she came to the conclusion that this was no place for an English mother to bring up her children. George had got into bad company in Philadelphia, she probably saw infinitely more horrendous ways in which he could be laid astray in Caracas.

Whether with justification or not, Joseph Lancaster too had begun to feel that his person, if not his life, was endangered. It is not easy to see why the situation, which on February 23rd was so full of promise should by March 5th have become so soured that Joseph Lancaster asked for passports to leave. Sir Robert says that he struck a lady who threw water on him during carnival and that this incident took place in the house of General Escalona. Such a breach of etiquette, especially by one of humbler birth, would not be forgiven. Joseph does not mention a blow, though the occasion was probably the same as the one he recorded; but he had never written or spoken of acts of physical violence in which he had been said to be involved. It does not seem unlikely that his temper was roused by what he felt to be a discourtesy to his newly married wife and, carried away in the hysteria of the moment, hit out in her defence.

If he had expected support from Bolivar he had gravely misread the Liberator's character. If Lancaster became a liability, Bolivar would be without pity. There would be no question of one whose ambition encompassed half the South American world stooping to champion a naive school master. Almost without realising it Joseph Lancaster had stepped into a world whose ways were alien and whose customs beyond his comprehension. With the arrival of Bolivar in Caracas, a city where when he had been absent many had been disloyal, the tempo of the times had changed; excitement and violence, fear and threats, ran very near the surface.

Perhaps there was disillusion on both sides. Joseph Lancaster was no Simon Rodriguez, the wandering scholar-gypsy of wide-ranging intellect and radical imagination whose image time may have superimposed on the plump Quaker from Southwark. Simon Bolivar had asked Sir Robert if this were indeed the famous Lancaster.

Whatever the truth there is no doubt that Joseph Lancaster felt himself threatened with physical harm. Passports were granted to him and his family, an act which immediately roused a swarm of hostile creditors. Bolivar had called for a strict review of the financial situation in Caracas, where incompetence and corruption held sway, and suspended payment of the vales, the Government promissory notes on different Customs houses, many of which had not been honoured for four years. There was speculation on a grand scale in these official pieces of paper. Lancaster was told that before he could leave he must account for the expenditure of the twenty thousand pesos and his passport was withdrawn.

Though Joseph had never received a peso of the twenty thousand, he had borrowed heavily from local merchants against the promise of the draft. His financial dealings with Colonel Stopford, who was himself deeply embroiled in debt, were intricately entangled. Lancaster had ordered goods with abandon from Britain and America; though many of the parcels of books that arrived were from friends who knew only too well that they had little alternative to making the contents a gift. The fonts for the printing press seem to have been paid for by Captain Ryan. No doubt the very mention of financial statements produced a panic reaction in Joseph Lancaster, bringing up memories of past disgrace. He replied haughtily that his time was too valuable to be wasted in attending to such details. In the circumstances it was not a tactful claim to make. The bitterness with which he looked back on this difficult moment must have been enhanced by the fact that he felt impelled to seek the help and protection of Sir Robert Ker Porter, the British Consul.

Sir Robert asserted that he would not return evil for evil, and was sufficiently just to admit that the money collected for the Topo settlers, though in his view misspent, had not been squandered by Lancaster for his own use. A balance sheet, which must have been worthless, was made out and, probably owing to the good offices of the Consul, Joseph's passport was returned and, according to Joseph, a formal requisition, against the debt, made on all the property in the schoolroom; a circumstance which was to result in accusation and counter-accusation for years to come.

On April 18th, as soon as the sun was up, Joseph Lancaster alone and in disguise, made his way out of Caracas. Official accounts may have been settled, but his private creditors were still unsatisfied. He took with him 'two books, a second coat and some linen', as well as three hundred and fifty dollars. He still had some friends and was concealed for two weeks in the countryside near La Guaira until, with the connivance of the Captain, he was smuggled aboard a packet for St Thomas in the Virgin Islands. He then crossed over to the island of St Croix, where he stayed for a while with friends and obtained fresh introductions to potential backers in America. In the beginning of June he stepped off the brig 'Shepherdess' at New Haven.

The situation of Mary Lancaster, left behind with her family in a strange country, afraid for lives and property, can be imagined. She had with her two young men, one of who was the Dane, Vigo Wadskiar, with whom she did not get on, and Joseph's servant Thomas. All the money in her possession amounted to fifteen dollars. She, in turn, applied for passports. At first the request was refused, but eventually, perhaps because some arrangement seems to have been come to with regard to the furniture, she was given permission to leave. She took with her one bedstead and bedding, some books and the printing press with its type. At this crisis a number of the Scots from Topo, who were in no doubt what they owed to her husband, came to the rescue. Three weeks after her husband had departed the settlers conveyed Mrs Lancaster and her children over the mountains to La Guaira. For this service they refused any kind of remuneration, and when they left her they sent a message to Joseph Lancaster;

'Tell our father that we hope yet to see him again before we die.'

A month later, under arrangements made by Sir Robert Ker Porter, the first contingent of the colonists left for Guelph in Upper Canada, where they eventually made a good life for themselves.

Mr Sprotto, a Hamburg merchant, gave Mrs Lancaster a hundred dollars, while the Customs seized her last remaining goods. Virtually penniless, thanks to the kindness of yet another sea captain, she and her children Mary, George and John, at last got passages for Philadelphia free of charge. The pattern for much of her married life was set.

In July Simon Bolivar left Caracas for Carthagena. He had only three years to live and was never to see Venezuela again.

'Faith and Knowledge'

Chapter 14
TWILIGHT

'Time is the only commodity I can use enough of. School is my element: the society of children my delight, and therefore I do all (1) do among them in a spirit that makes labour an enjoyment and industry a pleasure'. (Joseph Lancaster to Roberts Vaux)

The manner of Joseph Lancaster's departure from Caracas, and in particular the dissension over the draft from Bolivar and the seizure of most of his own and some of his wife's property, was to remain for years a matter of bitter resentment. Once again Lancaster felt betrayed. It was true that not all was lost. On June 20th 1827 a La Guaira merchant, John Harwood, sent forty-seven packages of Mrs Lancaster's goods by the 'Eliza Pigot' from Caracas to Robert Ralston's warehouse in Philadelphia. They duly arrived and were signed in. These boxes probably contained books, pictures, engravings and perhaps the printing press and type. At the same time John Harwood reported that he had sold a chest of drawers for twenty-two and a half dollars, which money was used to ship Vigo Wadskiar's trunk to St Thomas, where the latter stayed for six months before moving on to Cuba and eventually back to Caracas in about 1830. Whether any of Joseph Lancaster's 'philosophical instruments', globe and considerable library were returned is doubtful. Indeed Robert Hill, a kindly Scot and a provision merchant, whom Sir Robert Ker Porter called a 'notion monger', wrote in July that furniture and books had been auctioned, the 'electrifying instruments etc' to Mr Sprotto, the Hamburg merchant who had helped Mary Lancaster. The common law of Spain, under which the Lancasters had been married, reserved a wife's separate right to her own property, as also did the declaration which Joseph himself had drawn up on that occasion for both to sign. With some sophistry Joseph Lancaster argued that this marriage settlement assigned to Mary Lancaster all his own assets and property, "todas cosas", "all things" connected with or pertaining to education then belonging to Joseph Lancaster in Caracas.

Loss of possessions rankled; but over the accusation of misuses of money he felt again the gall of treachery. Joseph Lancaster had no hesitation in publicly accusing Simon Bolivar of dishonourable conduct. In 1829, when once more Lancaster was in desperate circumstances, he tried to get an appeal for funds printed in New York papers, which referred to his treatment by Colombian savages. The 'Evening Post' and the 'Morning Courier' were among those who accepted it; the New York 'Journal of Commerce' refused. Some months later the latter carried an anti-Lancaster article from a Caracas news sheet, which Joseph answered at length in yet another of his supposedly educational, but in reality self-justifying, publications, 'The True Friend', August 1829, four copies for one dollar, letters addressed to Joseph Lancaster to be post paid.

The article asserted that Lancaster had received payment for Bolivar's draft and used the money to cancel his debts before he left Venezuela. Joseph replied by reprinting the letter from Bolivar of March 1825 which offered the gift of twenty thousand pesos to be paid by the agents of Peru in London. He also pointed out the poverty of the Lancaster family in their last days and alleged that he had to approach Bolivar for passage money. That he never received financial reimbursement for the draft is certain, though he borrowed in South America on the strength of it. As though also conscious that honour had not been satisfied, when Bolivar died in 1830 his will directed that the twenty thousand be paid from his private resources out of the sale of the Aroa silver mines to a British syndicate. Of this money too Joseph Lancaster never saw a peso, though others, Vigo Wadskiar among them, tried to sue Bolivar's heirs for salaries and other debts unpaid.

The second accusation put forward by the New York 'Journal' was that Lancaster had neither established an Institution in Caracas, nor left a successor. On this Joseph was more vulnerable. His answer was that he had educated dozens of scholars and a young Danish professor. But Vigo left shortly after Lancaster himself, and there seems never to have been the emphasis on teacher training that was so important a part of other Lancastrian establishments. It would also be true to say that social conditions in Venezuela, and in Caracas itself, during those years, were hardly conducive to the spread of non-sectarian schools. Lancastrian methods may have survived in South America, but less because Joseph Lancaster himself taught there than because news of his educational discovery was disseminated like wildfire through the world when he was in his heyday and still working in London.

However, loyal friends remained. Robert Hill had written woundingly from Caracas, 'Your departure seemed to create emotion amongst none excepting those you owed,' but when Joseph Lancaster stepped off the brig 'Shepherdess' at New Haven John Lovell, the devoted disciple, was there to welcome him.

To greet his old Master, and secure an invitation from the New Haven School Committee for him to pay a formal visit to the institution which Lovell had so patiently built up in he image of that other Institution in the Borough Road, was the highlight of John Lovell's life. And whatever the traumas of the departure from Caracas, Joseph Lancaster did not disappoint him. For him too the pleasure of being once more in a well ordered school, run on his System by a young man whom he had trained, overrode all other feelings. At least for John Lovell he left behind an 'unforgettable impression'. He had also given John a strong feeling that in Joseph Lancaster's private life he was happy. Though curiously he seems never to have spoken of her by name, John Lovell knew that his Master had found himself a beloved wife and, being a young man of great sensitivity, he rejoiced in this.

Mary Robinson Lancaster, in spite of a difficult and stormy start to her second marriage, seems to have willingly accepted that it was her lot to provide an anchor for this wayward man, and to have shared with Betsy the view that he was not sufficiently appreciated by his own nation or the world. The one comfort John Lovell could not provide was money; 'money slips through my hands like water through a sieve – And you do not appear destined to make a fortune'. So when at the beginning of July Joseph Lancaster arrived back in Philadelphia, Mrs Lancaster, who had managed to collect a thirty-five dollar debt of her own since returning, had to pay the fare of the coach which brought him.

Almost immediately, driven as much by his own passion and optimism as by the urgent need to make a living, he was off again on a lecture tour. Both Robert Ralston and Roberts Vaux proved to be practical, as well as faithful, benefactors. The two men had seen Lancaster through ten years of varying fortunes, and Roberts Vaux had been closely concerned with him in the Philadelphia schools. For them his gifts as a man to whom education mattered transcended all his worldly incompetence and his foolish financial disingenurousness. Robert Ralston supported the family generously: Roberts Vaux never refused a request for assistance, he subscribed to Joseph Lancaster's magazines and helped to sell them, and he did what he could to provide contacts and arrange lectures.

Where others had fallen away, de Witt Clinton too remained staunch, and his intelligent and informed interest gave Lancaster a correspondent to whom, as he travelled round, he could propound his educational observations at length. It was a grievous loss to the community that the System should be taught by unqualified teachers. 'They come forth into the world as chickens hatched by artificial heat in the Egyptian ovens – alive and limping to be sure, but limping sadly at best, some wanting one leg and some one wing – from the unnatural manner of hatching . . .' He saw the need of a seminary for village teachers, so that well qualified masters would attract the offspring of the rich as pupils, and so make their fees cover the deficiency of other funds. In his own case this policy, which he was to put into practice later, proved disastrous, for affluent parents objected to having their children educated beside those from poor families whom Lancaster took in free. He would not compromise on the poor, so the rich withdrew their young people and left the school without sufficient financial support.

The importance of the character of the teacher was constantly stressed by Lancaster. Sometimes it came near to outweighing a lack of training. Of the school at Troy, in New York State, he wrote;

'The master is a kind of half qualified tender spirited and very respectable young man. He will make his pupils love him – perhaps he may be deficient in firmness of character but he really is that kind of young man whom I should delight to instruct and finish in his profession'.

Though he could be critical, where praise was due he was generous and admiring.

'There are many of the teachers in the New York schools who have a fine native character . . .'.

He wrote de Witt Clinton,

'The children too are a fine race of children – while I was in a school addressing them – whilst I was talking with my tongue, they were talking to me with their eyes – They looked at me and my words as if they were hungry to eat every one, and this occurred with little children of 4 and 5 years of age as well as the elder ones . . .'

The Lancastrian System, which was soon to harden into a mechanical device and fall into disrepute, was not in its Founder's eyes a method of education lacking in the potential for development. He had himself organised a school of hundreds with the active assistance of his pupils, at a period when trained school teachers were non-existent. But even then he had not seen the master as solely administrator, but as the vital source and essential exponent of all the knowledge that flowed through the veins of the school. Thirty years later, thanks in large measure to Lancaster himself, teachers were being qualified in increasing numbers. Joseph Lancaster saw this as a reinforcement to the System of major importance – but not one that abrogated the pupil's contribution. It was his genius to perceive that while teachers must be as well qualified as possible to teach, the energies of boys and girls should at the same time be harnessed to helping other boys and girls to learn.

Though it was hoped that lectures would bring some immediate ready money, the real object of this tour through the States of New Jersey and New York was to find a suitable place where Joseph Lancaster could settle with his family and open a school. Running a school was the only trade he knew, and school keeping was for Joseph Lancaster the heart and soul of his reason for existing.

It was not a particularly successful search. He was forty-nine years old and the era of Lancastrian excitement was passing. Ten years before many of the towns up the Hudson river had heard him talk when he came this way with Betsy shortly after landing in the United States. Times had moved on. In many places the interest in him was minimal and there was a marked reluctance to pay for the pleasure of listening to him. It was the fall, and both the heat and the harvest provided excuses for poor audiences. When he gave religious lectures the weather was always fine; when pay lectures always stormy. Still, his confidence in God remained unshaken. Nor was it easy to find a town where the local school board would welcome the arrival of such a well known intruder, or where essential financial support for any new educational venture would be forthcoming from the legislature. Joseph, furnished with a wife and a new daughter thought of a boarding school for the children of tradesmen and the daughters of merchants and farmers, who would be 'content without music dancing and the petite but useless accomplishments of fashionable life.'

He travelled up the Hudson to Newburgh, Catskill, Athens, Hudson itself; on to Albany, where he hoped to see de Witt Clinton, and Troy, along the line of Clinton's new canal to Utica and as far as Rochester. Then back down the river again to New York, and on the road to Philadelphia by way of New Brunswick and Trenton. It must have been a depressing journey, as one after the other his hopes were dashed, so that he began to speak of trying Canada where the Governor General, the Earl of Dalhousie, had been one of his London subscribers or indeed to return to England. He was severely ill in Utica and was left weak from dysentry. In Newburgh, on the return journey by steamboat, his baggage was left ashore by accident and he had to retrace his steps for twenty miles to find it.

But everywhere he wrote hopefully to his 'Beloved Wife', waiting quietly in Philadelphia, ready to join him the moment he indicated that his search had been successful. In all the years of marriage to Elizabeth Joseph had never addressed her by such an uxorious title. As he had to Betsy, so to Mary he reported his financial takings and what he spent the money on; as with Betsy, so he constantly overestimated future possibilities, and was then forced to apologise for his lack of ability to remit any money. Meanwhile, in an emergency, Robert Ralston would keep the wolf from the door.

There may not have been cash in any of the letters, but there was certainly affection. Not only to Mary Lancaster 'the wife of my bosom, the mother of our children, the dearest earthly friend of my soul', did Joseph Lancaster send the love of his heart; without reservations he sent it to her children too. Particularly to the naughty George.

'Tell him,' he wrote from Newburgh, 'Joseph Lancaster wants to hear that he's been a good boy . . . thou may tell him that I love him very dearly and thou may give him a basket full of kisses for me. PS . . . Tell George he has had his good wish for me "a pleasant journey" really with all his naughtiness he has a fine kind heart.'

And from New Brunswick;

'PS Tell George he's seen the Chief Justice and if George isn't careful of his behaviour he'll be carted out and whipped in the market by the constable.'

He hoped his precious Frances (Mary junior) was being very industrious against his return and sent 'unspeakable love', to Mrs Lancaster herself.

Then, on September 21st 1827, when he had been away nearly ten weeks, there was good news from Trenton, New Jersey.

In Trenton, quite near the State House, an old cotton mill was to let. It was small, but in good condition with four rooms, one of which had been a printing office. Adjoining it was a six room family house with a garden. The rent for the mill was sixty dollars a year, for the house eighty to one hundred dollars. Joseph Lancaster began instantly to make plans. He could have a day school and printing office, as well as a seminary for school masters. Once again he could 'take his proper rank as head of the system which is now usurped by a whole tribe of jackasses'. All that was needed was a loan of five hundred dollars and he had little doubt that this could be managed. It all seemed providential. There was no Lancastrian school in the town and existing educational establishments were inferior. The people were friendly and someone high up in the legislature had recommended the place.

By September 25th a handbill was being printed in Trenton, proclaiming that the Lancastrian school, near the State House, was ready to receive scholars. Mrs Lancaster came the thirty odd miles to look over the prospects, and Joseph was on the way back to Philadelphia to prepare for the move and to ask for assistance from Roberts Vaux. The steamboat passage cost about two dollars each. Robert Ralston had already given Mrs Lancaster an extra thirty dollars.

On October 4th, a Thursday, the whole family left by river for their new home. On November 1st the school opened in the cotton mill. About thirty children had paid three dollars a quarter in advance. The State Legislature promised a grant of twenty-two dollars a month for the education of seventy poor children, and a contract was entered into with the township's Committee of Public Schools. Joseph Lancaster was to look after the boys, Mrs Lancaster the girls.

On the 5th of November the House of Assembly of the State of New Jersey indicated that they would, collectively, be pleased to attend a lecture by Mr Lancaster.

It is hard to know what exactly went wrong in Trenton. In the beginning all the signs were propitious. The intake of pupils increased rapidly to between two or three hundred. Difficulties, however, were not long in surfacing. Fee paying parents objected to their offspring being taught in the same room as the children of the poor. They demanded separate accommodation. In the circumstances, with the school's finances balanced on a knife edge, this was not possible. The wealthy withdrew their sons and daughters, perhaps they also asked for their money back. The Committee of Public Schools agreed that Lancaster should fill their places with the poor. Joseph sent out a message for young brothers and sisters to come into school with siblings already there. They came, but the legislature refused to increase its grant, and the income both of the institution and of the Lancaster family was drastically reduced.

It was an ominous situation. Once again debts began to accumulate. The five hundred dollar loan that Joseph had so glibly anticipated never materialised. But Joseph Lancaster does not seem to have given this new venture any opportunity to succeed before deciding that it was a failure. Within a matter of weeks he was in New York, leaving Mary Lancaster once again to hold a crumbling fort. Was it the contract and the careful calculation of the legislature with their grant that roused his old antipathy to subordination? Yet he needed official support and had himself sought it. Though his affection for children was real, had he lost the ability to sustain the daily discipline of the schoolroom? There were enemies to whisper that this was so. Or did he, for once, when the fee paying pupils were withdrawn, see clearly before him the drearily familiar round of debt, disaster, perhaps disgrace, and lose his nerve?

The family was in desperate straits. In the autumn of 1827 they were all prostrated by fever, which left them weak and debilitated. Joseph departed to make a public appeal to the citizens of New York. He raised about four hundred dollars, to which the Corporation immediately added a grant of another five hundred dollars. Not content with this Joseph Lancaster was writing in February 1828 to the new Governor of New York State, Martin Van Buren, seeking for an independent foundation of at least one thousand dollars to be set up by the State legislature to enable him to provide for his old age and his children's education, and to settle on a small farm in the State of New York. De Witt Clinton had died on the 11th of February and his passing must have been a severe blow.

In spite of the generous donations to Joseph of nine hundred dollars, in Trenton Mary Lancaster was facing a situation fraught with calamity. She was in poor health, beseiged by creditors, and confronted by unpleasant innuendoes that her husband had absconded to escape his obligations.

In May there was a suggestion that Mr and Mrs Lancaster might be offered the charge of a new public school to be opened in New York. The friend who wrote of it hinted that Lancaster was now considered old fashioned as a teacher, but urged him to approach the school director. Nothing came of this kindly thought.

In July the Trenton school was finally given up, but Mary Lancaster stayed in the township until November, held there by the contract which the school committee refused to dissolve, and by her inability to pay accumulated debts. Not surprisingly both her nervous and her physical health were badly undermined.

Joseph meanwhile had travelled to Quebec in Lower Canada, lecturing, visiting schools and viewing the prospects, having conceived the idea that the climate of America was no longer one in which any of them could survive. By the beginning of October he was back in New York and had published another appeal in the New York 'Morning Courier' and the 'Evening Post', setting out the disastrous state of his family affairs and his own merits as the founder of a System which had profoundly benefitted education in New York. Once again the response was astonishingly generous. Thomas Ewbank wrote the very next day enclosing one hundred and ten dollars and offering part of his house rent free. The children of one of the New York Public Schools collected $12½ towards the fund. The money poured in. Joseph sent his wife $326, with instructions to pay the bills in her own name, and to get the receipts similarly. He was staying with friends, as indeed he had been most of that year, but hoped to find a little house for her and the children. She was to come at the beginning of next week. 'Cheer up my beloved darling we have cut the devils chain.'

Alas it was not so. To add to her misery the school at Trenton was broken into one night by a man and several boys who said they were trying to retrieve their own property. Mary Lancaster rose from her bed, crossed to the school building and called on them to come out. They defied her. She sent for help from the neighbours and Charles Ewing, Chief Justice of the Supreme Court, arrived and threatened the intruders with the law. He was a man of eminence in Trenton, and was very helpful to Mary Lancaster. As nothing was taken, and a prosecution would have cost money, there was no follow-up to this incident, but it shocked an already overwrought Mrs Lancaster and added fuel to Joseph's sense of persecution. Attacks on him were appearing in the Trenton papers.

By October 25th Mary Lancaster had still not left Trenton. All the bills were not yet settled, and she was finding the packing up of their property almost beyond her strength. Joseph continued to remit sums of money by every post, but a lobby against him had begun to form in New York and subscriptions were falling off. John Lovell went round his friends and scraped together ten dollars, which he enclosed with a letter saying, 'To me you are still Joseph Lancaster'. In this hour of trial he loved him.

Joseph was deeply unhappy. He remained optimistic about his ability to raise more money, but already was reduced again to borrowing ten dollars here, ten dollars there. It slipped through his fingers like water. On October 28th he wrote to Mary that she should come, even if all the bills were not paid. He did not see that it mattered, now that she had got the goods away. And it would be cheaper for her to take a private carriage to New Brunswick than to bring the family by stage coach.

On November 1st, exhausted and ill, she and the family arrived at last in New York. She had had a gruelling experience, and must often have had a fellow feeling for her predecessor, Elizabeth. But Mary Robinson Lancaster was made of sterner stuff. Like Betsy she believed that Joseph Lancaster was a great man. He abjured her never to throw away any of his papers. In spite of immense provocation she never did. She kept every letter he wrote her for posterity. At this time she made Joseph Lancaster very happy. Looking back often on his time in South America he wrote bitterly to friends in England of loss of money and property, and betrayal of trust; but he always added a rider. In Caracas he had found supreme domestic happiness, which had changed his life. He openly admitted his dependence on her; 'We are dunces in the world's policy – both of us – but I (happily) the greatest'.

In Mexico, meantime, Betsy was frantic. From the autumn of 1826, when he became involved with the Topo settlers, until January 1829, when the Trenton affair was finally over, Joseph did not write to his daughter. Or if he did the letters never arrived. In March 1827, and again in June and September, Betsy wrote in great anxiety at this silence. By September she had seen in the American papers that Joseph was back in the United States, and was urging him to think of his own comfort and return to England. Now that the Catholic question was about to be settled she felt that the climate was favourable to all that he had tried to do in Ireland. She and her husband were still going through a difficult time as the ebb and flow of political affairs in Mexico affected their own fortunes. Though truly concerned for her father, she did not hesitate to press him once again to use his influence to get Richard a vice-consulship. Richard, writing in October, repeated this request, adding, 'I do not know if you are rich or poor – but I have my fears as usual'. This did not stop him from asking for the present of a lady's saddle for Betsy, as he had heard they were cheap in the States. By August 1828 Betsy had still not heard from her father and thought herself almost forgotten. She had just discovered from a Baltimore friend that he was in Trenton and also that he was married to a lady from Philadelphia. She did not know what to think. She had sometimes thought he was dead. His small grandson, Joseph Lancaster Jones, spoke no English, only Spanish.

It was to be January 1829 before Joseph answered her. Perhaps, as well as being a reflection of his marital happiness, this long silence between himself and his beloved daughter indicated the depths to which, in his own heart, Joseph Lancaster felt himself to have sunk. For those less close to him he could still summon up optimistic hopes; to Betsy, who knew him intimately, he feared to reveal the collapse of many cherished plans. It was probably also true that Mary Robinson Lancaster had begun to fill Betsy's place as supporter and comforter quite early in the marriage. Certainly it is surprising to find, in a long letter to their old friend Lucy Edmunds in Southwark, also written in January 1829, that Joseph makes no mention at all of his daughter or her family.

To Betsy, however, he was full of assurances that no other lady would supplant her in his heart or alter his feelings towards her. He described his new wife and the happiness she had brought him, and the step brothers and sister whom Betsy had acquired, but once again, as with John Lovell, he made no mention of his wife's name. This mystery was to worry Betsy for the next five years. Even more curiously, she was to write in 1834 'Who is Mary Robinson?' – as though the name meant nothing to her and the dark days in Philadelphia had been blotted out. John Lovell himself had married in December 1828. He made no such mistake when reporting this important step to his Old Master. His wife was called Henrietta. She was young, amiable, intelligent and handsome, and John felt that he had very satisfactorily taken his friend's often repeated advice. Joseph, passing on the news to Betsy, made an ironic comment of John Lovell. 'He is still as poor a spendthrift as ever.'

The early months of 1829 were not easy for the Lancaster family. Though her father wrote bravely to Betsy that he was very glad to be in a city with access to literary institutes and publications, Joseph Lancaster's future was filled with uncertainty. He was fifty with greying hair and he had lost nearly all his teeth. His constant search for money, by public appeal, subscription list for pamphlet or book, or private begging letter brought in a trickle of dollars which very soon ran out into the expanding sea of debts and expenses. He wrote to General Andrew Jackson, President of the United States. No record of any reply exists. He wrote to the British Ambassador asking for free cabin passages for himself and his family to England. The request was refused, but the Ambassador sent a liberal donation. Joseph then tried the French Ambassador, on the strength of an acquaintance with his predecessor Hyde de Neuville and membership of the Lancastrian Society in Paris, to seek pecuniary aid to take himself and his ailing wife to a more temperate climate. The response was probably another small donation. Everybody he knew, or whose name was known, received a note explaining the Lancaster contribution to the world of education, retelling the financial iniquities of the Colombian disaster and asking for assistance towards a serene old age. Very many found it in their hearts and their purses to respond. John Lovell compiled an article for the press and did his best to gather a small sum from his own friends.

But Joseph himself did not know where he was going. He spoke of a serene old age, but it was not possible for him to give up active involvement in the cause of education. He wrote to Lucy Edmunds of new inventions that would put him back in the forefront of scholastic reform; but nobody now wanted him and his inventions were peripheral to his original creation, the System. To Betsy he spoke of a small farm and seminary on the banks of the Hudson north of New York, but Canada was also in his mind. He sighed even for an American Andrew Bell, remembering the great debates which had stirred England to an awareness of the importance of schools for the poor. He thought of a possible return to his native land.

To some of those whom he had looked on as enemies his attitude had softened. Correspondence had been renewed with others. With William Corston the old friendship was revived. Joseph had heard with concern, and no doubt with a particular sympathy, of the bankruptcy of Joseph Fry and sent his loving regard to Elizabeth who had been kind to him in his early days. He now accepted that there had been many excuses for Joseph Fox and Samuel Whitbread, of whom he had once written with venom on his pen. Illness had overset the minds of both, and the former had suffered also from the death of his wife. Even with John Pickton, who had contacted his old master, he looked to a future reconciliation. Only William Allen, to whom he had gone as a saviour and whose careful accounting had eventually brought down his house about his head, he could not forgive.

His brothers were all dead, and his sister Mary had passed away in the workhouse. Sarah, still alive and in poverty, was the last of his family. Towards her Joseph felt the guilt of a brother who had failed in his fraternal duty. When his new inventions came to fruition, he assured Lucy Edmunds, he would help her with money.

The world that Joseph Lancaster knew was changing. Pestalozzi was dead. Andrew Bell was close to a stroke which would leave him speechless and lead, two years later, to a tomb in Westminster Abbey. The National Society and the British and Foreign School Society in the United Kingdom were both well established and, in 1833, would receive the first Parliamentary grant to be given for education in Britain to be shared between them. Henry Brougham, Lord Chancellor of England, had gone over to the enemy and now advocated parochial schools. Appealed to for help by Joseph Lancaster in 1831, he refused with disdain. Young men looked forward critically to fresh endeavour: for the moment Joseph Lancaster looked back to what had now become the old ways. Some men have talents that change their times; for others the times extend their talents. The former move with the times they have created, the latter remain behind with the moment of history now discarded. Such was Joseph Lancaster.

Nostalgic he might be; he was not yet defeated. In July the New York 'Journal of Commerce' printed an attack on him, to which Joseph Lancaster replied with 'The True Friend'. Though Roberts Vaux did his best to circulate it, John Lovell was unhappy with the shape of this answer and what was intended to be a journal of educational matters never saw more than one issue. About the same time the decision was taken to remove the whole family to Canada. They were all still in poor health and feared another winter in the extreme American climate. The possibility of a return to England lurked in the background. In August 1829 they left New York for Albany. Here Mrs Lancaster and her youngest son, Don Juan la Grande to his step father, fell seriously ill and for a while the lives of both were in danger. They recovered, however, and in October 1829, in Montreal, Joseph Lancaster hired a small house and once again started a school.

The Lancastrian System was already well known in Canada. In Halifax, Nova Scotia, a Lancastrian school had been established in 1815, with a legislative grant of £200, and was so well thought of that even respectable families sent their children to it. The monitorial school in St John, New Brunswick, actually a National school, had been opened in 1818, and was patronised by the offspring of the provincial Governor. By 1824 there were thirty-nine National schools in the province of New Brunswick alone.

In 1814 the Reverend Thaddeus Osgood, a minister of liberal views, had gone to England excited about the Lancastrian System. He returned with enough funds to open the Quebec Free School with two hundred and fifty boys. Four years later a National school was also started in that city. In Canada, unlike the United States, the old sectarian rivalry straddled the Atlantic.

A National Free School opened in Montreal in 1819 – and in 1822 a British and Canadian School Society set up a school on the Lancastrian plan. In the same year a Roman Catholic Lancastrian school was founded in Quebec by the Education Society of that city. Monitorial schools of all persuasions were assisted by government grants.

Joseph Lancaster was to be four years based in Canada, Mary Lancaster much longer. The Governor General, Sir James Kempt, an ex-Peninsula officer, had served at the battle of Waterloo and Joseph left at once for Quebec to see him. He was gratified to be granted an immediate appointment, and even more so when Sir James agreed to order all Mrs Lancaster's baggage to be admitted duty free. Joseph was elated. Sir James had approved his plans and extended his patronage, had even given a £10 subscription to a new 'Journal of Education' still in the planning stage. There was hope of a government grant.

Sir James was coming to Montreal in four weeks time, Joseph wrote to Mary Lancaster, so they must make haste to acquire a home and get all in order. He wanted to institute a series of demonstrations using Don Juan la Grande as a little guinea pig.

Once again the future looked rosy. Mary Lancaster set up an exhibition of the prints she had inherited from her husband, and saved from Caracas, and sold four or five hundred dollars worth. Joseph, when he returned, borrowed '8 ignorant boys', from five to eight years old, from the Montreal British and Canadian School Society in order to show, by a kind of instant cramming, that he was genuinely the master of his craft.

Success might have lain within his grasp. The name of Lancaster and the prestige attached to it were still notably in his favour. Government made him a grant of £200; men of eminence and weight were prepared to interest themselves in him. Louis Joseph Papineau, Speaker of the House of Assembly, gave his support. A number of donations flowed in. But, though with considerable bombast Joseph publicised his school and announced that he brought new and astonishing inventions in the teaching of rapid reading and other pedagogical tricks, the hard fact was that he had no fresh ideas to distinguish his establishment from the recognised and respected Lancastrian schools already in the city. Indeed it is to be doubted whether he had any longer the commitment and the patience to seek solid results when teaching ignorant little boys as had once been the case when the school was the centre of his life and the entire focus of his attention.

He felt himself to be growing old; he was in his fifties and many of those who had been close to him were dead. Though he had made the name of Lancaster famous, the shades of personal obscurity were closing round him. He had collected vast sums of money for the purpose that ruled his life, but his family still struggled on the verge of poverty. Mary Lancaster may have become restive and concerned for her children's future. Often seemingly careless of their interests, Joseph Lancaster had always possessed a lively sense of familial duty. Good propaganda to ring the hearts of potential donors, he nevertheless relied on potential donors to save the family whom he loved. In 1830/31 he took up his pen to write to Henry Brougham, now Baron Brougham and Vaux, Lord Chancellor of England, founder of the new London University. Reminding him of Joseph Lancaster's just claims to be a national benefactor and explaining the reasons for his arrival in Montreal and the hope of once again being responsible for a resounding educational success, Lancaster then asked for a liberal grant of land in Canada, without fees.

Making some research into the business of land grants, Joseph had been told that the office fees sometimes exceeded the fee simple of the land. He had gone further and was able to pinpoint the land which might be suitable. On the other side of the St Lawrence from Montreal, at a place called La Prairie, were three thousand acres of common land belonging to the Crown. It had originally been given to the Jesuits for the purpose of education. Joseph Lancaster asked for one hundred acres to live on and start a seminary.

He enclosed a petition to the King, now William IV, for Brougham to pass on, and a flattering request for the gift of all the latter's printed speeches on the subject of education since the year 1812. No reply ever came from Henry Brougham.

Numbers in the new school never rose beyond fifty to sixty. Already in the summer of 1830, six months after the auspicious start in Canada, Joseph Lancaster was back in New York on a visit, clearly seeking for yet another fresh opening, and for news from England; and this although, as he himself admitted, his new monitors were too inexperienced to run the school properly.

Betsy had three sons now. John Lovell and Henrietta had produced Joseph Lancaster Lovell. The correspondence with Lovell continued, full of hints of success and happiness on Joseph's side, affection and gentle admonition on John's. But things were not going well. The printing press, which occupied half the house, was busy turning out fresh ventures in pamphlets, broadsheets, school lessons, many of which almost certainly had an adverse effect on the Lancaster reputation and failed to bring in any money. As always, when need other than his own obtruded itself, Joseph Lancaster began to take in free pupils and lose paying ones, and to hurry about the town helping with the claims of impoverished immigrants. Then in 1832 cholera struck.

For four months Montreal was in the grip of this plague. Lancaster's school had to close down. He and his family, however, did not leave the stricken city. Joseph turned his talent for eliciting subscriptions to the assistance of the victims and worked day and night to help where he could. When the epidemic subsided and life returned to normal, the Lancaster livelihood had once again melted away.

Things were going badly. The school was given up and Mrs Lancaster and the children moved to a cottage near La Prairie but without any land attached. Joseph Lancaster went to Quebec to try, unsuccessfully, to raise fresh support, and then to America. He was in desperate straits and news of his condition had filtered back to England. There some of his old friends decided to attempt to set up a subscription list to provide him with an annuity. An appeal was printed in the 'Morning Herald' and did not go unheeded. Among others the Duke of Bedford, Joseph Fletcher, Joseph Foster and Luke Howard subscribed. William Allen gave ten guineas. It was 1833 and the British and

Foreign School Society had just received half of the first Parliamentary grant ever given for education.

In New York Joseph Lancaster was writing furiously the 'Epitome of the Chief Events and Transactions of my own Life', which he hoped to sell at a dollar a copy, payable in advance, to three thousand subscribers. It was to be published in New Haven, with the help of the faithful John Lovell. In Ireland Maurice Cross appealed for his old master in the Belfast Press.

John Lovell had issued a warm invitation to Joseph Lancaster to stay with him. He wrote that he and his wife were entirely content and very comfortable in a neat little cottage. For a period Lovell had moved to Mount Pleasant School in Amherst, as Instructor in Elocution. It had been a two year engagement, but before the contract was up he was asked to return as Principal to New Haven, where the school had declined in his absence. In December 1833 he welcomed Joseph Lancaster to New Haven with undimmed friendship and admiration. Destitute and diminished in the eyes of the world, in John Lovell's eyes his old Master was still the man he had always been.

This visit to New Haven, to the school where his fomer pupil was an honoured and successful Master, moved Joseph Lancaster inexpressibly. He saw before him living proof that the claims he had so often made were true. He had indeed enabled many, perhaps millions, of children to read and write and through education opened to them a world of knowledge and opportunity. The bombast, the flourish of arrogance, the self-pity, fell away from him as he entered the schoolroom and he was, for some moments, speechless. A man who could cry, no doubt his eyes were full of tears. The scholars had collected thirty-seven dollars and a twelve-year old presented the gift with an address. Even at this moment of great emotion Joseph Lancaster replied with a joke. The address had spoken of him as a 'good man'. His father had told him that there were two kinds of good, 'good, and good for nothing'. He had tried to be good and do good. Now, looking round at all these happy children, educated in his System, it proved that he had not been quite 'good for nothing'.

But John Lovell did not confine his Friend's appearance to the school. He had arranged for a handsome tribute in the local paper, for publicity about 'Epitome . . .' and a public lecture at which he himself touchingly appealed for help for this great man. In every way he tried to show that in the hearts of some at least of his boys gratitude and affection remained unqualified.

But the battles were not over. From New Haven Joseph returned to Canada for the winter, where Mrs Lancaster was once more in a situation only too depressingly familiar; hounded for debts that she could not pay, engaged in acrimonious legal arguments about the ownership of her property. There were confrontations with a man named Miller and his lawyer Driscoll. Joseph Lancaster took Miller to court for alleged insult, and assaulting Mrs Lancaster on a public highway. When the case came before the magistrate Driscoll objected to Lancaster affirming instead of taking the oath. Though Driscoll was overruled, Joseph Lancaster had become very excited on this issue and made some exceedingly imprudent remarks about the lawyer. Driscoll chose to view them as libel and sued. He won, and fifty pounds damages was added to the Lancaster family debts.

Mrs Lancaster was fortunate at this point to find an attorney of her own, named McCord, who was to spend much time and energy on the tangled Lancaster affairs and in the end make no charge for his invaluable services. She needed this support for, soon after the Driscoll case, against which Joseph was determined to appeal, Lancaster himself left Canada for the last time. It was to be September 1837, nearly four years later, before his family followed him.

For both Joseph and Mary Robinson Lancaster these were to be years of estrangement and unhappiness. For Mary they were filled with disagreeable incidents and unpleasant brushes with the law. It was at this time that she met Joseph Burlingham, who was later to collect together as much material as he could towards a Lancaster biography. This does not look as though he despised Joseph Lancaster or thought him an insignificant figure, but his presence in Mary's life profoundly depressed the latter and caused him many pangs of jealousy.

For Mary, however the relationship may have developed, Joseph Burlingham was a lifeline. He paid the rent of the cottage, locked away the printing press and type in his own store, and fought her battles. Her patience with her husband was running out. He might escape from Canada, but burdened by three children, watched lynx-eyed by creditors, she did not see how she could. Nor indeed was there any reason to believe that the situation would be any better if she accompanied her husband. At least living in La Prairie was cheaper than in the

United States.

So she stayed, to have her goods seized by Driscoll. McCord pleaded that they were her own. Driscoll insisted on legal proof. Joseph, from a distance, wrote to Benjamin Butler, the American Attorney General, to ask if he could direct that a search be made in the law library of the United States Supreme Court for relevant passages in the common law of Spain, under which their marriage had taken place, and have copies made in Spanish. All this took time and extra expense.

By 1836 Driscoll, in need of money himself and no doubt tiring of this cat and mouse game, said he would withdraw the suit on a payment of twenty pounds sterling. McCord advised agreement. With the restoration of her goods Mary Lancaster could leave for the States. Mary Lancaster gave Driscoll her Note, to become due on receipt of the half-yearly annuity which Joseph Lancaster was now expecting from England. The goods were released. Her first thought was to put the miniature painted by John Robinson in safe keeping in case they were again seized. Meanwhile Driscoll, flourishing his Note among creditors still unpaid, raised the rumour that Mrs Lancaster had come into money. In fact the annuity had run into trouble. Another writ was issued and a second seizure took place. The cottage was stripped of everything except the beds; even the pot on the fire with the dinner cooking in it was taken. The creditors set up a table outside the cottage and ate the evening meal there with loud toasts.

It was not to be the last struggle over Mary Lancaster's ill-fated possessions. At last, in April 1837, Attorney McCord advised her to sell everything and so end the affair and find herself in a position to leave Canada. She did, and in September of that year his family joined Joseph Lancaster in Philadelphia.

In 1834, when he finally left Canada, Joseph Lancaster had first gone to New York. He still had one faithful ex-pupil there, C. J. Gayler, who had been helpful at the time of the Trenton debacle and now took him in. But de Witt Clinton was dead, and New York no longer contained men who were impressed by Lancaster the founder, or fond of Lancaster the man. Even his Quaker brethren wished to make plain their distance from one who had brought dishonour on the Society. After speaking in Meeting on First Day, a committee of elders waited on Joseph Lancaster and told him that, as he was not a member, his speaking was disorderly and he must keep silence. Few things could have pained him more than this rejection. In sorrow rather than anger he wrote to one of those who had judged him, William Waring.

'I also conceived that disowned persons repentant and sensible of their faults and fully acknowledging them, were – like convinced persons not admitted to membership – under the tender care of friends and elders to watch over for good – and not cut off from the tenderness and loving kindness of friends – to whom they themselves might feel the yearnings and meltings of tender bowels or the flowings of Gospel Love. But the treatment I have now received amounts to *proscription*, absolute and positive . . .

'I love silent worship in my own apartments. That must be my refuge. But does he who fills my heart with his love require me to put his candle under the bushel . . .

'I have acknowledged most fully every fault I ever committed to the monthly meeting to which I once belonged – not requesting membership but simply that they would accept my love and my society with their disownment . . .'

Joseph Lancaster was a man who needed to give and receive affection. He was deeply, and openly, unhappy at the separation from his wife and her children, though it seems never to have occurred to him that he bore any responsibility for it. Indeed he blamed them for not instantly leaving Canada to join him. The children, at least, wrote to him with love and forbearance, calling him father and showing towards him a warmth which leaves no doubt of the strong bond that had grown up between Joseph and his new family.

In 1835, when Lancaster was at last settled in Philadelphia and once again running a school, he had letters from all three of them. Mary Frances thanked him for five dollars and regretted that they could not send on the slates and lessons left in Montreal because they had been seized. She reproached him for blaming his family for staying in Canada, and spoke of the disgrace of living under threats and seizure. But her tone was mild and she rejoiced with him in the recovered friendship with William Corston. She was by now seventeen.

George, aged fifteen, thanking his stepfather for a letter, wished they were together for he loved him much. He then went on to give a vivid description of a sea serpent glimpsed in Lake

Ontario by a Captain Kellog. The latter had stated:

'. . . on June 15th about 7 o'clock, as he was making for Kingston Harbour . . . he saw something lying still on the weather bow that looked like the mast of a vessel. Observing it more Attentively, he was surprised and alarmed to see it in motion, and steering towards the schooner. Singing out to his hands to take care of themselves, he put the schooner to the wind lashed the helm a lee and ran up the main rigging, waiting for the monster to approach.'

It was an immense snake and it passed under the stern taking no notice of the vessel, about 175 feet, dark blue spotted with brown – tapered off at either end. In the middle the body was the circumference of a flour barrel. The head was peculiarly small and could only be distinguished by the direction in which it travelled. It swam with an undulating movement, keeping most of the body under water. For fifteen minutes the monster was in sight. It was last seen making its way down the St Lawrence. At the end of this tale George signed himself,

'Your affectionate son'.

As for Don Juan La Grande, he would have liked to have been eating plum cake and sugar candy with Joseph Lancaster; if he had not been obliged to stay in La Prairie. He was nine, and he had just finished reading the life of Thomas Spencer who was drowned at Liverpool, and had begun the life of Rowland Hill. He enjoyed reading the lives of eminent men. There were Siamese twins being exhibited in Montreal and a large white porpoise caught near St Helen's Island. Perhaps Joseph Burlingham had taken him to see them.

Joseph Lancaster wrote back with an equal mixture of anecdote and affection, larded with paternal admonition and religious instruction couched in simple, straightforward language. He was beginning now to get letters also from a grandson. Betsy's eldest, Joseph Lancaster Jones, a year older than Don Juan La Grande, was learning English and anxious to keep up a correspondence with his grandfather. By 1837 Betsy had five sons, three of whom had just had measles. 'Charles and Richard send love,' their elder brother wrote, 'Henry and Alfred cannot yet talk.'

Betsy continued to be agitated about the difficulties in communicating with her father. Times were still uncertain for the Jones family. In 1834 a turbulent political situation in Mexico deprived Richard of his position and closed down his flourishing institution of three hundred boys. He hoped that Joseph Lancaster might bring some influence to bear. Betsy by now had perhaps a juster appreciation of his real circumstances. She had seen rumours of the English annuity in the New York papers and wrote to her father in 1834 that this had 'relieved me in some degree from the painful anxiety which the state of thy pecuniary affairs had always occasioned'. She added that the time had come when she felt he should concentrate his efforts on helping himself.

The matter of the annuity had become a tangled one. In the early 1830's news trickled through to Britain that Joseph Lancaster was in sore financial straits. He had made no secret of his need when writing to his friends. It is unlikely that anyone was surprised, but the passing of time had allowed tempers to cool and passions to subside. His friends began to feel that it reflected shame on them to let the founder of an Educational System on which so much had been built face an old age in destitution and want. Perhaps too Andrew Bell's tomb in Westminster Abbey stirred feelings of guilt.

At the beginning of 1834 accounts were opened at various London banking houses and a subscription list begun to provide Joseph Lancaster with an annuity, on the initiative of Joseph Fletcher of Tottenham, an original supporter of the Borough Road school. An appeal was circulated to the newspapers.

'There are few persons who have not heard of Joseph Lancaster, the Founder of the New System of Education and not any who will deny that all Classes of the Community have been benefitted by his exertions . . . But who enquires, where is he? – how has he been rewarded? He has no reward! he is an exile!! he lives in poverty!!! – residing in Montreal, labouring for his existence and the hard maintenance of a wife and family . . . this ought not to be.'

Then, lest ghosts of old scandals should arise, the circular hastened to add that Joseph Lancaster's return was not advocated, that the cause was being undertaken solely to eradicate the blot of Joseph Lancaster in want.

But the past was not yet forgiven. Joseph Fletcher appealed to the Government for a contribution. They gave nothing. He reported bitterly that they feared the National schools and the Church would be in danger if any comfort were given to Joseph Lancaster. Henry Brougham refused to see the deputation which

waited on him. The B&FSS Committee disassociated themselves. Rumours were put about that the 'family' mentioned as
requiring education was non-existent, or that one was an idiot.
Joseph Fletcher was angered. He knew Joseph Lancaster intimately with his many faults;

'All of which sprang from his innate benevolence and under
that influence his expenditure for charity was always beyond his
means and now if ten thousand pounds were sent him he would
expend it all on schools and be as poor as ever.'

Nevertheless he considered that if the money collected matched
the obligation of humanity to Joseph Lancaster, then Lancaster
would be rich indeed.

Humanity did not respond. But the faithful few of those who
still considered themselves his friends did. Luke Howard contributed £50, the Duke of Bedford £25; William Allen sent his ten
guineas. In Belfast Maurice Cross worked heroically to raise
£100; and in Bristol George Cumberland took up the challenge.
By November £1150 had been collected, of which £40 had been
despatched to Joseph Lancaster via Quebec in the spring.

Correspondence flowed between Joseph Lancaster and Joseph
Fletcher, who naturally wished the remainder of the money to be
as well controlled as possible. Lancaster asked for it to be
invested in a joint annuity for himself and his wife. It was not
until 1835, when papers started to arrive requiring his signature,
that he began to have scruples about the manner of that
investment. He could not accept profits from Government bonds
which, like many orthodox Quakers, he considered to be 'war
and blood money'. Mary Lancaster, struggling in La Prairie and
seeing the lifeline of a steady income, however small, being
thrown to her across the Atlantic, was exasperated with him.
Joseph, bitter and unhappy about his family situation yet
genuinely fearing to trifle with his God and eternity, signed the
papers with the greatest possible reluctance but continued to
bombard Joseph Fletcher with remonstrances. He wanted him to
revoke the annuity and simply send a lump sum instead. The
battle see-sawed on until 1838, when Joseph Fletcher's patience
finally failed. He wrote that he was weary of Lancaster's scruples
and the subject must be dropped. The Trustees would not agree
to revoke the annuity. 'Every one knows that Joseph Lancaster is
not to be trusted with money of his own'. Whatever Joseph felt,
Mary Lancaster was glad to have a steady £50 a year, and had no

hesitation in making use of it.

In the middle of 1834 Joseph Lancaster had finally returned to Philadelphia. In that city there were still two men of means and influence who had never withdrawn their support from him, Robert Ralston and Roberts Vaux. The latter had retired from the Presidency of the Philadelphia School Board in 1831 and was to die in 1836, but he remained much respected in his community.

It was a sad return for Joseph Lancaster, without family, financial stability or fresh honours, to a scene where he had once insisted that his personal worth and advice were not properly appreciated. Yet, undeterred by circumstances which would have felled a man less single-minded, he started once more to establish a school. Robert Ralston lent him a room in which to make a preliminary demonstration of his new methods of rapid teaching with three small boys, the youngest four years old. He hoped to show that they could learn to read easily in five or six weeks. As usual he started a subscription list to support this new venture.

In a worldly sense he might be down and out; in his spirit he was far from being so. On October 5th he asked Roberts Vaux to get him the use of the court room in the State House for lectures, and he petitioned the Controllers of the Education Board to give him opportunities for further educational experiments. Use of the court room was granted. The Controllers refused, but:

'Whether the Controllers do anything or not – I cannot lose time but must persevere and improve every moment,' Joseph wrote to Roberts Vaux. 'Did I not feel that I have benefits to confer on any community much greater than I can ask or expect in return I should be quite discouraged, for really teaching in the assiduous cool and soul absorbing manner in which I teach – often leaves me at the close of the day too much worn down, to pursue the active duties of calling on persons and making an interest to add promptitude and sufficient aid to my experiments'. 'The souls of the people in the United States are not more absorbed in their political contests than I am in my education interests.'

Though in February 1835 Joseph Lancaster seems to have cast his eye on a position in Pottsville, ninety miles north-west of Philadelphia, the new Lancastrian Institute progressed reasonably well. In October of that year it had about fifty scholars, forty-two of them paying eight dollars; presumably a quarter. Fitting up a schoolroom was going on apace, the carpentry being done by three young apprentices who worked in the evenings. This activity absorbed all the ready money and there was little to spare for Canada. Joseph had asked John Lovell to send Mrs Lancaster ten or twenty dollars, a request that John had regretfully to refuse being himself in debt. In May 1835 his Henrietta had died in childbirth, leaving her heartbroken husband with two tiny children; but even this personal tragedy made no difference to the loving concern with which he continued to follow the fortunes of his Old Master.

By April 1837 Joseph was writing to Roberts Vaux's son Richard;

'The school continues the same, that is in a flourishing state – and there is now no doubt that if other resources cannot easily be found that it will finally create a sufficient small capital for all purposes of efficient demonstrations within the restricted space of its own walls and more ample room of parental hearts.'

To Mary Lancaster, in June, he wrote less optimimstically. Summer was a bad quarter. School attendance was thin. He was wretchedly uneasy about her. If she did not come soon he must give up and lose the fruit of three years labour. He could no longer go on alone.

At last, in September, the family arrived. Nothing was ready for them and 'as usual' Joseph Lancaster had no money. For four nights they all slept under their cloaks on the schoolroom floor. Then Mary Lancaster bustled about and took a small house, sensibly converting the front room into a store where prints and other articles could be sold. Prudently this venture was put in the name of Mary Frances Robinson, her daughter.

It was a difficult winter. Four years estrangement and, on both sides, experiences which carried bitter memories, cannot have made for easy readjustment. But there are signs that Joseph Lancaster had begun to enter a period of greater tranquility, when flamboyant extravagance no longer tarnished the essence of his gifts. In June 1838 the Philadelphia Board of Control minuted that Joseph Lancaster was to be assisted to visit the primary schools in the different sections of the city and to have a personal interview with the director of each, a very different attitude from thjeir uncompromising refusal to deal with him at all three years before. As a result Joseph published an open letter on Education, 'On teachers in the Public Schools of Philadelphia'.

It was generously appreciative, full of praise for the men and women of this new profession that he had helped to create. Over forty years his emphasis had shifted. Once the young teacher had ben virtually non-existent; his own pupils had shown the way, enabled to do so by the System he had devised. There was now a widespread demand in America for universal education. In Philadelphia the Public School system had become a permanent part of the city's activities and there were three infant school societies in addition. The citizens were already turning away from the Lancastrian System. Joseph Lancaster showed no sign of resenting this. His concern, as always, was for the greater issue; that all children should be given a chance to learn.

'Twenty years past, I visited the public schools in Philadelphia, I have lately revisited them all; it was a great sacrifice of time, but a work of pleasure, satisfaction and peace.

'The state of their infancy and their advancement forms a striking contrast – twenty years have increased the number of teachers and pupils and the liberal principle of public education, by taxation, has increasd the resources and magnified the great scale of their usefulness.

'It is a credit to the existing feeling between the directors and teachers, that a number of them have filled their stations for ten or twenty years – that during that time they have ripened in practical knowledge and gathered strength from experience . . . I often involuntary discern the state of the teacher by the state of the school and feel at once, whether I am with a children's friend or a stranger to their interest; whether my heart is at home and can be at home, or not, and I have had the satisfaction in all the school houses, to feel completely at home, and to be pleased, highly pleased, with seeing both teachers and scholars.

'Knowing, on the other hand as I do, the trying nature of a teacher's duty, and that they have to manufacture the raw material of singular, eccentric, and invisible mind, always presenting new and complicated difficulties – I can and do allow for many things which persons of less sympathy, to say nothing of experience would not be inclined to indulge, to see a fault by no means makes it indispensible to speak of it. One who will find the right way to the heart and the understanding, to induce the practice not to say the invaluable practice of self inquiry and self correction of errors, is in my esteem a person of attainments whom I should feel less likely in endeavouring to emulate, than in professing to equal – a visitor official or not, can never derrogate (sic) from a teacher's rank especially in the eyes or hearing of pupils without lessening himself as much as the Teacher. The duties of the instructors of youth, are really arduous and the more sincere, and pure, the actual attention of teachers, the greater very often will be their diffidence. The teachers of youth need much more cheering on their way, than they usually receive in this city or elsewhere . . . Touch human nature on the bright side and it will expand – touch it on the dark side and it will contract. The teachers of youth have to make a multitude of efforts for the good of their pupils, which can never be appreciated by human beings because unseen, except by their effect. When teachers are obviously at the post of duty, doing their very best encouragement is the paramount privilege of the visitor. When the teacher sees a person enter school whom he knows to be the teacher's friend, it is all delight – the visitors of schools in this capacity meet a cheerful welcome and teachers become more energetic when they find their exertions are properly noticed. My impression of the native character capacity and good intention of the great mass of the teachers of all the schools I have visited is highly favourable. There are a large number of hopeful young persons among them. The experience as well as the talent and the interest which they feel in their avocations all speak well of them . . . I found so many whose hearts were in their work – as if they were in love with it.

'In visiting schools, I have never held a teacher responsible for anything prescribed to him by those persons who employ him. In such a case he is no more responsible than the patient is for the prescription of his physician. His business is neither to make or mend, the composition of his medicine, but either take them or give up the character of patient. I hold a teacher responsible only for those things which are in his own power. His love to truth and rectitude. His tender but firm vigilance over ( ) conduct. The order, the cleanliness, the obedience, the happiness, and the endeavour to instruct his pupils, and improve his time and opportunities to the utmost.

'To such a teacher I am indebted for he is an active friend of man, he is diminishing the stock of ignorance. He is increasing the mass of knowledge in the human family. He is an ally and friend of moral principle working in that cause to which I have devoted my life and general fellow feeling alone, entitles him to my goodwill, my respect and my thanks in proportion to the purity of his motive and the energy of his exertions.

'When I speak of teachers I include the females who have charge in all the schools which I have visited.

'If the public edifices – do credit to this city the teachers hold a very honourable place in my esteem – may they deepen in the root and spread wide in the branches of instruction, and may the children of their hands and the plants of their care, rise up and call them blessed.'

In the first half of 1838 both teaching and printing went on apace. Joseph Lancaster was erecting a new schoolroom. He put out broadsheets seeking influential people to support cheap and economical publications of service to mothers teaching their own children, private tutors, farmers and their families, those in frontier settlements. The usefulness would consist in '1) brevity, 2) surprising bearing on the mass of our language'. He had a proposal to publish by subscription 'An Introduction to Orthography and Reading the English Language on an entire new principle'. Three bound copies, or four unbound, for every dollar subscribed. He had never learned the lesson that Americans were wary of this way of doing business. But perhaps some of them, for their part, had come to accept it as a means of helping a man who still had claims on their attention for the list attached, of those who had subscribed five dollars already, contained some illustrious names. It included John Joseph Gurney of Norwich, England, Daniel Webster, Senator, R. M. Johnson Vice President of the United States of America, Benjamin Butler Attorney General, Henry Becket Acting British Consul Philadelphia, James Polk Speaker of the House of Representatives in Congress and a number of Senators, including Henry Clay of Kentucky.

In September Joseph Lancaster was in New York on what he called, in a letter to William Corston, an 'apostolic visit'. He was making a report on the schools, in the same way that he had already done in Philadelphia. It was unlikely that the authorities in New York had requested this visitation, but equally certainly Joseph Lancaster would not have had free access to all their establishments unless the School Boards had given permission. When Lancaster wrote on September 21st he had seen sixty schools on Manhattan and hoped to visit one hundred and fifty more. When he entered them 'teachers, monitors and children shout "Here comes our father"'.

It seemed that, at last, he really intended to make a trip to England. 'My wife cheerfully gives me up to come and I have friends who will make the way easy.' He had hoped to sail on the 'Great Western' on October 8th. Perhaps the number of schools still left to see, and a public demonstration of teaching fifty ignorant boys to read which he planned, accounted for this arrangement being delayed. To William Corston at any rate he wrote with all his usual vigour and optimism.

On October 22nd 1838, crossing a street in New York, Joseph Lancaster was knocked down by a horse drawn vehicle and run over, sustaining broken ribs and a severely lacerated head. He was a month short of his sixtieth birthday. He died the next day, as sure of his faith as he had ever been, in the presence of C. J. Gayler, his pupil, and William Wagstaffe, a Quaker friend. John Lovell was so heartbroken he could not attend his funeral, which took place, almost unnoticed, in the Friends' burial ground in Houston Street. 'In my eyes', John Lovell wrote, 'he was always the good and great man, the best friend and kindest of fathers'.

There was another letter, dated August 14th, which Joseph Lancaster probably never received. It was from Betsy, assuring him that in spite of long silences between them nothing could ever change her affection. She wished he could see her Spanish-speaking boys. She had five sons, and was to produce eight, all brought up in the Roman Catholic faith. In this letter she enclosed another from Joseph Lancaster junior to his grandfather.

'My beloved Grandfather . . . I know English regularily and I am learning Latin with the hopes of learning soon Greek, French and Italian which is said to be a very beautiful idiom. I am now conjugating verbs and I am also in the second book of Triarte Grammar is a very good method of teaching boys . . . I believe along eight months I will write to you in Latin English and Espanish . . . I am also yours truly son Joseph Lancaster Jones. My brothers names are Charles Richard Henry and Laurence.

Please excuse the mistake I have made'

It was a fitting memorial for the man who loved children and longed to give them the key to knowledge.

BIBLIOGRAPHY

Life of William Allen Vol 1, Charles Gilpin, London 1846
Life of Andrew Bell Vol II, Rev Charles Southey Murray 1844
Life of Joseph Lancaster, William Corston, Harvey Darton 1840
Joseph Lancaster, David Salmon, Longman Green 1904
Autobiography of Francis Place, Ed. M. Thale, Cambridge University Press 1972
Life of Francis Place 1771-1854, Graham Wallas, Allen & Unwin 1925
The Life & Works of Sarah Trimmer, D. M. Yarde, Hounslow & District History Society 1971
Account of the Life and Writings of Sarah Trimmer, London 1814
Robert Raikes, Alfred Gregory, Hodder and Stoughton 1880
Life of Samuel Whitbread, Roger Fulford, Macmillan 1967
Pestalozzi, His Thought and its relevance today, Michael Heafford Methuen 1967
Memoirs of the Life of Sir Samuel Romilly, ed. by his sons, Vols I and II, Murray 1840
Lord Brougham & The Whig Party, A. Aspinall, Manchester U.P. 1927
The Letters of King George IV 1812-1830 Vols I & II, Ed. A. Aspinall, C.U.P. 1938
Correspondence of George Prince of Wales 1770-1812 Vol VIII, Ed. A. Aspinall, Cassell 1971
The Practical Parts of Lancaster's Improvements & Bell's Experiments, David Salmon, C.U.P. 1932
The Oeconomy of Charity or an Address to Ladies, Mrs S. Trimmer, 2 Vols, London 1801
The Education of the People, Mary Sturt, Routledge & Kegan Paul 1967
A History of English Education (from 1760), H. C. Barnard, Univ. of London Press 1961
History of the Elementary School Contest in England, Francis Adams 1882. Intro. Asa Briggs, Harvester Press 1972
A Short History of Education, J. W. Adamson, Cambridge U.P. 1922
History of Elementary Education in England & Wales from 1800, Chas. Birchenough, Univ Tutorial Press 1938
The Charity School Movement, M. G. Jones, Cambridge U.P. 1938
History of the Borough Road College, G. F. Bartle, Dalkeith Press 1976
The Year of the French, Thos Flanagan, Macmillan 1979

Sir Robert Ker Porter's Caracas Diary 1825-1842, Ed Walter Dupouy, Editorial Arts, Caracas 1966

Bolivar, Salvador de Madariaga, Hollis and Carter 1952

Birth of a World: Bolivar in terms of his people, Waldo, Frank Gollancz 1935

The Evolution of an Urban School System, New York City 1750-1850, Carl F. Kaestle, Harvard Univ. Press, Cam., Mass. 1973

Joseph Lancaster and the Monitorial School Movement, Carl F. Kaestle, New York 1973

Students as Teaching Resources, American Institutes for Research, Pittsburgh, Penn Oct 1973

Our Inherited Practice in Elementary Schools, S. Chester Parker, Univ of Chicago

Old New England Academies founded before 1826, Harriet Webster, Marr Comet Press Bk, New York 1959

Public Education in the United States, Ellwood P. Cubberley, Howard Mufflin & Co 1974

PAMPHLETS

An Account of the Progress of Joseph Lancaster's plan for the education of poor children . . . Lancastrian Royal Free School Press 1810 Dr W.

An Address to the Friends and Superintendents of 'Sunday Schools' on the Advantages that will result from introducing into them the Royal British System of Education 1809 Dr W.

An Appeal for Justice in the Cause of Ten Thousand poor and orphan children . . . London 1807 Dr W.

Improvements in education, as it respects the industrious classes of the Community Darton and Harvey 1803 Dr W. (also editions 1805, 1808, 1810)

Instructions for forming and conducting a Society for the Education of children of the labouring Classes according to the general Principles of the Lancastrian Plan 1810 Dr W.

Report of Joseph Lancaster's progress from the year 1798 . . . Royal Free Sch. Press 1811 Dr W.

Schools for all in preference to Schools for Churchmen only Jas. Mill 1812 Dr W.

A Comparative view of the plans of Education as detailed in the publications of Dr Bell and Mr Lancaster, Joseph Fox 1811 Dr W.

A vindication of Mr Lancaster's system of education . . . Joseph Fox 1812 Dr W.

Letter to John Foster Esq., Chancellor of the Exchequer for Ireland . . . London 1805 FL.

Oppression and Persecution . . . Joseph Lancaster Bristol 1816 Bristol PL.

Sketch of an economical plan for providing the public with good schoolmasters London FL.

Vindication of some truths contained in the Scriptures by the exercise of reason only . . . London 1807 FL.

A Comparative view of the new plan of education . . . Sarah Trimmer London 1805 FL.

Life and Travels of Joseph Lancaster. Proposals for publishing . . . J. Adlard FL.

Epitome of the Chief Events & Transactions of my own life Joseph Lancaster New Haven 1833 Bristol PL.

Lancaster in America Dr J. McCadden BR.

A Britisher Tours the Hudson New York History Society Dr J. McCadden 1851 BR.

David Holt Monograph 1843 RA.
An Experiment in Education . . . Andrew Bell 1797.
The Guayrians at Guelph in Upper Canada Edgar Vaughan Guelph Hist. Soc. Vol XVIII.

NOTES

Where the text makes names of correspondents obvious initials only are used in the references.

For Betsy Lancaster BL has been retained even after her marriage.

1 Where the reference is to printed sources appearing in the bibliography the author's name is written in full.

2 Pamphlets appear under shortened title and initials denoting library.
   FL – Friends Library
   Dr W – Dr William's Library
   LL – London Library

3 Mss sources are indicated by initials, as follows:
   AAS – American Antiquarian Society: Lancaster Papers
   B – The Bedford Estates
   BL – The British Library: Place Papers
   BFSS – British and Foreign School Society Archives Centre (West London Institute for Higher Education)
   Bristol PL – Archives, Bristol Public Library
   CU – Columbia University, New York: Lancaster Letters
   GC – Gratz Collection: Historical Society of Pennsylvania
   HC – Haverford College, U.S.A. Quaker Collection
   NPG – National Portrait Gallery, London
   RA – Royal Archives Windsor
   UCL – University College Library, London: Henry Brougham Papers
   UK – University of Keele: Fox and Wedgwood Papers
   WP – Whitbread Papers, Bedford County Record Office

References appear in sequence under page numbers.

Where all references in one page are from the same source only one reference is given.

REFERENCES

Chapter 1

pp
2   Epitome . . . 1833 (pamph)
3   JL Autobiog. AAS
3   JL Autobiog. AAS
4   JL Autobiog. AAS
5   JL Autobiog. AAS
6   Improvements . . . 3rd 1805 Dr W
7   JL Autobiog. AAS
8   JL Autobiog. AAS
11   JL Autobiog. AAS
12/16   JL Autobiog. AAS
16   4.11.1796 Josh Knight to JL AAS

Chapter 2

pp
20   Education . . . Sturt
24   Charity Sch . . . M.G. Jones
25   Life of AB Southey
27   JL Autobiog. AAS
29   Life of JL Corston
30   Life of JL Corston
31   Epitome . . . 1833(pamph)
    4.5.1800 FS to JL AAS
32   FL
33   Epitome . . . 1833 (pamph)

Chapter 3

pp
35   Improvements . . . 1st 1803 Dr W
37   Robert Raikes Gregory
38   Improvements . . . 1st 1803 Dr W
39   Improvements . . . 1st 1803 Dr W
    Improvements . . . 1st 1803 Dr W
40   Improvements . . . 1st 1803 Dr W
    Pestalozzi . . . Heafford
41   Improvements . . . 1st 1803 Dr W
42   Improvements . . . 3rd 1805 Dr W
43   Improvements . . . 3rd 1805 Dr W
    Improvements . . . 3rd 1805 Dr W
44   Salmon: Education Record 1913
    BFSS
45   Improvements . . . 3rd 1805 Dr W
46   Improvements . . . 3rd 1805 Dr W
47   Improvements . . . 1st 1803 Dr W
48   1.3.1803 EW to JL AAS
    Life of WA Gilpin
    21.11.04 JL to AB GC

50   20.6.04 TE to JL AAS
    Life of JL Salmon
51   Improvements . . . 1st 1803 Dr W

Chapter 4

pp
54   Improvements . . . 3rd 1805 Dr W
    Improvements . . . 3rd 1805 Dr W
    Life of JL Corston
55   Life of JL Corston
57   8.8.04 JL to EL GC
58   24.11.04 JL to ? AAS
    n.d. JL to TU GC
    21.11.04 JL to AB GC
    21.11.04 JL to AB GC
59   6.12.04 AB to JL Salmon
59   13.12.04 JL to AB Southey
61   13.1.06 AB to ST Southey
    13.1.06 AB to ST Southey
    14.10.05 AB to ST Southey
62   n.d. GC
    Life of JL Corston
63   19.8.05 JL to EL GC
    19.8.05 Salmon BFSS
    Holt Monograph RA
65   Improvements . . . 3rd 1805 Dr W
66   Sept? 1805 GC
67   Sept? 1805 GC

Chapter 5

pp
68   Life of AB Southey
69   Oeconomy of Charity Trimmer
70   1.10.05 ST to AB Southey
    21.4.04 PW to JL AAS
    1.10.05 ST to AB Southey
71   1.10.05 ST to AB Southey
    Improvements . . . 1st 1803 Dr W
72   1.10.05 ST to AB Southey
    1.10.05 ST to AB Southey
    24.9.05 ST to AB Salmon
73   28.9.05 AB to ST Southey
    28.9.05 AB to ST Southey
    14.10.05 AB to ST Southey
    1.10.05 ST to AB Southey
74   Oeconomy of Charity Trimmer
75   Oeconomy of Charity Trimmer
    A comparative View . . . .ST FL

76   A comparative View . . . .ST FL

Chapter 6
pp
81   Salmon: Education Record 1912
BFSS
83   JL to LD 1805 GC
84   JL to M of B 1805 GC
      19.4.06 FL
      25.12.05 JL to TS GC
85   25.12.05 JL to TS GC
      1.1.06 JL to TS GC
      11.11.09 RO to JL AAS
86   10.2.06 WG to RH AAS
      22.8.08 WG to JL AAS
      29.11.09 WG to JL AAS
      29.9.07 JL to RH GC
      19.10.06 JL to pupil HC
87   25.5.08 GC
      28.10.07 JL to HH GL
88   7.7.08 HH to JL AAS
      17.10.08 HH to JL AAS
      8.11.07 JL to TS GC
      1.1.07 JL to TS GC
90   n.d. JL to Ldy H GC
      JL to JF 1805 FL
91   JL to JF 1805 FL
      9.10.06 JL to JF Belfast PRO
92   20.10.06 JL to DofB B
      20.10.06 JL to DofB B
93   8.11.06 JL to DofB B
      31.12.06 JL to WC Corston
      24.11.06 JL to DofB B

Chapter 7
pp
97   Life of JL Corston
      n.d. RL to JL GC
98   n.d. JL to RL GC
      n.d. JL to RL GC
99   26.07AB to SW (pamph 37)LL
      Life of JL Corston
101   26.2.08 JL to Mr Phipps Corston
102   Life of JL Corston
103   n.d. JL to ? GC
104   26.2.08 JL to Mr Phipps Corston
      23.11.07 JL to WC Corston
105   26.2.08 JL to Mr Phipps Corston
      16.11.07 JL to WC Corston
      6.12.07 JL to WC Corston
      10.12.07 JL to Birtill Bristol PL
106   27.12.07 Bristol Mercury
      2.1.08. Bristol Mirror
      27.12.07 JL to WC Corston

107   6.1.08 Thos Foster to Jas Harford
      AAS
      18.1.08 JL to WC Corston
      22.1.08 BFSS Minutes BFSS
108   24.1.08 JF to WC/JL Corston
109   Life of JL Corston
      Practical Parts Salmon
110   Oppression & Presentation (pamph)
      FL
      15.6.08 B&FSS Minutes BFSS
      Life of WA Gilpin
111   29.7.08 BFSS Minutes BFSS
      29.7.08 BFSS Minutes BFSS
112   Life of WA Gilpin
      WA to J Foster Gilpin
113   WA to J Foster Gilpin

Chapter 8
pp
116   Improvements . . . 4th ed Dr W
117   QR vol VI 1811
118   5.5.09 JL to WC Corston
119   29.4.10 JL to EL GC
      18.11.10 JL to WA BFSS
120   5.12.10 JL to WA BFSS
      15.3.09 JL to Fox GC
      18.11.10 JL to WA BFSS
      28.11.10 JL to WA BFSS
      18.11.10 JL to WA BFSS
      5.12.10 JL to WA BFSS
121   20.11.10 JL to WA BFSS
      28.11.10 JL to WA BFSS
      5.12.10 JL to WA BFSS
      14.3.11 JL to WA BFSS
122   18.11.10 JL to WA BFSS
123   10.3.09 JL to Fox GC
124   3.7.10 Dublin PRO
      ? 12.10 JL to WA BFSS
125   1.12.10 JL to WA BFSS
      16.5.09 JL to RL GC
      28.11.10 JL to WA BFSS
126   9.10.09 BFSS Minutes BFSS
      16.7.10 BFSS Minutes BFSS
128   14.12.10 Gilpin
129   16.1.11 JL to WA BFSS
130   16.1.11 JL to WA BFSS
      24.1.11 JL to WA BFSS
      24.1.11 JL to WA BFSS
      11.2.11 Gilpin
131? WA to Reynolds Gilpin
      23.2.11 JL to Trustees BFSS
132   18.2.11 JL to WA BFSS
      18.2.11 JL to WA BFSS
      18.2.11 JL to WA BFSS

133   11.7.10 JL to RL GC
        5.1.11 JL to Parents GC
        Report of JL's Progress . . . (pamph)
        Dr W
        16.5.09 JL to RL GC
134   n.d. JL to Parents GC

Chapter 9

pp
136   26.8.11 SP to PR RA 18458-9
        23.10.11 Arch of C to Col McM RA
137   n.d. JL to WWP Dublin PRO
        7.11.11 JL to WWP Dublin PRO
138   9.11.11 JL to WWP Dublin PRO
        19.11.11 JL to WA BFSS
        1.2.12 JL to WA BFSS
139   12.4.12 JL to WA BFSS
        24.4.12 JL to Magrath BFSS
        12.4.12 JL to WA BFSS
140   12.4.12 JL to WA BFSS
        9.5.12 Diary WA Gilpin
        9.5.12 Diary WA Gilpin
141   ? 8.12 WA to RR Gilpin
142   ? 8.12 WA to RR Gilpin
        7.12.12 Diary WA Gilpin
143   29.8.12 WA to Brougham UCL
        12.8.12 GLS to JL AAS
144   11.8.12 JL to ? BFSS
        10.7.12 JL to SB BFSS
        10.10.12 BFSS Minutes BFSS
        9.11.12 JL to SB BFSS
145   22.6.13 to Comm. Ireland BFSS
        Report of Trustees 1812 FL
146   20.2.13 DH to JL AAS
147   8.5.13 Diary WA Gilpin
        24.2.11 JL to Trustees BFSS
149   22.7.13 DH to JL AAS
        7.7.13 Education Record Salmon
        BFSS
        10.7.13 Education Record Salmon
        BFSS
150   11.7.13 Education Record Salmon
        BFSS
151   17.7.13 Diary WA Gilpin
        23.7.13 JF to SW WP
152   Place Papers BL
153   7.8.13 JH to SW WP
        13.8.13 Diary WA Gilpin
154   15.8.13 DofK to WA Gilpin
155   11.9.13 JH to SW WP
156   17.9.13 DofK to DH RA
157   Place Papers BL
        Place Papers BL
        16.11.13 Fox to Wedgwood UK
        10.11.13 Report BFSS 1814 Dr W

Chapter 10

pp
158   4.12.13 WA to ? WP
159   n.d. WA to ? WP
160   Place Papers BL
161/166   Place Papers BL
166   Place Papers BL
167   Place Papers BL
        Report BFSS 1814 Dr W
        Report BFSS 1814 Dr W
168   RA
169   BR
171   27.8.14 EL to JL AAS
        27.8.14 EL to JL AAS
        27.8.14 EL to JL AAS
172   13.8.14 BC to JL AAS
        6.9.14 JL to RL GC
        1.9.14 JL to RL GC
173   n.d. RL to JL AAS
        9.9.14 RL to JL AAS
        8.9.14 JL to RL GC
        28.9.14 JL to RL GC
        28.9.14 JL to RL GC
174   28.9.14 JL to RL GC
        ?1.15 Diary WA Gilpin
185   18.8.15 JL to RL GC
176   2.6.16 JL to BL GC
        Broadsheet 1816? Bristol PL
        19.11.16 JL to G Cumberland
        Bristol PL
177   Oppression and Persecution
        (pamph) FL
179   9.11.16 BR
180   3.6.17 JL to EL GC
181   9.10.17 LE to JL AAS
        n.d. Holt Appeal NPG
        6.4.18 JL to BL GC
        ?.4.18 JL to Bl GC

Chapter 11

pp
185   11.11.18 JL to deWC CU
186   22.10.15 EB to FP Place BL
        22.10.15 EB to FP Place BL
        22.10.15 EB to FP Place BL
187   n.d. BL to EL AAS
190   Evolution . . . Kaestle
        3.9.18 JL to EL GC
191   29.8.18 HO to JL AAS
        15.7.18 JLo to JL AAS
192   1.9.18 WmS to JL AAS
        17.9.18 JL to deWC CU
193   7.9.18 JL to deWC CU
        9.9.18 JL to EL GC
194   15.10.18 SE to RV BR

196 11.11.18 JL to deWC CU
198 1.1.19 JL to RV BR
     n.d. JL to TS GC
     12.1.19 McCadden BR
199 23.1.19 BR
     30.1.19 (6.2.19 HO to JL) AAS
200 26.1.19 JL to RV McCadden BR
     n.d. RV to JL AAS
201 9.2.19 JL to RV McCadden BR
     4.3.19 McCadden BR
     12.3.19 JL to RV McCadden BR
     18.3.19 McCadden BR
     5.4.19 JL to deWC CU
202 25.5.19 JL to RV McCadden BR
     27.5.19 McCadden BR
     3.6.19 RV to JL McCadden BR

Chapter 12
pp
204 11.6.19 JL to BL GC
205 17.6.19 BL to JL GC
     17.6.19 BL to JL GC
206 21.6.19 BL to JL GC
     24.6.19 JL to BL GC
207 21.7.19 BL to JL GC
     2.7.19 JL to BL GC
208 2.7.19 JL to BL GC
     14.7.19 BL to JL GC
     14.7.19 JL to BL GC
     10.8.19 JL to BL GC
209 16.9.19 BL to JL GC
     19.8.19 JL to RJ GC
210 21.6.19 EL to JL GC
211 29.7.19 JL to BL GC
     13.11.19 JL to BL GC
     n.d. EL to JL GC
212 24.8.19 JL to BL GC
213 18.9.19 JL to BL GC
     21.12.19 JL to B Bassett AAS
215 6.1.10 JLo to JL AAS
     13.2.20 JLo to JL ASS
216 1.2.20 JL to BL GC
     3.2.20 JL to BL GC
     3.2.20 JL to BL GC
217 1.3.20 JL to BL GC
     17.2.20 JL to EL GC
     17.2.20 JL to EL GC
     11.3.30 JL to EL GC
219 18.11.20 C Coote to JL AAS
     15.8.20 JLo to JL AAS
     22.8.20 JLo to JL AAS
221 29.3.22 RO to JL AAS
     14.2.23 JLo to JL AAS
     14.2.23 JLo to JL AAS

Chapter 13
pp
222 29.8.26 JL to SS NPG
223 5.5.23 JL to SB Vaughan
224 3.11.23 JL to deWC CU
225 20.1.24 BY to JL AAS
228 n.d. GC
230 5.5.25 R Ackermann to JL AAS
     29.8.26 JL to SS NPG
     29.8.26 JL to SS NPG
     28.7.25 JL to J Robinson GC
231 5.2.25 JL to Geo IV GC
232 17.1.25 M Foster to JL AAS
233 29.11.25 Porter Diary Dupouy
234 28.12.25 Porter Diary Dupouy
     29.11.25 BL to JL GC
235 29.11.25 RJ to JL GC
     29.11.25 BL to JL GC
     29.4.26 BL to JL GC
236 1.11.26 RJ to JL AAS
     6.6.27 RJ to JL AAS
237 19.10.26 JL to deWc CU
239 20.5.26 JL to deWC CU
     19.5.26 Porter Diary Dupouy
     25.5.26 JL to deWC CU
241 1.7.26 JL to MR GC
242 1.7.26 JL to MR GC
243 1.7.26 JL to MR GC
244 19.10.26 JL to deWC CU
245 n.d. JL to ? GC
     n.d. JL to ? GC
246 4.9.26 Porter Diary Dupouy
247 23.10.26 JL to Dr M GC
     23.10.26 JL to Dr M GC
     23.10.26 JL to Dr M GC
     23.10.26 Porter Diary Dupouy
248 1.11.26 JL to GW GC
249 1.1.27 Porter Diary Dupouy
250 10.1.27 Porter Diary Dupouy
252 JL Autobiog AAS
253 26.2.27 Porter Diary Dupouy
256 Epitome. .1833 (pamph)
     Vaughan

Chapter 14
pp
258 10.10.34 McCadden BR
259 3.7.27 RH to JL AAS
260 3.7.27 RH to JL AAS
     15.7.27 JLo to JL AAS
261 18.12.27 JLo to JL AAS
     8.8.27 JL to deWc CU
262 8.8.27 JL to deWC CU
     17.9.27 JL to deWC CU

263   8.8.27 JL to deWC CU
264   22.8.27 JL to MRL GC
       24.7.27 JL to MRL GC
       19.9.27 JL to MRL GC
       21.9.27 JL to MRL GC
267   14.10.28 JL to MRL GC
       30.8.28 JLo to JL AAS
268   18.9.29 JL to MRL GC
       5.10.27 RJ to JL AAS
269   Jan 1834 BL to JL AAS
       28.1.29 JL to BL AAS
272   Epitome . . . 1833 (pamph)
275   Epitome . . . 1833 (pamph)
278   ?.3.37 JL to WW McCadden BR
279   21.7.35 George to JL AAS
       17.6.37 JLJ to JL GC
280   2.1.34 BL to JL AAS
       n.d. NPG
281   3.3.34 JF to G Cumberland
       Bristol PL
282   18.4.38 JF to JL AAS
       5.10.34 JL to RV McCadden BR
       10.10.34 JL to RV McCaddden BR
283   4.4.37 JL to RVjnr McCadden BR
284   n.d. GC
286   2.6.38 GC
287   21.9.38 JL to WC Corston
       21.9.38 JL to WC Corston
       21.9.38 JL to WC Corston
       30.10.38 JLo CG Gayler AAS
       15.8.38 JLJ to JL AAS

INDEX